CHARACTER IS CAPITAL

CHARACTER IS CAPITAL

SUCCESS MANUALS AND MANHOOD

IN GILDED AGE AMERICA *Judy Hilkey*

The University of North Carolina Press • *Chapel Hill and London*

© 1997 The University of North Carolina Press
All rights reserved
Manufactured in the United States of America
The paper in this book meets the guidelines for permanence and
durability of the Committee on Production Guidelines for Book
Longevity of the Council on Library Resources.
This book was set in Janson Text by Tseng Information Systems.
Book design by Mary Mendell.
Library of Congress Cataloging-in-Publication Data
Hilkey, Judy Arlene, 1948–
Character is capital : success manuals and manhood in Gilded Age
America / by Judy Hilkey.
p.   cm.
Revision of the author's thesis (Ph.D.)—Rutgers University, 1980.
Includes bibliographical references and index.
ISBN 0-8078-2353-8 (cloth : alk. paper). — ISBN 0-8078-4658-9
(pbk. : alk. paper)
1. Success in business—United States—History.   2. Masculinity—
United States—History.   3. Competition—United States—History.
4. Industrialization—United States—History.   5. Ethics—United
States—History.   6. Social classes—United States—History.
I. Title.
HF5386.H522   1997   650.14—dc21   96-51450   CIP
01   00   99   98   97   5   4   3   2   1

To the memory of Warren I. Susman

CONTENTS

A section of illustrations appears following page 30.

ACKNOWLEDGMENTS

This book began in 1974 as a dissertation topic emerging from Warren Susman's graduate seminar in cultural history at Rutgers University. Over the years, many friends and colleagues generously have read various versions of this work and offered valuable advice and encouragement. Thanks especially to Daniel Bronson, Susan Bronson, Paul Buhle, Joseph Cady, Harvey Green, Leon Fink, Sue Levine, Norman Markowitz, Jan Rosenberg, Gerald Sider, Fred Siegel, Martin Waldman, Daniel Walkowitz, Allis Wolfe, Irwin Yellowitz, and members of the Columbia University Seminar in American Civilization.

I would also like to acknowledge those who have helped in other special ways. I am grateful to my parents, Arlo and Marvene Hilkey, for providing material and spiritual support at critical junctures along the way; to Warren Susman for teaching me to look for meaning in what is commonplace; to George Bush for helping me overcome my hesitation in pursuing this project; to all of my colleagues at the City College Center for Worker Education but especially to Leonard Kriegel, Stephen Leberstein, Karl Malkoff, and Ed Quinn for believing that college administrators can and should pursue their intellectual interests and for making it possible for me to do so; to Lewis Bateman at the University of North Carolina Press for demonstrating the persistence and patience that any success writer would applaud; to Katherine Malin at the Press for expert guidance on the last leg of the journey from manuscript to book, to Janis Ruden for research assistance, to Josh Brown and Emily Bronson for photography, to the staff of the New York Public Library General Research Division for unfailing and courteous assistance; and last but not least, to my daughter, Robin Xinping Hilkey, for the love and levity that makes everything worthwhile.

This research was supported in part by a grant from the Professional Staff Congress–City University of New York Research Award Program.

INTRODUCTION

If this book shall serve to rouse to honorable effort any young man who is wasting his time and energies through indifference to life's prizes, — to cheer, stimulate, and inspire with enthusiasm any one who is desponding through distrust of his own abilities, — or to reveal to any one who is puzzled to discover the path to success and usefulness the art of "getting on" to the goal of his wishes, — the author will feel himself abundantly repaid for his labors. — William Mathews, *Getting On in the World, or Hints on Success in Life*

A CULTURAL HISTORY OF THE SUCCESS MANUAL

In the years between 1870 and 1910, a special, new type of book became commonplace in millions of homes across America. These new books were typically large, elaborately bound, illustrated volumes boasting such titles as *The Way to Win*, *Pushing to the Front*, *The Royal Path of Life*, and *Onward to Fame and Fortune*.[1] These "success manuals" were didactic, book-length works of nonfiction literature that promised to show men how to find success in life. Written primarily by ministers, educators, and publicists, most success manuals were produced by the subscription book industry, marketed door-to-door by traveling "book agents," and sold for the considerable sum of two to four dollars, depending on choice of binding. They were marketed with a rural and small-town market in mind and addressed to an audience of native-born Protestants of moderate means and modest education. Individual success manuals sold in the tens of thousands and in some cases even hundreds of thousands of copies, and each decade between 1870 and 1910 brought dozens of new titles to a seemingly insatiable market. Year after year certain success manuals were reprinted, and new editions were issued. By the turn of the century, there were well over one hundred different titles in print and millions of copies in circulation.[2] These volumes are still a commonplace on the shelves of used book shops, and most libraries have at least a modest collection in some dusty, little-frequented part of the stacks. Despite its former prominence, the success manual, this artifact of popular culture, has received little attention as such. Neither its popularity nor its place in the cultural history of the period has been fully investigated heretofore.

A number of important studies have explored the idea of "success" in American history as it has appeared over time in a variety of written sources, both fiction and nonfiction.[3] By studying patterns of upward mobility in different times and places and among different classes and ethnic groups, social historians have looked at the degree to which Americans have been able to achieve success.[4] However, this book is neither an intellectual history of the idea of success nor a study of social mobility. It is rather a cultural history of the success manual, one particular genre of nonfiction success literature that emerged and flourished in the years 1870–1910. I made the assumption that a cultural phenomenon that could be demonstrated to have wide popularity in a specific period—if scrutinized carefully—might reveal something about the society in which it emerged. I have treated the success manual as a cultural form, attempting to look at not only what these books said but also what they looked like, the ways in which they were similar, who wrote them, how and where they were published and distributed, their circulation, and their audience.[5] I have examined the success manual as a literary genre, as an artifact of popular culture, as a mass market commodity, and as a treatise embodying a special view of the world.

Irwin Wyllie's book *The Self-Made Man in America* (1954) first alerted me to the existence of a large body of nonfiction work on success in the Gilded Age. Although Wyllie used a variety of sources—including speeches, sermons, and articles—he coined the term "success manual" for the book-length didactic works he examined and suggested the enormity of the circulation and popularity of these books. Wyllie wrote in the 1950s, when the "consensus" school dominated the interpretation of United States history. Historians of this ilk stressed what they saw as a homogeneous, harmonious "American way of life," uniquely devoid of serious dissent or conflict. The American ethic of success came to be seen as the popular expression of a broad political and ideological consensus.[6] My study revisits success manuals with the benefit of the last thirty years of postconsensus scholarship in social, intellectual, and women's history. We now have a keener sense of the conflict and upheaval of Gilded Age America: waves of economic boom and bust, unprecedented extremes of poverty and wealth, labor strife, farm revolt, transformation of work, revolutions in women and men's roles, social and ideological conflict about the very future of the nation.[7] Against this backdrop, the contradictions within the literature of success stand out in sharp relief, and make it possible to interrogate success manual texts for their multiple meanings in a way that was not possible before. It is possible, for example, to look at the dialectic of pessimism and optimism in this literature and at the paradox of a boom in success books among buyers who were being marginalized by the new economic order that these books seemed to celebrate.

Similarly, the new wave of women's history published in the 1960s and 1970s, particularly the work of Barbara Welter on the idealization of women, sensitized me to the possibility that an analogous idealization of manhood might exist.[8] When I first began reading success manuals in 1973, the "genderized" and "sexualized" language, unexamined by an earlier generation of scholars, seemed to leap off the page and demand some kind of explanation.[9] I argue here that rather than being a quaint or quirky reflection of nineteenth-century prose, the success manual's linguistic and symbolic equation of success and manhood is essential to understanding the American ideology of success. Women's studies seems to have spawned a new and parallel field sometimes referred to as manhood studies, which looks at men's roles and gender expectations and how they have changed over time.[10] By taking gender into account, this study contributes to a growing body of literature that looks at how gender and ideas about gender shape how we view the world.[11]

THE AMERICAN IDEA OF SUCCESS

The idea of success, in one form or another, has been a part of the American discourse from the very beginning. Four centuries of writers and exponents have defined success in terms of the pursuit of individual, material well-being. Within this broad definition, different generations have provided variations on a familiar theme. In 1707 the Puritan divine Cotton Mather preached that every Christian was "called" to pursue some special business so that he might glorify God "by doing of *Good* for *others*, and getting of *Good* for *himself*." [12] Mather would have been shocked by the purely secular self-help advice of Benjamin Franklin's *The Way to Wealth*, published only fifty years later. Likewise, the modest early-nineteenth-century yeoman ideal of success—emphasizing competence, respect for honest labor, and economic self-sufficiency—clashed with the rags-to-riches stories of Horatio Alger's juvenile fiction. In 135 Alger titles published in the second half of the nineteenth century, luck as much as pluck won down-and-out boy-heroes a chance at great wealth.[13] The salesman ethic and psychological orientation of the early twentieth century, culminating in the 1936 publication of Dale Carnegie's best-seller *How to Win Friends and Influence People*, would have either offended or baffled the authors of most Gilded Age success manuals, who believed that *character*, *willpower*, and *manhood* (the inner core qualities of the man himself) rather than *personality* (the skill of projecting and selling himself) was the key to success.[14] In 1952, the Reverend Norman Vincent Peale published his winning combination of pop psychology, self-help, and Christian faith in *The Power of Positive Thinking*, an upbeat gospel that was superseded by the Machiavellian success books that dominated the best-sellers list in the 1970s. The titles told all in works such as Robert Ringer's *Winning through Intimidation* and *Looking Out for Number One* and Michael Korda's *Power: How to Get It and How to Use It*. In the 1980s, best-selling self-help books ranged from the pseudo-scientific, do-it-yourself psychotherapy of L. Ron Hubbard, put forth in *Dianetics: The Modern Science of Mental Health*, to the financial advice of self-made multi-millionaire Charles Givens in *Wealth without Risk*. In the 1990s, after the book had enjoyed 13 million sales, billboards in New York City subway stations still promoted *Dianetics* with the question "What's Your Success Potential?" while Charles Givens published a sequel to his work, entitled *More Wealth without Risk*.

From Mather's *A Christian at His Calling* to Givens's *Wealth without Risk*, it comes as no surprise to find that American taste in success literature and self-help advice has shifted with the temper of the times. What remains is the extraordinary persistence of the idea of success itself and the popularity of generation after generation of literature that seems to promote and celebrate it.

The popularity of the success theme in the oratory and literature of American history has often been taken as evidence of a broad national consensus about the American Dream and, implicitly, as a sign of faith in the dominant social order that presumably made opportunity and success possible. The Gilded Age success manuals explored in this study reveal a different picture and call for a different interpretation. These works were dedicated as much to shoring up faith in the American Dream as to celebrating its preeminence. Rather than providing evidence of a preexisting consensus, this particular genre of success literature can be better understood as part of the process by which that consensus—or at least the appearance of consensus—was created.

Despite their upbeat, "how-to" titles, Gilded Age success manuals offered neither practical business advice nor a simple celebration of the American Dream of opportunity and success. Rather, they presented a dire picture of a difficult and uncertain new age in which life, as they described it, was a brutal struggle for survival, and they assumed that some young men were in danger of losing hope. In prefaces and introductions, success writers dedicated their books to the "discouraged," the "doubters," and the "faint-hearted," to those who had lost courage or had become disenchanted with the promise of success.

The success manuals offered reassurance and inspiration to Americans who had become anxious and uncertain about their prospects for success in Gilded Age America. They articulated a moralistic view of the world that projected the values and virtues of an earlier preindustrial era as the means to success in the new age of industrial capitalism. By the diligent application of virtues such as honesty, frugality, industry, reliability, and loyalty, buttressed by the force of character and true manhood, any poor boy could find a "way to win." In the world depicted in the success manual, "character was capital" and "manhood was everything." Success writers defined character and manhood not only as the *means* to success, but as *success itself*, a nonpecuniary notion of success in which the "worthy"—be they rich or poor, capitalist or laborer—might be joined together in a common set of beliefs about what it meant to be a man and what it meant to be a success. This definition of success not only excluded women, it equated success and manhood in a way that depended on the corollary equation of failure and the feminine. Success writers associated failure with women and effeminacy and used a pejorative form of the feminine as a way to shame men who did not measure up.

Though the success writers' moralism can be taken as a critique of what seemed to many a harsh and immoral new age, the implications of their advice had a variety of other meanings and perhaps some unintended consequences. For example, their advocacy of the individual virtues of a pre-industrial age of self-employment and small-scale entrepreneurship as the key to success had radically different ramifications in an industrial age of wage and salaried labor. Paradoxically, despite the bravado concerning the celebration of manhood and manliness, success manual advice helped to define a new economic man who was a mere shadow of the powerful and independent entrepreneurs and statesmen that these works also canonized. This new economic man was an employee, idealized from the point of view of the employer: his preindustrial work habits selectively applied in a white-collar world made him the man who would identify his interests with the dominant industrial order without demanding too large a stake in it and who would willingly conduct himself in ways that were consistent with the triumph of that order.[15]

Though we know a good deal about the success manual audience, there is no way of knowing with certainty what readers thought of what they read or whether or not success manuals shaped the way readers acted or looked at the world. The success manual cannot be viewed as the kind of evidence that constitutes "proof" of a particular belief or point of view among its readership or even among its authors. On the other hand, the success manual can be seen as a kind of evidence that does shed light in a subtler, less direct way. In the first instance, the fact that millions of people were willing to spend as much as a quarter of a week's wages to buy a book that promised to teach them how to achieve success in life is testimony to the fact that they did not feel successful. They were worried either for themselves or for their children; they didn't know how to get on or stay on the bandwagon of opportunity and the American Dream. This was the assumption of the success manual authors, when they addressed their volumes to the worried, the discouraged, and those who had lost hope. Further, when we look at the kind of advice that is standard fare in this formulaic literary genre, at the problems these writers repeatedly address, the success manuals provide a window onto the underlying conflicts of the age; they offer a perspective on what people were worried about. Finally, when we look at the answers success writers offer to what they present as the pressing issues of the day, we get a unique amalgamation of ideas, admonitions, and moral philosophy that constitutes a view of the world that had broad political and ideological implications. Even if we do not know to what extent readers embraced this view of the world, we do know that it was a perspective that was available to a great number of people through the success manual, a medium they embraced with great enthusiasm. Success manuals constituted an important voice in the debate about the new industrial order as well as a source of advice about how to cope with its vicissitudes. As such, this seemingly not-so-serious form of popular culture deserves to be taken seriously by historians and others as one kind of evidence of the underlying issues and tensions that confronted ordinary Americans in the country's transition to corporate capitalism.

THEORETICAL ASSUMPTIONS

The argument I make about the interrelatedness of Gilded Age views of success, manhood, and the legitimation of the new industrial order builds on two propositions well-established by the work of other scholars. Though my research provides data that help show the usefulness and accuracy of these propositions, it is not the goal of this book to prove them. I take them as givens; they are underlying assumptions that together provide the analytic constructs and the context through which to interpret the success manual.

First, I assume that a particular social, political, or economic order partly achieves and helps maintains its hegemony or dominance by the complex and subtle cultural process of legitimation—winning the consent, or at least the acquiescence, of the governed.[16] This is especially true in modern democratic states, where violent political force is not a visible, everyday reality for most people. The electoral process and a welter of public and private, commercial, cultural, and social institutions help establish a sense among the general population that fundamental, underlying social arrangements—such as class relations, the functioning of the economy, the structure and operations of government—are normative, legitimate, and above serious challenge. For societies in which power relationships are already well-established, the legitimation process may result in the simple, tacit agreement not to question fundamental social, political, and economic arrangements. Societies in crisis or in transition to a new social order, as the United States was in the Gilded Age, witness more active and overt operations of this ideological process. In such situations, those who identify their interest with an established order defend themselves, their institutions, and their view of the world against the challenge of critics, dissenters, and naysayers or against the threat of social change that seems to undermine traditional values.

I believe that the success manual can be seen as part of the cultural apparatus that helped legitimize and establish the hegemony of the new industrial order that emerged in the Gilded Age. Success writers addressed those whom they viewed as in danger of losing faith in the industrial age, and they offered advice and a view of the world that encouraged readers to reconcile themselves to the uncertain, sometimes unpromising possibilities it represented. Yet I do not see the writers of success manuals as self-conscious ideologues in the service of the plutocrats of the new industrial order. In general, success writers were small-time but ambitious ministers, educators, and publicists who were in a good position to take the pulse of those in the American heartland. They discovered a market for advice about how to get on in life, and they no doubt hoped that by meeting this demand through the sale of advice books they might win for themselves success of the pecuniary sort while offering much-needed encouragement and reassurance to their public. These writers' roots were in preindustrial Jeffersonian America, and their message contained a critique as well as a defense of the new order. Their individualism, their celebration of a producer ethic, their attack on inherited privilege, their advocacy of success in nonpecuniary terms coexisted uneasily with a celebration of the possibilities for success in the new order.

Insofar as success manuals ultimately helped to legitimize the new industrial order, it was most likely the unintended consequence of authorial activity that had as its primary concern rather different and more immediate goals: namely, to reach an ever larger audience and achieve success of their own through the sale of advice books while carrying the torch of the values and virtues of a bygone era to a new generation. Success writers' enthusiasm for the possibilities of the new order is consistent with their own identification with its hopes and promises. The moralistic view of the world that they presented, one in which individual willpower held sway, was not unlike the view that many other Americans held. Americans of the Gilded Age generally lacked the conceptual tools and experience needed to grasp the degree to which the power to affect one's own destiny had been removed from the individual, the family, and the local community and concentrated in a complex maze of interdependent, impersonal forces. Success manual readers apparently welcomed guidance about how to weather the storm of change and find a way to prosper, or at least to hold on to what they had. Whatever their personal motivations, neither the writers nor the readers of success manuals were in a position to see clearly the larger implications of embracing the values of an earlier era as the key to success in a new world of industrial capitalism.[17]

My second assumption has to do with symbolic language, and particularly with gendered language. I assume that language has symbolic as well as literal significance; furthermore, that *gendered* language can be a way of expressing meanings and legitimizing power relationships that may not be primarily or directly about gender; and finally, that the power and meaning of important unitary concepts are often established by their sometimes unspoken or presumed opposite. This perspective, outlined by Joan Scott in her *Gender and the Politics of History* and other works, provides an interpretive framework for two central features of the success manual: the tendency to masculinize and even sexualize success and the tendency to portray a bipolar, "either/or" world. In language that now often seems humorous, success manuals presented a "sink or swim" world in which "potent spirits" and "erect and constant character" could bring success to the truly manly man. Scott argues first that meaning is made through "implicit or explicit contrasts" or "binary oppositions," and second, that gender is a way to signify and legitimize power relationships or concepts of power even when they "are not always literally about gender itself." In summary, she writes: "[C]onceptual languages employ differentiation to establish meaning[,] and sexual difference is a primary way of signifying differentiation. Gender, then, provides a way to decode meaning and to understand the complex connections among various forms of human interaction."[18] The masculinized, bipolar worldview articulated in the success manual constitutes such a conceptual language. A close reading of this language shows that the concept of manhood and manliness was used as a way to make distinctions among men, to identify a particular type of man with success in the new order, and to promote a particular set of behaviors as appropriate for the new age. In this sense, the success manuals, in their obsession with a potent type of manhood and, by implication, obsession also with fear of its opposite—that is, inadequacy, failure, loss of manhood, effeminacy— suggest one of the ways in which men learned to accept and internalize the discipline of the new order. Manhood became a form of *self-discipline*, a new code of behavior enforced by stigmatization of those who failed to practice it. The hopes and fears associated with the concept of manhood may be part of what Norbert Elias has explained as the "civilizing process." [19]

In the success manual, "manhood" and "manliness" signify the man who is dominant over all other men by virtue of behaviors and attitudes that are consistent with legitimation of the new industrial order. [20] The success of this special type of self-disciplined manhood became one and the same with the dominance of the new order. Simultaneously, the fear of failure became the fear of loss of manhood. Gender or genderized language in success manuals thus became a means to establish the dominance of ideas and ideals that had little to do with gender. [21] But the use of gender to legitimize nongender concepts usually also has at least indirect roots in and implications for gender. The genderized concept of success built upon, reinforced, and elaborated existing stereotypes about sex roles and gender relationships. [22] The conceptual power of the equation of success and manhood was based on the opposition inherent in the two terms: success versus failure and manliness versus womanliness. To put it another way, the power of the linkage of success with manhood was underwritten by the power of the less overt linkage of failure with womanhood. Insofar as the equation of success and manhood became normative, it became difficult to imagine a successful woman who was not "manly" or to believe that a woman could be "a success" in the world of work and politics outside the home.

THE HISTORICAL SETTING

The years in which success manuals emerged and flourished—1870–1910— were watershed years during which a new industrial order emerged and established its hegemony in all aspects of American life, cultural and social as well as economic and political. In a wrenching, all-encompassing process that Alan Trachtenberg has called "the incorporation of America," a "changed, more tightly structured society with new hierarchies of control" emerged, consisting of "not only the expansion of an industrial capitalist system across the continent, not only tightening systems of transport and communication, the spread of a market economy into all regions of what Robert Weibe has called a 'distended society,' but also, and even predominantly, the remaking of cultural perceptions this process entailed," that is, the emergence of "a changed conception of that society, of America itself."[23] These were the years in which Americans became painfully aware of the fact that the much-heralded industrial age had the capacity to punish as well as to reward.[24] Rapid economic growth and rising per capita wealth coexisted with international depression from 1873 to 1896. A Wall Street crash in 1873 induced an epidemic of bankruptcies and failures in the United States, 6,000 businesses closing in 1874 and as many as 900 a month in 1878. A perilously erratic business cycle continued for more than twenty years, touching all sections of the economy: inexplicable surpluses and declining world prices, tightening credit, and foreclosure for farmers; wage reductions, layoffs, irregular employment, and deteriorating conditions, even starvation, for industrial workers.[25]

Also in these years it became obvious that the tremendous growth and transformation of the American economy brought with it—even in the best of times—a wide range of social consequences, some of which were far from beneficial. The fascination of some people with the well-reported doings of the Astors, Carnegies, and Vanderbilts was tempered by the growing awareness throughout society of a class of desperately poor. Such visible extremes of wealth and poverty raised the specter of a two-class society in which opportunity for the average man might be curtailed. Along with these forebodings came the fear of corruption and vice, focusing especially on the city—the suspected refuge of foreigners, Catholicism, political "bossism," gambling, liquor, prostitution, socialism, and all forms of ungodliness. For the middling sort of native-born, Protestant, small-town American, such fears may have been a displacement of other anxieties closer to home, where everything from the decline of self-employment to the rise of the New Woman and the advent of Darwinism threatened to change the way people worked, lived, and believed. Whatever the specific focus, some Americans, even those who enjoyed the gains in prosperity and life-improving advances brought by industrialization, were apprehensive about what they saw or experienced as the social consequences of the industrial age, changes that might jeopardize the American tradition of individual opportunity, undermine the moral order of the nation, or threaten the legitimacy of the social order.

Because turmoil was so widespread, no one was totally immune from the crisis of the Gilded Age. Americans were confronted with important questions about where their interests lay and with whom they would identify. For some, the answer to the question would be shaped by the concrete economic and social changes that swirled around them. For others, answers would come from their interpretation of those changes, their view of the world, which pivoted about their view of the new industrial order and how they saw their own place within that new society. Success manual readers were most likely to have been native-born, Protestant, rural and small-town farmers, mechanics, clerks, and storekeepers of modest means—people at the epicenter of economic shock produced by the new industrial order. In their ideology of self-reliance and self-sufficiency, they were the social incarnation of American yeomanry, and they represented a sector of the population whose prospects would be radically narrowed and redefined in the new age. They were the lower echelon of what C. Wright Mills called the "old middle-class" of independent, self-employed property owners.[26]

Competing interests vied for the attention and allegiance of those in this broad American mainstream. The same family who might entertain a book agent selling success manuals that hailed the virtues and victories of the man who could "go it alone" might also attend a huge, open-air meeting to hear a speaker from the Farmers' Alliance explain the advantages of joining others in a cooperative movement to defeat or bypass the bankers, merchants, and railroad and grain elevator operators who they believed robbed them of their profits. The same population from which critics of the new order such as the Knights of Labor, the People's Party, and the Socialist Party recruited membership was also the market for the new magazine and mail-order industry that provided readers a glimpse of the consumer comforts and enticements of an idealized middle-class home, providing both evidence of what the new industrial order could provide and a preview of the life that could be enjoyed by those who succeeded in it.[27] Then again, these same families may have studied one of the most famous Sunday school tracts of all times, *Our Country* (1886), Josiah Strong's vision of America imperiled by materialism, immigration, Catholicism, Socialism, and intemperance.[28]

Americans who felt uncertain or caught in the middle expressed their views on the larger social questions about the legitimacy of the new industrial order de facto, in the answers they accepted to a myriad of concrete and pressing personal questions and anxieties. Most demanding of the attention of young men and of the parents seeking to guide their sons were questions and anxieties about how to earn a living, what to believe, how to behave, and how to be a man. The fact that so many Americans confronted a new range of perplexing questions and anxiety-producing decisions helped to create a market for information and advice of all kinds, especially for advice of a general nature about how to get on in life. The success manual was one source to which Americans might turn to find answers to their questions and doubts. How the success manual answered these questions and addressed these doubts is the subject of this book.

1

The Success Manual of the Gilded Age

☞

The Royal Path of Life is the best book (aside from the Bible) I ever saw.
— The Reverend J. W. Wharf

THE SUCCESS MANUAL AS CULTURAL FORM

Books that told how to get on in life were not new in the Gilded Age, but success manuals took on a special significance. They were not the works of a single author—a Benjamin Franklin or a Horatio Alger—but were produced by many different authors. And yet success manuals were as much or more alike as the products of any one author could possibly be. In this sense, the success manual genre was a formulaic literature, like those of popular fiction genres such as westerns, mysteries, and gothic novels. Like these fiction genres, success manuals faithfully reproduced a structure of elements and conventions that constituted a standardized pattern or formula.[1] Many of the themes and ideas of success manuals were prefigured in the sermons, speeches, commencement addresses, newspaper and magazine articles, and pamphlets published in the 1850s and 1860s.[2] A handful of book-length works suggestive of the later success manual format were also published in these midcentury decades.[3] But in the 1870s, the success manual emerged as a distinct, recognizable, and easy-to-duplicate literary form: a large, didactic, nonfiction volume offering advice on how to succeed in life.[4] Certain ideas and values of the 1850s and 1860s had been distilled into a commodity. This commodity was then offered for sale in a market much expanded by the work of traveling book agents, who sold success manuals by subscription the length and breadth of the land, reaching even the most isolated homesteads and frontier settlements. The success manual was a special type of book that by the turn of the century had become a standard item to millions of Americans.

Success manuals had more in common than their familiar literary formulas and conventions. These books looked alike—they shared certain characteristic physical and structural elements of size, binding, organization, and layout. They are artifacts of their particular culture and can be studied as such. Furthermore, they had in common the specific historical and social circumstances of their emergence and growth into a widely popular genre: they were the product of a unique stage in America's industrial transformation, they were addressed to a specific audience, written by a particular type of author, produced by a certain sector of the book industry, and sold through a special new marketing system. The same structure of elements, the same message, was duplicated in many individual works and in turn distributed widely throughout the country. Year after year, more and more people bought these books. Commercial success stimulated further production, distribution, and even higher sales. Taken together, this entire range of shared elements—literary, physical, socioeconomic, and ideological—constitute the distinct entity that defines the success manual. It can be understood not only as a popular literary genre in its own right but as a singular cultural phenomenon, a cultural form that expressed something of importance to the society in which it emerged.[5] Taken together as a body of works and considering all of their elements from the most basic to the seemingly trivial, success manuals provide a window on the social psychology of a society moving toward a new industrial order. In their advice—telling people what to do, what to believe, and how to behave in a changing world—they offer a special glimpse of the underlying hopes and fears, tensions and ambiguities of the age. The success manual constituted a popular cultural form through which a wide range of often contradictory ideas, values, and beliefs were expressed, systematized, and ultimately harmonized.

Everything about the success manual—from its elaborate binding and size to its sweeping promises, from its personalized sales techniques to its high price—conveyed the sense that *here* was a book of substance and importance. In certain respects, the success manual was like the most serious and popular of all works, the Bible. Like the Bible, the success manual was imbued with a sense of right and wrong; the Bible gave commandments, the manual offered precepts. The success manual had, in the form of self-made men, "apostles" whose lives set examples for others to follow. And though the success manual offered a secular gospel, the goal of which was to achieve success in life, ultimately its definition of true success, like the Bible's definition of true righteousness, made material achievement secondary to a loftier calling—the development of true character and manhood. Finally, many success manuals looked like Bibles; some were actually published by "Bible Houses." Such qualities may have contributed to the success manuals' appeal. The Reverend J. W. Wharf stated this point of view simply in his endorsement printed in the back pages of one of the most popular of all success manuals: "*The Royal Path of Life* is the best book (aside from the Bible) I ever saw."[6]

THE SUCCESS MANUAL AS MASS-MARKET COMMODITY:
THE SUBSCRIPTION BOOK INDUSTRY

The success manual was a commercial as well as a literary phenomenon. It was a commodity designed for a particular audience, produced and distributed by an aggressive new sector of the book publishing industry, and offered for sale in a vast new marketplace. The circumstances of the success manual's appearance as a commodity destined for mass distribution is an important part of its story.

The book trade in the Gilded Age was plagued by a number of difficulties that impeded its growth. Many publishers regarded their work as a "career" rather than a "business" and were motivated more by a sense of commitment and devotion to bringing out "good" books than by the drive to maximize profits. This attitude did not generate innovation in business methods and techniques. Unlike the more successful newspaper and magazine publishers, many book publishers made little effort to address a wide audience or to appeal to popular tastes. These publishers were slow to adopt advertising or other promotional methods, and most paid little attention to marketing and distributing their books effectively. Furthermore, overproduction kept profits low. The industry published many new titles each year; given the fact that the only way to make a profit was to distribute the nonrecurring production costs over a large number of copies of individual works, and given the fact that most books were not promoted in any way, the chances of a publisher even breaking even on most books was very slim.[7]

Few publishers, however, could long afford to assume a stance that exalted intellectual ideals over the expedience of making a living, particularly in an age in which such ideals competed with the flowering of entrepreneurial talent and opportunity. But even for publishers who were more businesslike in their approach, a major obstacle to the book trade's development into a modern, mass-production, mass-distribution industry was the wide geographic distribution of the American consumer in small towns and rural areas all across the country. In 1870, 28 million people, almost two-thirds of the population, lived in areas defined as "rural territory," places with less than 2,500 inhabitants.[8] Bookstores, on the other hand, were located in the large towns and cities and were the last kind of business to migrate to newly settled areas.[9] In 1859, there were 843 locales with bookstores. By 1914, that number had actually dropped to 801.[10] For this reason, enterprising publishers sought other means to market books. One alternative was to sell through jobbers to other retail outlets, such as stationers, news dealers, and dry goods stores. Dealers in toys, paper, fancy goods, notions, drugstore items, and pictures and picture frames were all likely to handle books as well.[11] Another alternative to bookstore sales was mail order. Through advertising in newspapers and magazines and the distribution of circulars and catalogs a publisher might reach a book-buying audience directly without incurring the cost of a middleman.[12]

But the method that proved by far the most effective in getting books into the hands of the American public, and the method responsible for the majority of success manual sales, was subscription selling.[13] The key to this system was the book agent: a traveling salesman who canvassed door-to-door, soliciting "subscriptions" or orders for the purchase of a particular volume. The publisher provided the agent with a prospectus that was a dummy of the book being offered for sale. It included table of contents, selections from the book itself, testimonials of satisfied customers, and order sheets to list the names of those who had already subscribed. This was bound in one of the more elaborate versions of the bindings available with purchase. An order received constituted a contract between the buyer and the agent. When the agent had collected a number of subscriptions, he ordered the requisite books from the publisher. He collected payment from the customer when he returned and delivered the book.[14]

The subscription trade had its heyday in the half century after the Civil War.[15] Publishing houses devoted exclusively to subscription sales depended for their profits on the size of their corps of book agents in the field. At the close of the war they recruited large numbers of demobilized soldiers, who greatly expanded the book-selling business.[16] The effectiveness of these veterans was enhanced by the nature of the works many peddled in these years, for some of the best-selling subscription books were histories and memoirs of the war itself. Joseph T. Headley's *The Great Rebellion* sold 150,000 copies, and Horace Greeley's *American Conflict* sold 250,000.[17] This experience demonstrated to the publishing industry as a whole both the effectiveness of subscription selling and the vastness of an untouched market for books in the rural part of the country.[18]

In the 1860s and 1870s, some twelve firms devoted exclusively to the subscription trade made Hartford, Connecticut, the center of the subscription industry. Together these twelve houses were estimated to have employed

50,000 agents in any given year.[19] In subsequent years, subscription houses and general book agencies for distributing books by subscription grew up in major cities across the nation. Much of the "regular" or "legitimate" trade held the subscription trade in low esteem. They considered themselves above such peddling and anticipated the demise of subscription sales with urbanization.[20] But to the dismay of bookstore owners, who were passed over by the subscription publishers,[21] regular publishers began to employ book agents to sell some of their titles, and the subscription business grew rather than declined. By the 1890s, the annual sales volume of the subscription trade amounted to more than $12 million, and most large publishing houses had established separate subscription departments that employed a regular staff of book agents.[22]

The subscription industry addressed the very problems that impeded sales in the regular trade. They concentrated on titles that they believed would have a wide general appeal,[23] especially items that might capitalize on that little-exploited market of aspiring middle-class Americans. In addition to success manuals, the subscription trade specialized in Bibles and devotional guides; one-volume encyclopedias and dictionaries; collected biographies, histories, and travel accounts that focused on sensational events; and practical treatises on housekeeping, gardening, livestock, medical care, legal transactions, and letter-writing.[24] Most subscription books were nonfiction, although many of Mark Twain's novels and a few sets of European classics were also sold by this method. Subscription publishers took few risks; they looked for books with sure sales potential, at times picking up titles that had already demonstrated high sales in the regular trade.[25] By identifying certain types of works with good sales records, subscription houses were able to publish large editions of a relatively small number of titles with fair assurance of a good return.[26]

In addition to the rationalization of such crucial production decisions as which books would sell widely, the strategy that most enabled the otherwise slow-moving book industry to expand its market and increase sales was the door-to-door canvass. One scholar has estimated that as many as 90 percent of book buyers in the late nineteenth century never entered a bookstore.[27] A book sold in a bookstore was at a disadvantage not only because of the limitations in number and locations of the stores but also because this kind of retail selling depended entirely on the motivation of the customer, who had to want a book in the first place, seek out a store that sold books, and then select, usually unaided, from among hundreds of different titles.[28] The book agent, on the other hand, greatly multiplied the sales potential of each title. He reached customers who lived far from the large cities, those who in many cases had no other access to reading material. The agent not only brought the books to the customers, he sold the idea of buying books to people who otherwise might not have perceived the need.[29]

Book agents were aided by small handbooks containing tips on how to sell, which were provided to them by the subscription houses. These little booklets provide an inside glimpse of the industry, its aims, and its methods. They show, for example, that the *idea of success* was central to the subscription method and to the pitch that agents developed. Subscription publishers attempted to appeal to the aspirations for success of their agents and through them to their potential customers. This was clear from the use of the word "success" in titles of some of these booklets, for example, "The General Agent's Guide to Success" or "Success in Canvassing, A Manual of Practical Hints and Instruction Specially Adapted to the Use of Book Canvassers of the Better Class."[30] Some agents' handbooks included a few pages of success maxims in the front or back pages,[31] and their model sales pitch was designed to play on people's hopes for success and fears of failure. According to one guide to canvassing, the question a book agent must ask a potential customer to consider was not "Can I afford it?" but "Can I afford to be without it?" The pitch continued:

> I am aware that many people would have no particular use for such a library, but I was of the opinion that you would appreciate its advantages. . . . In professional, mercantile or mechanical life a man's growth is in proportion to the amount of knowledge and nerve force he brings to bear upon his work. It is not a question of size or physical strength; nor is it scarcely a question of age—we see very young and very old people break forth into success. It is a question of knowledge and mental *acumen*.[32]

The book agent's success was further enhanced by the fact that he did not travel with a whole *list* of works, but rather focused on one or two volumes at a time.[33] By devoting his power of persuasion to a single book, he avoided confronting potential buyers with what might have been a difficult choice, and even further enhanced the chances of high sales for the one title he was promoting. In 1879, *Publishers' Weekly* commented bitterly on the effectiveness of this method:

> It cannot . . . be denied that an insistent book agent of the orthodox type, pushing with all high might and main at a single book, and invading, if necessary, the sanctity even of the back kitchen, has it in his power to sell more copies of that book, which for the moment he backs against the whole body of literature, sacred and profane, than

the dealer who handles and pushes a general stock, expecting people to come to him instead of going to them.[34]

One final element that helped to assure the wide distribution of titles sold by subscription was the fact that each was sold by many different agents simultaneously in different parts of the country. The American Publishing Company, a subscription house in Hartford, printed 223 prospectuses between November 1878 and December 1879 for a success manual by Mathew Hale Smith entitled *Successful Folks*.[35] Since each agent needed only a single prospectus, it is likely that the company planned to send 223 agents into the field on behalf of this one book. Some general agencies are known to have employed as many as 5,000 agents overall, while *Publishers' Weekly* reported in 1894 that there were 20,000 independent book agents in Chicago alone.[36] All of these special advantages that the subscription industry enjoyed over the regular book trade meant that there was no better way to sell a book in late-nineteenth-century America than by subscription.

Most success manuals were sold by subscription. There are three features that identify a book produced for the subscription trade: an inscription on the title page reading "Sold by Subscription Only"; a distinctive size, quality, and format typical of subscription books; and the name of the publisher, as some companies can be identified as subscription publishers. The best single resource for identifying subscription publishing houses is the Library of Congress collection of book agent's handbooks, which were published by subscription firms to teach their agents how to sell. However, since all books that were *sold* by subscription were not necessarily *produced* by and for the subscription industry, it is impossible to identify them all. Some books produced by regular publishing houses were sold both in bookstores and by subscription. Nonetheless, many success manuals are identifiable as subscription books using the methods just described. Moreover, those with the best sales records are known to have been subscription books. Finally, subscription was known to be the major book sales method of the period. These facts are the basis for claiming that the majority of success manuals were sold by subscription.

The subscription industry helped to turn the success manual into a mass-market commodity, making it available to many more people than would have been possible without the door-to-door canvass. But the subscription industry did not create the success manual or establish it as a popular genre. The fact that subscription publishers selected success manuals as one of the kinds of works to handle is evidence that this genre had already attained a measure of popular acceptance before it was revamped and turned over to the skill and persuasion of the book agent. Success manuals published early in this period and sold through the regular trade, at least in their earliest edition—such as Smiles's *Self-Help* (1860), Mathews's *Getting On in the World* (1873), and Whipple's *Success and Its Conditions* (1871)—established the genre and provided the model that was duplicated in later success manuals prepared for the subscription trade. By the end of the 1870s, the success manual was well-established as a commercially viable product and was to become one of the mainstays of the subscription trade through the 1880s, 1890s, and early 1900s. The subscription sales method was important in promoting success manuals, but it cannot alone explain their popularity. Subscription selling could not create "best-sellers" out of books that no one really wanted. Many people had to want these particular books, or at least want what these books seemed to represent. Success manuals sold well and became important as a popular form of literature because they had a special appeal. Just by looking at the prospectus of a book such as *Masters of the Situation* or *Pushing to the Front* or any one of dozens of similar titles, millions of people saw something that struck a chord within, and they were moved to invest handsomely to own such a book for themselves and their families. The sheer number of such sales makes it clear that the success manual in some way represented ideas and themes that had special meaning for a large sector of the American population during this period.

Sales and Circulation

Even as early as 1890, years before success manual production and sales peaked, so many different success manuals had already been published that success writers felt a need to justify the presentation of yet one more volume of this type. Tilley prefaced his *Masters of the Situation* with the following explanation:

> Truth is as old as the world. As no two, however, see exactly the same rainbow, so no truth presents itself to all alike. So much has been written, we are told, that it is no longer possible even to appear original. Yet all will agree that the manner of presenting old truths is of the first importance. . . . Many of us can understand the feeling which prompted him who failing to find in his library the book he wanted, went to work and made one. On the other hand, at rare intervals we have found the books we wanted, as well, only to rise from its perusal with a keener appetite for others like it. One can hardly read certain books without instinctively wishing for more like them. . . . Of such there cannot be too many.[37]

At least 13 success manuals were published in the 1870s, 25 more in the 1880s, another 38 in the 1890s, and 68 more in the first decade of the twentieth century, totaling 144 different success manuals known to have been published between 1870 and 1910.[38] Tilley might have been even more defensive had he realized that his success manual would be only one of the more than thirty-eight published in that decade. But in fact even then he need not have worried about this apparent glut, for the American market for success manuals was far from saturated in 1890.[39] Sales and circulation were never higher. This was the decade in which Orison Swett Marden published his *Pushing to the Front*, a success manual that went through 250 editions, and this was just the first of his thirty success books and pamphlets.[40] These success manuals joined others published in the 1870s and 1880s that were still selling strong. The "best-seller," Haines and Yaggy's *The Royal Path of Life*, first published in 1876, was building toward its sales total of 800,000 copies.[41] The works of the Scottish self-help writer Samuel Smiles were published in this country and became what Frank Luther Mott considers "better sellers." ("Best seller," by Mott's definition, sold a number of copies equal to at least 1 percent of the U.S. population in the decade of publication; "better sellers" sold slightly less than this number.) Taken together, Smiles's books, *Self-Help* (1860), *Character* (1871), *Thrift* (1875), and *Duty* (1880), sold over one million copies in the United States.[42]

Success manuals generally had long and vigorous selling lives, which in turn encouraged more and more would-be success writers to enter the field. In 1873, financial writer and University of Chicago professor of rhetoric and English literature William Mathews published *Getting On in the World, or Hints on Success in Life*, based on a series of self-help articles he had written for the Chicago *Tribune* in 1871.[43] *Getting On in the World* went through at least seven editions in its first year of publication, and by 1882 Mathews's publisher claimed to have printed 50,000 copies. New editions continued to appear through the turn of the century.[44] In 1883, Presbyterian minister and temperance reformer Wilbur F. Crafts published *Successful Men of Today*. Just four years later, 38,000 copies were in circulation.[45] Jerome Paine Bates's *The Imperial Highway* (1881) and Harry A. Lewis's *Hidden Treasures, or Why Some Succeed While Others Fail* (1887) both went through multiple editions in the first few years following initial publication, and both were still in print for the 1902 and 1912 compilations of the *U.S. Catalog of Books*.[46]

Multiple imprints made it possible to circulate any given success manual by more than one publisher simultaneously, thus boosting sales even higher. *Hidden Treasures*, for example, was sold by publishing companies in Chicago, Cleveland, Indianapolis, Meadville (Pennsylvania), New York, and Springfield (Massachusetts) in the same years. Year after year these and dozens of other success manuals were reprinted, and new editions were issued. The spectacular sales of certain titles, the generally good sales, multiple editions, and long selling lives of many if not most, coupled with the publication of dozens of new titles each decade meant that by the turn of the century there were well over one hundred different success manuals in print and several million copies in circulation.

Audience

Although it is impossible to know exactly who bought and read success manuals, it is possible to learn a good deal about the intended audience by what the manuals say in prefaces, text, back-page endorsements and advertisements, and from the advice in book agents' handbooks about where, how, and to whom to sell. With this information—along with circumstantial evidence provided by price, demographics, and knowledge of the subscription book industry that produced and distributed most success manuals—it is possible to make some reasonable generalizations about their actual audience. In general, it can be said that the audience for success manuals was a rural and small-town population of native-born Protestants, people of modest means and modest educations, yet people of some aspiration, not the destitute or the dispossessed. Furthermore, success manuals were most clearly targeted for an audience of young men and the parents of sons who were anxious to provide them guidance.

Part of the evidence that the success manual was essentially a rural, small-town phenomenon is that the subscription trade that produced and sold most success manuals specifically targeted this untapped market. In 1890, nearly two-thirds of the United States population still lived in rural areas.[47] Book agents deployed by regional supervisors reached even the most isolated homesteads and distant frontiers. In many thousands of instances they provided their customers' only contact with reading material.[48] The book salesman followed the circuit rider and the district schoolmaster, bringing "civilization" to the great American hinterland.[49] Subscription publishers alerted their book agents to the special advantages of this rural market in sales instruction booklets such as the Success Company's *Work Plans and How to Work Them*:

> Canvassing country territory is the ABC's of agency work. Social conditions are simpler, the time of country people is not so much distracted by this or that, there is less competition from stores and other solicitors, and the democratic and hospitable traditions of country people render it very much easier to secure a sufficient hearing than in

any other field. Country people are thrifty, they are good pay, they are ambitious for their children and they are more susceptible to the influence of testimonials and the orders of others than any other class.[50]

The location of subscription publishing companies also suggests access to a broad rural market. Publishers established subscription houses in almost every section of the country—from Hartford, Connecticut, to Portland, Oregon, from Chicago to Kansas City and Dallas. The largest concentration of subscription publishers, especially toward the end of the nineteenth century was in the Midwest as opposed to the eastern cities of Boston and New York, which were the strongholds of the regular trade. Cities such as Cincinnati, St. Louis, Indianapolis, and Kansas City, as well as Chicago, had thriving subscription companies and made practical locations from which to dispatch agents into the surrounding countryside.[51]

Finally, the texts of success manuals reveal an attempt to address concerns of a rural and small-town audience. Time and time again, success writers celebrated the farm over the city and the valuable lessons learned in rural life. In *The New Day*, Russell Conwell praised what he called that "substratum of character and principle which saves the cities from utter ruin . . . the firm moral and religious beliefs held by the largest and most successful part of the city population, most of whom were reared, at least to youth, on a farm."[52]

Success writers exalted that which belonged to the everyday experience of ordinary people as key to success, praised the values of rural life, expressed contempt for all that was alien and urban, and generally seemed to try to keep the boys home on the farm. William Mathews claimed that 99 percent of those coming from the country to the city failed.[53] William James Tilley insisted that the city "created wants" the farm dwellers could not imagine, and he worried about the "great hordes of young men making [their] way to the city not knowing how to live on small pay."[54] For those bound and determined to join this migration, Edward Bok advised young men to choose smaller cities,[55] and John T. Dale, in a chapter entitled "How To Get Rich," assured his readers that opportunities for wealth were "all in the rich, unoccupied country we still have only partially developed."[56]

Had success manuals been aimed at an urban or foreign-born audience in this period, references to the immigrant experience or some appeal to ethnicity might have been expected. Instead, such references were rare, and when they did occur, it was in a nativist context. "Foreigners," to one success writer, were the "refuse" of Europe.[57] In general, the foreign born, when mentioned at all, were associated with radicalism and with the lazy, spendthrift ways of the irresolute. Consistent with the nativism was the explicit Protestantism of these works. Protestant clergyman were a strong presence in success manuals, as authors, endorsers, and quoted authorities. The warnings against the evils of liquor, tobacco, and intemperance of all kinds; the emphasis on Christian character, church membership, and observance of the Sabbath; as well as the anticity, antiforeigner rhetoric all suggest a literature designed with a world of rural, native-born Protestants in mind. This is not say that success manuals did not appear on the shelves of city bookstores and in other retail outlets, nor is it to say that the success manual was an exclusively rural phenomenon. Rather, it is to suggest that in a time when a large majority of Americans still resided in small towns and country territories, it was they who were the target population for success manuals and accounted for a large majority of their sales.

Within this general definition of the market, success manual sales were more narrowly targeted for a sector of the population sometimes referred to as the "middling sort." They were aimed at farmers, skilled workers, tradesmen, and small proprietors, people of moderate incomes who had ambitions for something better—an "aspiring middle-class" who had both much to be anxious about and much to hope for with the emergence of a competitive new order. The likely buyer was well-off enough to afford such a book yet not so well-off as to be indifferent to advice about finding success; educated enough to read but not so educated as to be able to scrutinize too closely or critically. The advice in the book agents' handbook confirms this logic:

> Farmers, mechanics, clerks, intelligent laborers and factory operatives, miners, small shopkeepers and men of moderate means in general, are the best buyers of subscription books in the world. To pass these by, for the doubtful chances of larger sales among the wealthy and more highly educated classes will almost invariably prove a most serious mistake.[58]

Everything about the subscription sales method was designed to capitalize on this market. The book agent's handbook instructed him to establish a territory and begin canvassing by first visiting the respected members of the community—the ministers, the teachers, the businessmen—in order to solicit testimonials that might impress others in the region and convince them to subscribe. The model sales pitch made a direct appeal to ambition and status anxiety:

> It is too true that many mechanics do not hope or care to become masters; many clerks have no ambition to grow into proprietary merchants, and many people in general are not ambitious to go to the top in their lines of thought or action; but in your case it is different, and

you must also know the price of superiority along your line. . . . If any of us go to the top in our lines, we must avail ourselves of the modern facilities for success; that is, we must keep up with the times. If others were not getting this work you would stand an equal show with them without it; but improvement forces itself upon us in thought as well as in machinery.[59]

This pitch suggests a class-divided social order — "mechanics" and "masters," "clerks" and "proprietary merchants" — but one in which upward mobility appears possible. In this view of the world, each individual was arbiter of his own fate; the class line was permeable.

Though success manuals were clearly not designed for a well-to-do or sophisticated reader, neither were they aimed at the poor and destitute members of society. This is suggested not only in the advice to book agents about to whom to sell but also by the price of success manuals. The typical price range for success manuals sold by subscription was two to four dollars, depending on the choice of binding, and some were as high as five dollars.[60] In 1890, this represented one-quarter to one-half the weekly earnings of the average wage earner,[61] thus the purchase of a success manual represented a considerable investment for most families. The price is even more significant when one considers that many other books of the time were available to consumers at a fraction of this price. For example, the average price of a good-quality clothbound volume in a bookstore was one dollar to one and one-half dollars.[62] Lower prices like these were also typical of some of the more modest earlier editions of success manuals, which were not specifically designed for the subscription trade. Furthermore, in the years between 1870 and 1891, certain books were available for a fraction of even the bookstore prices, for this was also the era of the so-called "cheap book." These cheap books included serial libraries of the European classics, largely fiction, that sold in paper covers by mail and through newsstands for from ten cents to fifty cents a volume. With the exception of the works of Samuel Smiles (apparently also regarded as a European classic), success manuals were not available in this form. The low cost of the cheap books was made possible in part by the absence of an international copyright law until 1891. European works published before 1891 could be pirated by American publishers without incurring royalty or publication right fees.[63] When the *Sears, Roebuck and Company Consumers' Guide* offered to "fill your library with seventy-three titles for $20.44," Smiles's *Self-Help*, *Character*, and *Duty* were among the titles listed as part of the set (they were also available individually for twenty-seven cents).[64]

For most Americans, however, buying a success manual meant investing several dollars in a copious and elaborately bound volume. Possibly those who bought success manuals by subscription had no idea how expensive these works were compared to reading materials available from other sources; possibly the high price was part of the appeal—one of the symbols of value. In any event, Americans at the bottom of the socioeconomic scale were unlikely to have had either the cash or the hopefulness to have purchased an advice book of this type. The success manual was addressed to those on the lower rungs of a fragile middle class and the petite bourgeoisie, people of modest incomes and education who aspired to higher things and those who worried about how to hold on to what they had.

The texts of success manuals provide other clues that suggest authors and publishers were addressing more specifically an audience of young men. Dedications and introductions were typically addressed to "youth" and "young men." A few stressed the relevance of their message to those of all ages, and a few were addressed to "boys and girls," but in the chapters themselves the appeal is to young men who will soon have to earn a living for themselves. Success manuals emphasized starting out in life, cultivating the virtues that would help one succeed, building manhood, selecting a vocation, and the like. This does not mean, however, that young men were necessarily the primary purchasers of success manuals or even that they were necessarily the ones that a book agent might first approach. In a door-to-door canvass, it was quite unlikely that the "youth" or "young man" would be the family member to receive the solicitation or make the decision to purchase such a costly item. The book agent had to be prepared to deal with the woman or the man of the house. Thus success manuals, especially those designed for subscription sales, addressed parents and their concern about the future of their children, especially their sons. Testimonials urged "parents who could afford it" to add this or that success manual "to the attractions of the center table," and press notices recommended these volumes as invaluable aids for the inspiration and instruction of the young.[65] Furthermore, the subscription trade developed a sales approach and pitch designed specifically with parents in mind. The "educational canvass" began when the book agent met with the school superintendent and the teacher of a particular area, with the goal of obtaining a sale, a testimonial, and information about the pupils and their parents. With this accomplished, the agent next canvassed families in the area one by one. At each door he first announced that he was calling in regard to their son whom he mentioned by name, related some flattering comments the schoolteacher had made as to the boy's talents, and then invited himself in. Once inside, the model pitch began like this:

A boy's success does not depend so much upon what his parents teach him as upon the ambition his parents may succeed in instilling into him. . . . The fact that other parents have found out and are practicing these modern methods, which are of a kindergarten nature and which insure a steady growth of the child from the earliest period of perception, makes it all the more important for every parent to take advantage of these opportunities. The demands of the modern age are increasing; the same advantages that might have enabled us to succeed would not be sufficient to insure the success of children growing up in this rapid age. Success in life is undeniably a struggle between man and man for supremacy in thought and accomplishment. Some will be more successful, some less. If your boy is to stand equal show with those living in his age, he must avail himself of the same advantages which they utilize.[66]

This sales pitch not only illustrates an effort to play on fears and uncertainty, but reveals certain assumptions about what prospective customers might be anxious about. The question posed here was not only "Will my son do well?" but also, given the demands of the modern age and given the possibility that what once worked to bring success may no longer work, "Can my son compete with those who may have some special advantage?" Stated more broadly, the producers and marketers of success manuals and other subscription books assumed their audience was anxious about the prospects for themselves and their sons. They assumed that this population was worried about what to do and how to behave in a fast-moving, competitive new social order, and they capitalized on these fears through both the products they created and through their marketing techniques. They broadened their sales potential by addressing not just young men, but young men and boys within a family context. Many success manuals, especially those designed for subscription and especially those known to have sold well, combined their advice to young men on getting ahead with hints on etiquette and manners, essays on marriage, family and home life, and admonitions about moral conduct. Such material, along with use of illustrations, gave the success manual the status of a family book, enhancing its marketability among those who were not big book-buyers and to whom an appeal of "something for everybody" could be made.

Finally, though the success manual reached a broad geographic market in the Northeast, Midwest, and West, it was more a northern than a southern phenomenon. The fact that many success manual illustrations depicted Civil War battle scenes in which the North was victorious certainly suggests a northern market (see Figure 1). Second, the Southeast is the one section of the country not represented as a place of publication on success manual title pages. And finally, the population of the post–Civil War South would not have looked promising to either the subscription trade in general or the purveyors of success manuals in particular. The general postwar devastation and the extent of farm tenancy and sharecropping meant that fewer families in this region of the country fit the profile of the aspiring middling sort of independent proprietors, farmers, tradesmen, and clerks who most often bought success manuals and other subscription books.

Once purchased, to what extent did people actually read success manuals? Though it is impossible to know with any real certainty, the well-worn covers and tattered pages of remaining copies, the high sales figures and the longevity of the genre, the claims of some success writers of having received thank-you letters from satisfied readers, as well as the fact that so many of the success manual maxims still have a familiar ring today, all suggest that these works were widely read and that their message as well as their form became a part of the culture of the period. The fact that some volumes were personalized in special ways indicates that success manuals held a special place in their purchasers' esteem. One copy of *Pushing to the Front* was inscribed "Howard G. Mitchell from his Mother" and included a newspaper clipping pasted on the first page, an article entitled "Put Snap Into Your Work." A copy of *Getting On in the World* was inscribed "A. C. Dixon, Nov. 16th—G.T.R.R.—1877 Returning from Chicago—Underhill, Vermont." Pressed in its pages were two four-leaf clovers. Here was a man who was hedging his bet that a "pound of pluck was worth a ton of luck."

THE SUCCESS MANUAL AS ARTIFACT

Success manuals were generally imposing-looking volumes. Many were massive, elaborately bound works of 600, 700, even 800 pages. Even more modest versions of 300–400 pages had a look of authority and importance about them, with their gold-embossed titles, filigree designs, and leather or leather-like fabric covers in black or deep hues. The impressiveness of these books apparently contributed to their sales; some of the best-selling success manuals were the largest and most elaborate. One edition of the *Royal Path of Life*, reported to have sold 800,000 copies,[67] measured three inches thick at the spine, had a cover nine by seven inches, contained over 600 pages, and was bound in black leather with gold-engraved lettering and trim. The page edges were decorated with a marble design, and the inside covers were lined in glossy paper printed with a peacock-feather design of gold, scarlet, and royal blue. Even the high price of these works may have added to their appeal. The fact that a beautiful book on such an important subject could cost as much as four or five dollars—several day's wages for many people—was one measure of its value.[68] Such a volume was no ordinary reading material but a possession that appeared, even at a casual glance, to be something of considerable substance and worth (see Figure 2).

The size and binding were not the only way in which "success" was written on the covers of these works. The easiest way to tell a success manual at a glance was by its title. They all professed a central concern with finding success in life but typically did so in a way that left the meaning of success open to any number of interpretations. Did success mean wealth and fame? Personal happiness? Social respectability? Moral and spiritual rectitude? In titles such as Mathews's *Getting On in the World, or Hints on Success in Life* the meaning was not immediately apparent. The ambiguity carried over into the texts themselves, and the fact that readers might to some degree emphasize the interpretation that suited them no doubt added to the appeal of the success manuals. In addition to this generalized theme of "getting on in life," as in titles such as Dale's *The Way to Win* and Bates's *The Imperial Highway*, most full titles actually contained the word "success." This may seem an obvious point, but in literature considered in the success tradition and published before this period, such as Benjamin Franklin's *The Way to Wealth* (1757) or Freeman Hunt's *Worth and Wealth* (1856), the word "success" was rarely used in titles or in the text itself.[69]

Turning the first page of a success manual would reveal a title page that contained a good deal more than the title, though in some cases the title itself might take up a large share of the available space. Consider, for example, the full title of William James Tilley's volume: *Masters of the Situation or Some Secrets of Success and Power: A Volume Designed to Awaken in Its Readers by Precept and Example a Realizing Sense of the Vast and Inspiring Possibilities of Human Achievement Which Lie within the Reach of All*. From the title page, one would also learn the author's name, something of his occupation or qualifications, perhaps that he was a pastor or professor, his college degrees, or his other publications related to the success theme. In addition, one might see a brief quote or two from a famous person; a declaration of the number of illustrations included; possibly a statement that the book is "sold by subscription only"; sometimes a claim as to the number of editions already printed; the name, date, and place or places of publication, at times listing five or more different cities; occasionally a mention that the publisher was a "Bible House"; some kind of decorative engraving; and possibly a portrait of the author or an elaborate engraving of some kind on the opposite page (the frontispiece), separated by a page of tissue. In short, the title page was packed with information; it served as both a description of and an advertisement for the contents within.

After the title page came the table of contents and a list of illustrations. These listings could cover up to ten pages, because some success manuals had over 100 short, essay-like chapters (a format that seemed designed to appeal to the reader who might not have the time or inclination for prolonged periods of reading) *and* over 100 illustrations. Not all success manuals were illustrated, but the more popular ones—especially the ones known to be published and sold by subscription houses—generally were embellished with a variety of woodcuts, engravings, and portraits. This fact was boasted prominently on the title page: "Seventy-five Superb Portraits and Numerous Other Illustrations" or "Profusely Illustrated from Original Designs." [70]

The iconography of success manuals may be the single most revealing element of their physical makeup; these illustrations not only mirror im-

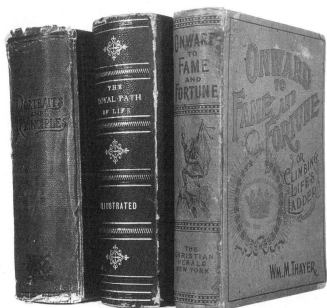

Figure 2. Books of substance and importance: *Portraits and Principles* by William C. King, *The Royal Path of Life* by Thomas L. Haines and Levi W. Yaggy, and *Onward to Fame and Fortune* by William M. Thayer. The ornate physical aspects of success manuals are easy to miss in library research, because the original volumes often have been rebound for preservation or microfilmed and destroyed. (Author's private collection, photograph by Josh Brown)

Figure 1. "Admiral Farragut Forces His Way into the Harbor of Mobile." Civil War battle scenes like this depiction of a Union victory illustrate both the importance of the battle metaphor and the success manuals' appeal to a northern market of subscription book buyers. (William M. Thayer, *Onward to Fame and Fortune*; courtesy General Research Division, New York Public Library, Astor, Lenox, and Tilden Foundations)

Figure 3. "Pizarro, on the Island of Gallo, Spurs His Comrades to the Conquest of Peru." Historic illustrations of combat and military conquest conveyed powerfully and graphically the imperatives of "the battle of life." (Thayer, *Onward to Fame and Fortune*; courtesy General Research Division, New York Public Library, Astor, Lenox, and Tilden Foundations)

Figure 4. "Gladiatorial Combat in the Arena." The one-on-one confrontation of the prizefight or the arena had special poignancy in success literature, which focused on individual achievement in a dog-eat-dog world. (Thayer, *Onward to Fame and Fortune*; courtesy General Research Division, New York Public Library, Astor, Lenox, and Tilden Foundations)

portant themes in the text but also provide clues about the intended audience of these works and may help account for part of their appeal. Pictures made the success manual a "family book," a book that the youngest member of the family as well as the oldest could enjoy, a book that could both edify and entertain regardless of the "reader's" level of literacy. Insofar as it was a large book with lots of pictures and insofar as it had something for everybody, it was a practical investment, a good buy at any price.

The subject matter of success manual illustrations was generally one of three types: battle scenes, portraits of famous men, and scenes of domestic life. Each type of illustration reinforced ideas that can be seen in the texts and in other aspects of these works. The idea that "life was a battle" was central to the success manual's worldview: success required a soldier-like stance to enable one to emerge the victor in the battle of business. Success manual illustrations took this idea out of the realm of the metaphoric and placed it squarely in the realm of the literal with historical scenes of warfare, combat, and military conquerors drawn from all times and places. In *Onward to Fame and Fortune*, for example, readers would find engravings of everything from Civil War battle scenes such as the fiery depiction entitled "Admiral Farragut Forces His Way into the Harbor of Mobile" and the imperialist "Pizarro, on the Island of Gallo, Spurs His Comrades to the Conquest of Peru," to the violent "Gladiatorial Combat in the Arena" (Figures 1, 3, and 4).[71] Though these illustrations almost always had titles that both identified the historical scene and conveyed the inevitability, indeed the urgency, of battle, they were not explained further in the text, nor was there a direct relationship between the illustrations and the text in which they were placed. In some success manuals, illustrations were scattered throughout in what appeared to be a random manner. Despite claims on some title pages, it is likely that most success manual illustrations were not "originals" prepared or designed especially for the particular volume in which they appeared. Most were probably borrowed from other types of books produced by the same publishers, such as popular histories, encyclopedias, and collected biographies. Such "borrowing" would be consistent with the strict cost-accounting methods employed by the subscription book publishing houses; their financial success was based on keeping production costs low as well as using aggressive marketing techniques.

The second type of illustration—portraits or engravings of famous men—shared certain characteristics of the battle scenes, in that many of them also were probably borrowed from other genres and represented a net cast wide in terms of the historical and geographic scope of their subject matter. The frontispiece of Orison Swett Marden's *Rising in the World, or Architects of Fate* featured a portrait of Columbus with the caption "Sail on, Sail on." William Makepeace Thayer's *Onward to Fame and Fortune* also pictured Columbus, this time in an engraving titled "The Night of October 11, 1492," depicting the explorer on board a sailing ship, staring intently out into the distance with charts in hand (Figure 5). William D. Owen's *Success in Life, and How to Secure It: or Elements of Manhood and Their Culture* began with a portrait of Sir Isaac Newton and the quotation "I have succeeded by putting my mind unto it."[72] William King's *Portraits and Principles* adopted the device of presenting composite portraits of men who had achieved prominence in particular fields, ranging from "Leading Bankers," "Prominent Manufacturers and Merchants," and "Great Railroad Men," to "Eminent Preachers" and "Sunday School Leaders," and including also "Great Statesmen," "Lawyers of Fame," "Honored Soldiers," "The World's Poets and America's Favorites," "Prominent Inventors," novelists, journalists, writers, educators, historians, and even a page of "Famous Women." Each of the composite illustrations featured reproductions of nine to twelve portraits, arranged as cameos surrounded by hand-drawn scrolled frames and nameplates (Figure 6).

A popular variation on the "great man" theme in success manual illustrations was the depiction of a well-known "self-made man" in his formative years. In an illustration entitled "Enterprise," Harry A. Lewis's *Hidden Treasures* pictured the young Cornelius Vanderbilt rowing his boatload of produce across the Hudson to the New York market (Figure 7). Another illustration, entitled "Determination," offered a rendering of Henry Clay in his youth: a small boy standing on a stool in a barnyard practicing the art of oratory to an attentive audience of cows, horses, and chickens (Figure 8).[73] These illustrations not only provided models, especially for young readers, but provided accessible models. They presented famous men in ways that the common man might be able to identify with. And they reinforced the idea of the "self-made man" by associating the names of the great with feats of individual virtue—"enterprise," "determination," and so forth—feats presumably within the capabilities of men of otherwise perhaps limited means. Making this connection may have seemed especially important to the producers of success manuals, because these illustrations are the ones that appear the most likely to have been "original designs," conceived and commissioned specifically for the success manual. Not only was their subject matter more specific to the context, but they were often crude woodcuts rather than the finely detailed engravings that seem likely to have been borrowed from encyclopedias or other works. Making certain points through illustration may have been important enough to warrant the commission of original artwork but not so important as to justify the expense of original professional-quality engravings. The quality of certain

Figure 5. "The Night of October 11, 1492." Many success manual illustrations not only described the qualities that would lead to success but also provided readers easy access to information about historic personages and events. This rendering of Columbus discovering America appeared opposite a chapter entitled "Perseverance." (Thayer, *Onward to Fame and Fortune*; courtesy General Research Division, New York Public Library, Astor, Lenox, and Tilden Foundations)

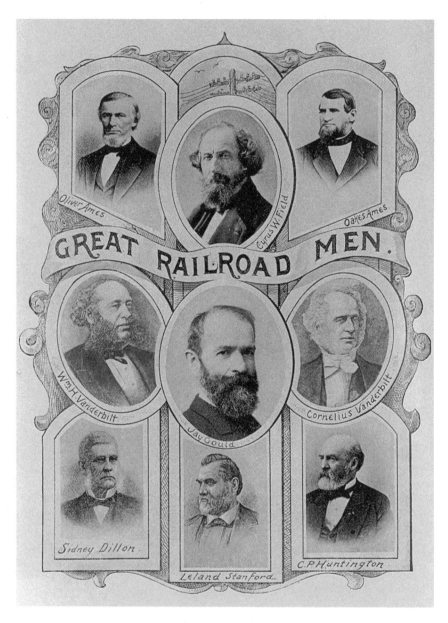

Figure 6. "Great Railroad Men." The title page of William C. King's *Portraits and Principles* boasted of "over 400 photo-engraved portraits of the World's Great Men and Women." These portraits of "Great Railroad Men" were joined by "Great Merchants," "Eminent Preachers," "Prominent Inventors," "Modern Writers," and others successful in many other categories and endeavors, providing a kind of pictorial who's who for the layperson. (Author's private collection, photograph by Josh Brown)

Figure 7. "Enterprise." This engraving represents the young Cornelius Vanderbilt rowing a boatload of produce across the Hudson River, presumably demonstrating the individual virtue upon which a great shipping empire might be built. (Harry A. Lewis, *Hidden Treasures*; courtesy General Research Division, New York Public Library, Astor, Lenox, and Tilden Foundations)

Figure 8. "Determination." This engraving rendered Henry Clay in his formative years on the family farm, practicing the oratory skills that would one day make him famous. (Lewis, *Hidden Treasures*; courtesy General Research Division, New York Public Library, Astor, Lenox, and Tilden Foundations)

success manual illustrations that appear "original" suggests the work of apprentice artists (to one observer, they looked as if they had been "engraved with a tablespoon"). Here, no doubt, was another concession to the profit-consciousness of the subscription book industry.

The third type of illustration—scenes of domesticity—suggested a very different world from that of combat or business. Here was the realm of the family and the hearthside, of peace and security. It was not only the place where the boy at mother's knee was set on the path of virtue and character-building that prepared him for the battle, it was also the refuge from that hostile world. Pastoral scenes of the proverbial vine-covered cottage, cozy front-room scenes of happy families, a collage representing the stages of life from childhood and schooling to old age and death—all spoke of these themes (Figures 9, 10, and 11). Furthermore, the juxtaposition of the domestic world with the world of battle suggests another important undercurrent in both the message and the appeal of success manuals: namely, parental anxiety about how their children would fare in the battle, how their offspring would do in a new, fast-moving, competitive order unlike that in which the parents had grown up. Illustrations dealing with the stages of life suggest this concern with the younger generation. The frontispiece engraving in *The Royal Path of Life*, titled "The Past and The Future," depicted a small boy in the lap of an old man (Figure 12). Another illustration, entitled "Leaving Home," showed a youth saying good-bye to his parents as he is about to set off down the road (Figure 13). Yet another, entitled "Trials of Life" and set in a chapter of the same title, conveys the difficulty of confronting the setbacks and failures in life; it depicts a man in grave conversation with a concerned-looking woman (Figure 14). The text does not mention women, but instead focuses on how hardship builds manhood and self-reliance. The illustration that best captures this sense of parental concern for the children's prospects is an engraving in Lewis's *Hidden Treasures*. It shows a mother looking worriedly over her small, sleeping son. The import of the picture comes across in its title, "Anxious Thoughts," and in its placement opposite a chapter entitled "Why Some Succeed While Others Fail" (Figure 15). All of these illustrations symbolize a world in which help in the form of instruction and family concern was needed in order to win victory in conflict, to acquire and preserve a life of comfort, security, and respectability, and to guide the younger generation in unknown paths.[74]

Taken together, all three types of illustration—battle scenes, portraits of prominent men, and scenes of home and family—provide clues about success manuals, about their message, and their appeal. They suggest that these works offered not only advice for the young man on how to succeed but guidance and reassurance for parents about helping their children (read

Figure 9. "Life in the Country." Illustrations like this one offered readers a happy and prosperous-looking view of rural life, quite unlike the reality experienced by most farm families and agricultural communities in the Gilded Age. (Jerome Paine Bates, *The Imperial Highway*; courtesy General Research Division, New York Public Library, Astor, Lenox, and Tilden Foundations)

Figure 10. "A Happy Home." This parlor scene featuring the unmistakable trappings of an upper-middle-class lifestyle appeared in Bates's *The Imperial Highway*. Book agents selling success manuals were advised to pass by homes that would have looked like these in favor of the homes of farmers, tradesmen, and those of modest means. (Courtesy General Research Division, New York Public Library, Astor, Lenox, and Tilden Foundations)

Figure 11. "Life." This composite engraving of the stages of life appeared as the frontispiece of Bates's *The Imperial Highway*. Such illustrations helped broaden the appeal of success manuals as family books offering something for everyone, something for every situation. (Courtesy General Research Division, New York Public Library, Astor, Lenox, and Tilden Foundations)

Figure 12. "The Past and the Future." This illustration captures the sense of old and new generations and reminded prospective book buyers of the grave responsibility parents have in providing guidance and inspirational reading material for their children and grandchildren. (Haines and Yaggy, *The Royal Path of Life*; courtesy General Research Division, New York Public Library, Astor, Lenox, and Tilden Foundations)

Figure 13. "Leaving Home." Illustrations like this expressed the central theme and subject of success manuals: concern about the young man who must go forth to make his way in the world. (John T. Dale, *The Way to Win*; courtesy General Research Division, New York Public Library, Astor, Lenox, and Tilden Foundations)

Figure 14. "Trials of Life." Despite the prominent role of the female confidante and comforter in this illustration, the success manual chapter it accompanies focuses on how hardship builds manhood and self-reliance; it makes no reference to women, even as wives, mothers, sisters, daughters, or friends. (Haines and Yaggy, *The Royal Path of Life*; courtesy General Research Division, New York Public Library, Astor, Lenox, and Tilden Foundations)

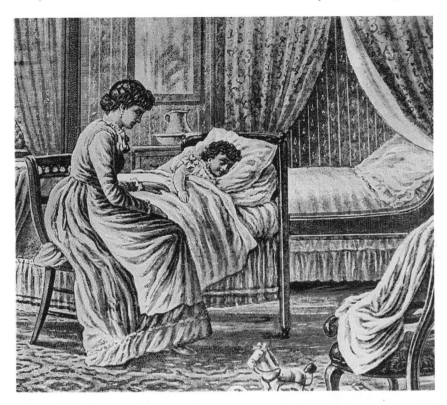

Figure 15. "Anxious Thoughts." The significance and meaning of this engraving lies as much in its title and placement as in its content; this tender mother-and-child bedtime scene appeared opposite the beginning of a chapter entitled "Why Some Succeed While Others Fail." (Lewis, *Hidden Treasures*; courtesy General Research Division, New York Public Library, Astor, Lenox, and Tilden Foundations)

sons) to succeed. In both cases, they help to confirm a theme that is threaded throughout the success manuals, namely, that these writers were addressing an audience they believed to be anxious and ill-prepared about the coming of a new age. In this regard, the success manual's appeal, like that of encyclopedias, can also be understood in terms of their potential for general education. Portraits of great men and illustrations of historic battles offered a passing introduction to the larger world for a less-than-bookish audience. Success manuals and their illustrations provided a source of information, a chaotic catalog of people and places accessible even to nonreaders, couched in the promise that this knowledge might inspire and instruct in ways that would contribute to one's future success or the success of one's sons.

The final elements of the success manual's physical form were the assorted advertisements included in the back pages of many volumes. Some

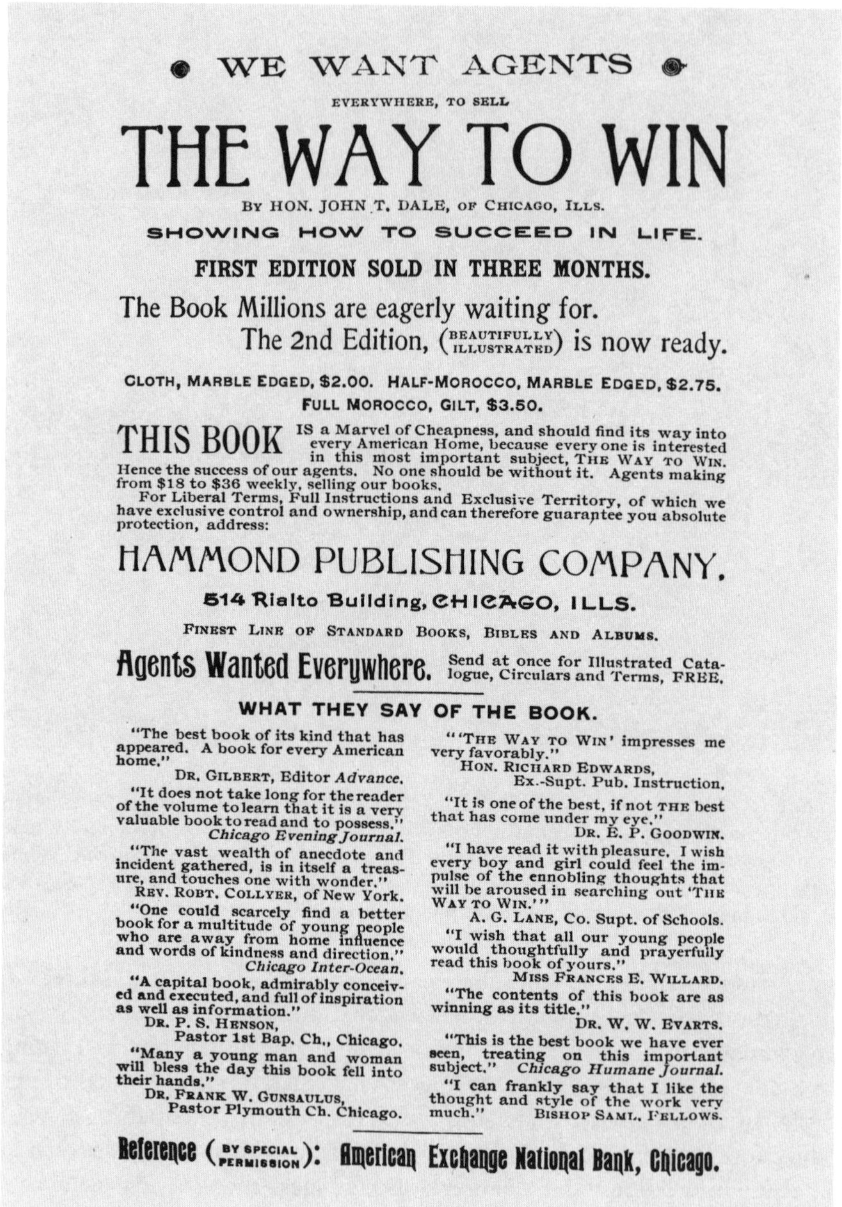

Figure 16. This advertisement for traveling book agents was on the back page of Dale's *The Way to Win*. Both its placement and the advertisement itself offer a glimpse into the marketing strategies of the subscription book industry that sold most success manuals. (Courtesy General Research Division, New York Public Library, Astor, Lenox, and Tilden Foundations)

WHAT IS SAID OF IT.

Dr. C. H. Fowler, Editor of "The Christian Advocate," New York, says:

"'The Royal Path of Life' is open before me. Its *practical* and *suggestive* subjects invite attention, and the manner in which they are handled retains it. Its principles and suggestions applied will secure success.

"One idea to a man in the beginning of life is worth *many books*. This one book will *furnish many ideas*. Brother man, read it."

President W. H. Allen, M.D., LL.D., of Girard College, Philadelphia, says:

"I have examined 'The Royal Path of Life,' and noted its direction, the lands through which it passes, and the end to which it leads. It is a straight path, and the young man who walks in it will not go astray in crooked ways. It is a safe path, and the young woman who walks in it will not be caught in a snare nor fall into a pit. It is the path of wisdom, in whose right hand is length of days, and in her left hand riches and honor. In a word, the book is full of wise precepts for the conduct of life, gathered from numerous sources, and clothed in a perspicuous style."

J. Grier Ralston, D. D., LL.D., Principal of Oakland Female Institute, Norristown, Pa., says:

"I am much obliged to you for calling my attention to 'The Royal Path of Life.' It is a book of rare excellence. I have read it with interest and profit, and think it will be found attractive alike to the old and young, to the grave and gay. The subjects of which it treats are all practical, and are so discussed as to furnish lessons for daily use. The spirit of the book is eminently Christian, its doctrines evangelical, its style crisp and lucid, its language direct and vigorous, and all its teachings pure and elevating. It does not contain a dull or prosy page. Any one who reads the first four chapters will want to finish the book.

"While I give it my hearty indorsement, I cordially recommend it to the general reader as highly entertaining and instructive, and especially to the young as a judicious counsellor, a safe guide, and a discreet friend."

L. Marks, D.D., Pastor of the Hanover Street Presbyterian Church, Wilmington, Del., says:

"'The Royal Path of Life' embraces a large number of important topics discussed in a brief but able manner. The work abounds in noble sentiments well expressed, and deserves a place in every family library. The publishers have done their part of the work well. The book will doubtless meet with a ready sale, and be read with interest and with profit. It affords us pleasure to give it our hearty indorsement."

W. M. Stanford, M. S., Pastor of the Fulton Street Evangelical Church, Pittsburgh, Pa., says:

"In journeying observingly along 'The Royal Path of Life,' a number of marked excellences strike the attention: First, the quite successful blending of the theoretical with the practical. Secondly, the natural order of the many subjects, as so many steps in 'The Royal Path,' exhibits mature judgment in selection and exceptional wisdom in arrangement, one step always preparing the traveller for the next above it. Thirdly, in the treatment of these subjects we notice the beautiful blending of two indispensable qualities, namely, *brevity* and *perspicuity*. It gives *the kernel without the hull, the wheat without the chaff*. Finally, its thought is ever pure, fresh, and vigorous, presented in the most pleasing, clear, and forcible diction, leaving with the careful reader a lasting impression and strong resolutions to reach a higher plane of life.

"The 'Royal Path' should be in every family, and would be a happy substitute for much of the trifling and corrupting 'Book-Furniture' that to-day decks the centre-tables of so many American homes."

O. C. Pope, Editor of "The Baptist Herald," Houston, Texas, says:

"I most cordially and heartily commend 'The Royal Path of Life.' It is a book that will be read by the great masses of the people, and, next to the Bible, is the most valuable book ever printed in the English language. It is a thoroughly practical guide in the every-day walks of life."

Figure 17. This page of testimonials in the back of Haines and Yaggy's *The Royal Path of Life* was the first of eight such pages. Testimonials were part of the prospectus that helped traveling book agents sell books by subscription. (Courtesy General Research Division, New York Public Library, Astor, Lenox, and Tilden Foundations)

solicited readers to become book agents to sell the particular success manual in hand or for the subscription trade generally. An ad for *The Way to Win* announced the second edition of "the book millions are eagerly waiting for" and urged readers to apply as agents. The ad claimed that the book was "a marvel of cheapness, (at $2–$3.50 depending on choice of binding), and should find its way into every American Home, because everyone is interested in this most important subject, THE WAY TO WIN" (Figure 16).[75]

Some works included mail-order advertisements for other success manuals by the same author or for other types of books. *Masters of the Situation*, for example, advertised a pictorial family Bible, the "White House" cookbook, a history of pioneer heroes and heroines, a "young folks" Bible, an anthology of poetry, and a "cyclopedia of live-stock."[76] Finally, as mentioned above, some manuals included endorsements from educators and ministers, testimonials from satisfied customers, and press notices, all of which lauded the worth and usefulness of the volume. *The Royal Path of Life* contained eight pages of endorsements at the back of the book (see Figure 17 for an example). Each of these elements in its own way contributed to the overall impression of a valuable work, a book of substance and importance. This feeling was effectively summed up in one of the endorsements for *The Royal Path of Life*. The Reverend C. W. Garoutte of Easton, Ohio, concluded his testimonial with the following benediction: "May God bless the mission of this *jeweled* treasure, and may it have a welcome into every home where it knocks for admittance."[77]

But not all readers, and certainly not all reviewers, held the success manual in such high esteem. These advertisements, endorsements, testimonials, and the manuals themselves came from men who were addressing a new American audience for whom buying and reading books was not a common part of everyday life. They were both catering to and helping to shape a popular taste for a special type of reading material that differed substantially from the tastes and standards of traditional and established producers, reviewers, and consumers of books. Indeed, in the case of the success manual sold by subscription, it was often the very features that most completely broke the rules and undermined the standards of the literary establishment that distinguished the genre and gave it its appeal. This becomes apparent from the criticism of success manuals made by publishers and bookstore owners from the "regular" or "legitimate," as opposed to "subscription," book trade, who were cut out of this lucrative business. Their bitter complaints provide some of the most vivid descriptions of these books. The following critique appeared in the trade journal *Publishers' Weekly*. It suggests the emergence of a *new* taste, however alien or despicable to these commentators:

A gorgeous binding, usually in very bad taste, thick but cheap paper, outrageously poor wood-cuts, the largest type with the thickest leads, add up into a very big, gaudy book which a glib tongue or persistent boring cheats folks into buying at five dollars, when the reading matter which it contains, if worth anything, would make about a dollar-and-a-half book in the regular trade.[78]

Criticism came from other quarters as well. By the early twentieth century, librarians were setting up subscription book committees in order to establish criteria for the evaluation (and one might guess, the elimination) of these works. In judging a book's appearance, for example, one such guide urged potential buyers to consider the following points:

(a) Binding. Substantial, plain binding, or showy, imitation leather with much gilt?
(b) Paper. Good quality or cheap? India paper? India paper is most unsatisfactory for library use. Are there deckle edges, i.e., the rough, untrimmed edges?
(c) Type. Clear and legible, or broken and blurred as if printed from wornout plates?
(d) Illustrations. Are they up-to-date and truthful? Clear, or broken and blurred as if made from wornout plates? . . . Do they really illustrate?[79]

The furor of criticism over the subscription book only heightened a more central issue: whose standards appeal to what audience? The subscription trade was designed to put books in the hands of those quite unlike the librarians who established such standards. For those living in the great American hinterland where any kind of illustrated material was a welcome source of family entertainment, for those who might never frequent a library or a bookstore, for those removed in both spirit and space from cultured literary concerns, who was to notice that certain illustrations were not of the highest quality, or that the type was at times imperfect? Furthermore, who really was to say if a thing was elegant or gaudy? Was not worth, as well as beauty, in the eye of the beholder? Whatever the establishment criticism, the record of sales made clear that the subscription book generally and the success manual in particular were satisfactory to a less sophisticated, less literate audience. Frank Bliss, the one-time manager of the American Publishing Company, a major subscription house of this period, reflected on this situation: "People in those days would not pay for blank paper and wide margins. They wanted everything filled up with type and pictures."[80] Though by some standards subscription books were unscrupulously padded, they projected what Bret Harte called "that intrinsic worth of bigness and durability which commends itself to the rural economist who likes to get a material return for his money."[81] It is thus not surprising to discover that when the more modest success manuals handled by the regular trade were prepared for the subscription business, they were illustrated, expanded in size, and elaborately bound. S. C. Griggs and Company, for example, published an unembellished 374-page version of *Masters of the Situation* in 1887 that underwent a dramatic transformation in preparation for the subscription trade. When the subscription house N. D. Thompson Publishing Company published their edition of this title in 1890, to be sold exclusively by traveling book agents, they added forty-eight illustrations and twenty-five new chapters, making a copious 769-page volume enclosed in a fancy gold-engraved binding. Here was a book that had the appearance of substance and importance, of culture, refinement, and value. It was meant to be taken seriously and thus deserves the same consideration from those who wish to understand the culture of this period. It was part of a genre whose emergence gave evidence of a new kind of popular taste, and a new kind of nonfiction genre.

THE SUCCESS MANUAL AS GENRE

Success manuals not only looked alike, they read alike, and in many cases, certain aspects of their contents were quite literally the same. Success manuals were presented as single, unified works, but in fact most were compilations and adaptations of (usually) unacknowledged essays, sermons, and speeches drawn from a variety of sources: newspapers, magazines, moral philosophy textbooks, and other success manuals. Anecdotes, quotations, and entire paragraphs seen in one success manual routinely reappeared in others. To put it bluntly, success writers cribbed, pirated, and plagiarized lavishly and unabashedly.[82] The result was that success manuals tended to say almost the same thing in roughly the same way—chapter by chapter within each work, as well as among all works within the genre. Though success writers rarely credited the specific sources from which they garnered material, neither did they claim originality. So common and accepted was this borrowing that in prefaces and introductions some writers acknowledged that they had "freely drawn from the thoughts and experience of others, more gifted" or "gathered posies from other men's flowers."[83] Others made repetition a virtue, suggesting that old truths arranged in a new way might provide fresh insight and inspiration.[84] Such also was the message of the quotation on the title page of *Getting On in the World*:

"Do not shun this maxim as commonplace. On the contrary, take the closest heed of what observant men, who would probably like to show originality are yet constrained to repeat. Therein lies the marrow of the wisdom of the world."[85]

It was exactly this sameness found within so many ostensibly different works that made the success manual a distinctive, recognizable genre. Again, characteristics that the literary establishment found the most offensive seemed to most please a popular audience for whom familiarity rather than originality had the greater appeal. Success manuals were nonfiction, but they had an epic, folktale quality in which the form itself depended on the retelling of a familiar and satisfying story. The saga of the self-made man who triumphed despite difficulties took on the character of the central drama. Here was a fantasy made real because it embodied so many half-truths and was set in recognizable surroundings. In the same way that westerns, mysteries, and gothic novels represent for readers a consistent and predictable world, so also the success manual came to be marked by the repetition of familiar themes, sentiments, and perspectives.

This repetition also has appeal for cultural historians. The fact that the same structure and message was replicated in dozens of different works that in turn were purchased by millions of people over a forty-year period provides evidence that success manuals and what they said had some special meaning to a significant portion of the population. The sameness of these works makes it possible to look for clues about their meaning by isolating and examining the particular common elements—such as style, language, dramatic convention, and literary device—and to look at how they were routinely woven together into a story line that was duplicated in every work. In short, it makes it possible to discover and to study the formula of this popular genre.

The most immediate and obvious element of the success manual formula was a characteristic style of presentation and writing that can be described as didactic, moralizing, and inspirational. Like the Bible, success manuals meant to teach, and they taught through precepts and parables, examples and maxims, all delivered in a ministerial and declarative tone of address. Though these works were "how-to" manuals, purporting to teach how to get on in the world, they were surprisingly devoid of practical, "worldly" business advice or instruction. Despite what at first glance appeared to be a grounding in the material world, suggested by titles such as *Onward to Fame and Fortune* and their canonization of the self-made man, there were no chapters about starting a business, accounting methods, or sound investment principles. An earlier type of success book, the mercantile handbooks published in the 1850s such as Edwin T. Freedley's *A Practical Treatise on Business or How to Get Money* (1852), were also moralizing in tone, but their preachments were scattered through chapters on buying, selling, lending, credit, interest, banking, speculation, and calculation. Some success manuals did include chapters with titles such as "Business Habits," but the focus was on the cultivation of the individual virtues they claimed were necessary for business success: the "habits" of "application," "manner," "observation," "tact," "accuracy," "industry," and "punctuality."

The success manuals' moralizing and inspirational style can scarcely be separated from their subject matter. This fact was apparent even from the tables of contents, which read like shopping lists of virtues, vices, and self-help maxims. Typically, the first chapter or two had titles that stated the problem or posed the question, such as "Success and Failure," "Success, a Slow Growth," or "What is Success?" These chapters emphasized opportunity and assured readers that the race of life was not only worthy, but open to all runners. The last chapters usually had titles that suggested the nonpecuniary aspects of success, for example, "True Success," "Rich Without Money," and "The Bible in Business." The titles of chapters between these conventionalized beginnings and endings comprised a very long list of the attributes and imperatives considered key to success. Some common titles were "Luck and Pluck," "Self-Reliance," "The Right Vocation," "Character," "Duty," "Industry," "The Advantage of Difficulty," "Manhood," "True Genius," "Physical Culture," "Manners," and "Bad Habits." To this basic fare, many success manuals, especially the longer ones, broadened their appeal by adding chapters relating more specifically to home and family, morals and manners. These might include titles such as "Courtship," "Marriage," "Children," "Dress and Decorum," "Make Home Attractive," "Reading: Use and Abuse," "The Drinking Habit," "The Tobacco Habit," "Faith," "Health and Happiness," "Family Prayer," and "Christian Love." Overall, the most striking aspect of success manual style and content was the focus on individual virtue. Each manual and each chapter identified and described important personal attributes, pressed the need to cultivate said virtue, and provided examples and illustrations from the lives of other men to demonstrate how these virtues might be applied in order to achieve success. Together, these virtues made up *character*, and it was character, not business-specific know-how, that made the successful man.

The biographical sketch, another of the conventionalized elements of the success manual, provided the perfect format for demonstrating the workings of virtue in individual lives. Typical subjects of these sketches were nineteenth-century American statesmen and businessmen, such as Clay, Webster, Grant, Lincoln, Garfield, Astor, Girard, and Vanderbilt. The sketches revealed little about the lives of their subjects that did not conform to a pattern easily identified as a formula for the self-made man. The stereotypical character was born in poverty and obscurity, or at least in modest circumstances, usually in a country home. He "raised" himself through the diligent application of virtues such as industry, self-reliance, frugality, perseverance, and willpower. Though he endured periods of suffering and self-sacrifice to gain his goal, he was ultimately rewarded for his efforts by fame, wealth, place, or some combination thereof. This vignette typically ended by emphasizing the subject's personal and public qualities. He was a man of character, a family man, and a church member. He made some important contribution to society either through his work or through his benevolence. The one American entrepreneur whom success writers hesitated to defend in these terms was financier Jay Gould of Wall Street scandal fame. But Gould's life, like the rest, was presented as an instructive example providing lessons useful in the pursuit of success—what to avoid as well as what to emulate.

The biographical sketch was only one of the ways in which success writers evoked the names and deeds of the famous. They routinely began chapters with inspirational quotations and maxims from great men and otherwise made mention of their names and related anecdotes that both revealed why they were famous and likened their struggle to succeed to the endeavors of young men starting out. The extent and scope of this device were truly vast: some success writers cited as many as 100 different eminent persons in a single chapter; quotes were taken from a range of individuals that included Napoleon, Jesus, Burke, Confucius, Longfellow, Goethe, Luther, Clay, Lowell, Emerson, Disraeli, Franklin, and Richelieu. A chapter in one success manual, entitled "The Will and the Way," began with this set of quotes and maxims:

There are men whose cant is simply can't. [uncredited]

Success in most things depends on knowing how long it takes to succeed. —Montesquieu

Our greatest glory is not in never falling, but in rising every time we fall. —Confucius

Valour is stability, not of legs and arms, but of courage and the soul. He that falls obstinate in his courage, si succederit de genu pugnat; if his legs fail him, fights on his knees. —Montaigne[86]

Such quotations from the famous not only offered instruction and inspiration, but lent an authority to the proclamations, warnings, and advice of the less-than-eminent success writers. The writers thus buttressed their arguments and enhanced their own status by cloaking themselves and their words in the mantle of eminent men. Within the texts the famous were discussed in a way that both provided a bit of instant erudition about who these personages were and what they did and at the same time linked these men, their lives, and their deeds to the hopes, fears, and struggles of ordinary folks. Note, for example, these lines from a chapter entitled "Practice Secures Perfection":

> No one ever wrote an immortal poem, painted a great picture, or delivered a famous oration without serving his apprenticeship, and doing what we may call the drudgery of his art. . . . Even Titian and Raphael had to begin by drawing straight lines; Beethoven and Mozart by picking out notes one by one; and Shakespeare himself had to learn the alphabet before he wrote Hamlet and King Lear.[87]

Scenarios from the lives of the rich and famous were interspersed with stories of the turning points and great moments in the lives of everyday citizens. Tales of lifesaving illustrated courage, examples of recovery from business failure provided lessons in perseverance, and anecdotes from the life of the man who endured great hardship in order to perfect his invention or to bring an original idea to fruition showed readers the power of will. Success writers used accounts of individual failure as well as triumph to teach the right and the wrong ways of doing things. The lazy man was contrasted with the diligent, the man of "pluck" was shown to be the victor over he who waited for "luck," and the "manly" and "stalwart" were raised over the "spineless" and "weaklings." The failure of those who put their hopes in inherited wealth, who indulged in spendthrift ways, or who succumbed to the temptations of liquor, tobacco, gambling, or imprudent entertainment were carefully cataloged.

A final and striking element of the success manual's standard makeup was its characteristically rich, figurative, and symbolic language. Similes and metaphors, aphorisms and analogies abound. Most figures of speech can be related to one or more of four ideas—*nature, the machine, competition,* and *manliness*—all of which were important themes in the overall success manual formula.

Metaphors of *nature*—such as "the stalwart oak" and "the trembling sapling," "the sea of life" or "the drone in the hive of industry"—evoked the familiar and suggested the preindustrial world of rural and small-town America. The image of *the machine*, represented in maxims such as "A man without a will is like an engine without steam" or "Better to wear out than to rust out" suggested the fast, new world of industry and enterprise with which readers were then being confronted. *Competition* — "the battle of life," "the race of life," the "contest," or the "arena" — symbolized the dangers of a fierce world of winners and losers, and the necessity of arming oneself for the fight. And finally, the idea of *manliness*, "manhood" or "true manhood," represented the solution to the problem of achieving victory in a danger-ous new industrial age. "Manhood," in a word, summarized the individual virtues, character, and willpower that made for success. The language of manhood often combined metaphors from nature, the machine, and war-fare, and in some cases a none-too-subtle phallic symbolism. For example, not only did success writers refer to "manly vigor," "manly character," and "that layer of metal that made manhood," they likened a man's power of will to the cannon or the steam engine and warned that "without will, a man would be like the soft, flabby, nerveless mollusk or shell-fish in the ocean."[88]

The chapters that follow explore the meaning of these specific symbols and metaphors having to do with battle, the machine, and manliness. But in general, the use of symbol, metaphor, and analogy in success manual language — as with the use of the biographical sketch — can all be seen as attempts to instruct by making one kind of reality understandable by ref-erence to another that is presumed to be more familiar. The study of this language thus provides clues about what success writers thought it was im-portant to stress *and* about what they assumed would have familiarity and meaning to their audience.

Together, all of these conventionalized aspects of the success manuals — their repetitiveness; their didactic, moralizing, inspirational style; the stan-dardized scenario of the self-made man; their evocation of the names of the famous; their focus on individual virtue; and their use of rich, sym-bolic, and figurative language — when arranged in a predictable way, make up a distinctive and recognizable story line or formula.

The summary of a single chapter illustrates how these elements fit to-gether to make up the formula characteristic of success manuals generally. A representative chapter in a typical success manual, "The Will" from William James Tilley's *Masters of the Situation*, began with the maxim, "Where there's a will there's a way," followed by inspirational bits from the writings of Goethe and Confucius. The point of the first few pages was to define and proclaim the importance of this particular virtue, "the marvelous power residing in human will." Willpower, according to Tilley, was "that mysterious form of mental energy which makes the difference between the great and the insignificant." Anecdotes from the lives of the Duke of Wellington, Pitt, and Napoleon were offered as illustrations of this quality. The chapter then shifted to a statement of problem, claiming that young men of the day lacked the "inclination for continuous exertion" and that they looked for an "easy life, an easy way." Tilley denounced this practice as both "impolitic" and "unmanly" and insisted that the mass of men were "too easily conquered by circumstances."

This problem was not dwelt upon long before a solution was offered—the application of manhood and willpower: "What's needed today is men who are so strong and vigorous and courageous that they are ready for anything that comes to hand, and able to accomplish what they undertake. . . . These are the men who conquer and control circumstances, who win the prizes in the race of life." This claim was buttressed by the words of President Garfield, "A pound of pluck is worth a ton of luck," along with Mirabeau's "Law of Success": "Nothing is impossible to a man who can will." In other words, the solution came in the form of a promise that success was within the reach of all who applied themselves.

But the chapter also contains some contradictory assertions that qualify the scenario outlined above. Tilley claimed that some were "born to lead and command and others to follow and obey" and that to "struggle against this inevitable inequality was useless." In his view, "Every time one man meets another, this difference is recognized—one is master." This conflict between individuals was pervasive, according to Tilley, and could be seen even among children in the nursery. Because of these innate differences, a man should study his strengths and weaknesses carefully so that he might endeavor only that in which he might reasonably expect to achieve success. This was a substantial qualification of the claim that anything was possible for the man of will. It pointed to ambiguity about whether willpower was an innate or a cultivated virtue and further raised the question about how success was defined. In fact, this loose, ambiguous definition of success was key to the success manual formula. As long as a success writer's definition was a broad and varied one that included not only wealth and fame but alternative, nonpecuniary varieties of success ("mastery" in a lowly calling, character, and manhood), he could finesse the tricky problem of promising success to all who were willing to abide by the precepts presented in the manual.

This particular mixture of elements—the didactic, moralizing, inspirational style; the biographical sketch; the figurative, symbolic language; the predictable story line—complete with its contradictions and ambiguities, recurs in manual after manual, within individual chapters, within different works, and across the genre. It constitutes the basic literary formula of the success manual.

2

Success Manual Authors and Their World

☛

He was an interpreter of men's souls to themselves.
—Margaret Connolly, *The Life Story of Orison Swett Marden*

The most striking fact about the authors of success manuals is their anonymity; though they created an enormously popular genre that included
some of nineteenth-century America's all-time best-sellers, only traces of
the lives of many of these authors are left to scrutinize. There are important exceptions. Detailed information is available about men such as Orison
Swett Marden and Russell Conwell, both of whom achieved fame as success writers. Biographical data are also available about those authors who
were known for other achievements and whose writing of a success manual
was incidental to an otherwise celebrated career, men like P. T. Barnum
and Edward Bok. But more often than not success manuals were the work
of relatively unknown ministers and educators, many of whose names do
not appear in biographical dictionaries of authors, educators, and divines
and whose books are not listed in encyclopedias of literature.[1] One might
guess that those success writers who seem to have disappeared from the
record did so because the particular works they published did not become as
popular or circulate as widely as those of more well-known figures. But this
hypothesis is discredited by the fact that Thomas L. Haines and Levi W.
Yaggy—authors of the success manual that sold more than any other, *The
Royal Path of Life* (1876)—are among those who go unrecognized.

There are two related explanations for the relative obscurity of many of
the men who wrote success manuals. First, writing a success manual was
not considered a "legitimate" claim to fame in the world of letters. When
authors of national reputation, such as Edward Everett Hale, were written
up in biographical dictionaries of the time, the titles of success manuals

they had written were often omitted from the list of their published works.[2] Authorship of a success manual, especially ones published for the subscription trade, would be more apt to earn scorn than recognition from the traditional publishing and literary establishment that determined which books and which authors merited notice, unless, of course, a writer or lecturer was so prolific and so energetic—like a Marden or a Conwell—that he was impossible to ignore. We have already seen examples of the disdain with which subscription books were regarded by the contemporary regular book trade and library establishment. The same contempt is apparent in the remarks of later observers. Frank Luther Mott, historian of best-sellers, deserves the credit for discovering that the subscription success manual *The Royal Path of Life* was one of the greatest best-sellers of the nineteenth century, but his description mirrors the attitude of the contemporary establishment's view of this type of book. Of its authors, Haines and Yaggy, Mott writes: "We should call them compilers rather than authors, for they did little more than put together tags and quotations; the whole has an effect of perfect triteness in the worst style of Victorian sentimental morality." Meanwhile, Mott is unable to provide any more information about the authors than what can be found on the title page of their book, namely that Haines was a teacher and Yaggy was a preacher.[3]

The second explanation for the relative anonymity of many success writers has to do with the profit-consciousness of the subscription book industry. From the point of view of a subscription publisher, a little-known author with the right credentials (a minister, teacher, or college professor) was preferable to a prominent author. Well-known authors demanded and got lucrative advances in this period, an expense that could be spared by contracting instead with a relative newcomer to the field.[4] Furthermore, given the relatively unlettered audience to which success manuals were addressed, the chances of an author's name recognition being a selling point were slim. Presumably it was the perceived merit of the success manual rather than the eminence of the author that generated sales.

Despite the lack of ample, detailed information about many of the success manual authors, one can develop a rough profile of these authors by combining data from success manual title pages and library card catalogs with more complete biographical material where available. Linking this profile with what is known about men of these general circumstances in the period, it is possible to make some generalizations about who these success writers were and about some of the forces that more than likely shaped their thinking, their actions, and their writing. The first section of this chapter presents a series of brief biographical sketches of several success manual authors about whom information is available; the second section presents a composite profile of the success writer; the third examines some of the educational, intellectual, and literary forces that almost certainly helped to shape these men; and the last describes the commercial world in which these authors operated.

The best known and most prolific success writer was Orison Swett Marden (1850–1924), whose own life was a model of self-help. Born in poverty in Thornton, New Hampshire, he was orphaned as a small boy and endured five different, unloving foster families. He nonetheless worked his way through school and by 1882 had earned two bachelor degrees and three graduate degrees—one in oratory, an M.D. from the Harvard Medical School, and a law degree from the Boston University Law School. According to Marden's biographer, the "greatest event of his youthful life" was his reading of Samuel Smiles's *Self-Help*, which he discovered in the attic. But despite this early inspiration and his elaborate education, he did not find his own secret of success until relatively late in life, when he took up Samuel Smiles's example, quite literally. At the age of 46, after an uneven career in the hotel business and three years of service on the Nebraska Board of Trade, Marden returned to Boston and "devoted himself to the literary effort of encouraging young people to make an earnest endeavor for success in life."[5] His first success manual, *Pushing to the Front* (1894), was a blockbuster. It went through twelve editions in the first year, and by 1925 had gone through 250 U.S. editions and been translated into twenty-five languages. It sold a million copies in Japan alone. Over the next thirty years, Marden wrote fifty success books and pamphlets (thirty were book-length) and became the founder and publisher of *Success Magazine* in 1898. But none of his works achieved the popularity of *Pushing to the Front*. Marden believed that the title—an idea he got from an African American barber—made this work successful.[6] Indeed, there was a directness and simplicity to this title that captured in a single phrase the idea of upward mobility and the aggressive stance deemed necessary to achieve it. He retitled his subsequent book, *Architects of Fate* (1897), with the punchier and more success-oriented title *Rising in the World, or Architects of Fate*.[7] In any event, it is clear that Marden had a special sensitivity to his public. The publisher's foreword to a 1911 edition of *Pushing to the Front* claimed that "[t]he author has received thousands of letters from people in nearly all parts of the world telling how the book has aroused their ambition, changed their ideals and aims, and has spurred them to the successful undertaking of what they before had thought impossible."[8]

Russell Herman Conwell (1843–1925) was another who came to national prominence through his efforts to broadcast a gospel of success. Like Marden, he too was raised in the economically depressed New England countryside. Born in South Worthington, Maine, he spent his early years on "a small sterile farm" and only through great frugality was able to attend the academy at Wilbraham, Massachusetts. In 1860 he entered law school at Yale, but left at the beginning of the Civil War to serve as a captain in the infantry. He completed his law degree in private study while in the army and at the close of the war set up law practice in Minnesota. He was a foreign correspondent to the New York *Tribune* and later to the Boston *Traveler*, toured the world for two journals, traveled with Bayard Taylor, returned to the East Coast and practiced law in Boston in the 1870s, was ordained as a Baptist minister in 1879, and in 1881 became the pastor of Grace Baptist Church of Philadelphia, famous for its 4,000-seat temple. In 1888, he founded Temple University. Here was a man whose life illustrated the tendency toward multiple careers of those who wrote success manuals, particularly careers that put them in touch with the public and public sentiment. Conwell is still best remembered not for founding Temple University or for his ministry at Grace Baptist Church but for a spellbinding, inspirational lecture entitled "Acres of Diamonds," which revealed how to discover success in life. Having written this lecture in 1861 and delivered it to a few hundred people in a little Methodist church in Westfield, Massachusetts, Conwell reportedly delivered it 6,000 times over the next 64 years of his life. "Acres of Diamonds" earned Conwell fortune as well as fame; it was the proceeds of his lecture tours that enabled him to found Temple University. He expanded his remarks from "Acres of Diamonds" into a number of success manuals, including *The New Day, or Fresh Opportunities: A Book for Young Men* (1904), *Present Successful Opportunities* (1902), and *What You Can Do with Your Will Power* (1917).[9]

Marden and Conwell achieved national reputations as success writers. There were certain other men—already established and well-known as writers, editors, and publicists—who at some point in their career turned their talents to the writing of one or more success manuals. Notable were Edward William Bok, William Makepeace Thayer, Edward Everett Hale, and William Mathews. Edward William Bok (1863–1930) was editor in chief of *Ladies' Home Journal* (1889–1919) and vice president of Curtis Publishing Company (1891–1930). He won the Pulitzer prize for American biography in 1921 for his autobiography, *The Americanization of Edward Bok.* Born in the Netherlands in 1863, his family suffered financial reverse, emigrated to America in 1870, and settled in Brooklyn, New York. At age thirteen, he began work for Western Union Telegraph, first as an office boy, then as a stenographer. He read about and corresponded with successful men—Hayes, Grant, Sherman, Emerson, Holmes, Longfellow. Evenings he worked as a reporter for the Brooklyn *Eagle*. When financier Jay Gould took over Western Union, Edward Bok became his stenographer. From Western Union, Bok went to the publishing firm of Holt, Scribner's and Sons. Meanwhile, as his biographer explains, "he studied current tendencies in the news and magazine fields, especially turning his practical mind toward discovering new channels through which popular reading tastes could be gauged and served." Some of Bok's innovations were his syndicated press, with weekly letters from Henry Ward Beecher, articles from notable women writers, and the original "woman's page." He became editor of *Ladies' Home Journal* at the age of 26, doubled the circulation in a few years, and, after a long and successful career, retired at age 56 to become an important benefactor, endowing funds for civic service.[10] In 1895, in the midst of this illustrious career, Bok wrote a success manual entitled *Successward: A Young Man's Book for Young Men*, published by a subscription publisher. A few years later, he personally took his message on the road in a popular 1898-1900 lecture tour featuring an address called "The Keys to Success." Not only did the tour augment the sales of *Successward*, but his lecture, published in pamphlet form, was circulated widely.[11] Given Bok's interest in popular reading tastes, it seems certain that he would have been quite familiar with Russell Conwell's famous lecture tours and books. It is also likely that he was aware of the two or three decades of popular success writing that preceded his efforts. He especially was in a position to know a sure publishing bet when he saw one and to know how to duplicate that success.

Edward Everett Hale (1822-1909), also an author of national reputation, was a Unitarian *and* Congregationalist clergyman, an active promoter of the Chautauqua Movement, and editor of the ten-volume *Modern Achievement Series* (1902). He was born into a literary Boston family, entered Harvard at age thirteen, and graduated in 1839. He published stories in *Atlantic Monthly* in the 1850s and 1860s and was the author of many books, including *Ten Times Ten Is Ten* (1870), *A New England Boyhood* (1893), *James Russell Lowell and His Friends* (1899), and the two-volume *Memories of a Hundred Years* (1902). In addition to these and other works, Hale wrote a success manual entitled *What Career?* that was reissued for over thirty years.[12]

William Makepeace Thayer (1820-1898), born in Franklin, Massachusetts, was a Congregationalist clergyman, temperance leader, editor, and writer. He was editor of *The Home Monthly* (1858-62), *The Nation* (1864-68), and *Mother's Assistant* (1868-72) and was a widely published author best known for his biographies of "self-made" politicians and businessmen designed for young readers. *The Poor Boy and the Merchant Prince: The*

Life of Amos Lawrence (1857) and his "Log Cabin to White House Series" were typical of these. Forty years later, he was still writing on the success theme and producing collected biographies of the successful: *Success and Its Achievers* (1891), *Ethics of Success: A Reader for the Middle Grades of Schools* (1894), *Men Who Win* (1896), and *Women Who Win* (1896), to name a few. Next to Horatio Alger Jr., there was no better known or more widely read nineteenth-century writer of juvenile literature on the success theme than William Makepeace Thayer.[13] But Thayer did not address only juvenile audiences. In 1893 he wrote a book that more properly fits the formula of the success manual, *Onward to Fame and Fortune, or Climbing Life's Ladder,* and accounts for Thayer's inclusion in this study.[14]

When William Mathews (1818–1909) wrote a success manual called *Getting On in the World, or Hints on Success in Life* (1873), he had already practiced law, founded a literary and family magazine called *The Watervillonian* in his hometown of Waterville, Maine (later published in Boston as the *Yankee Blade*), held a librarianship and then a professorship in rhetoric and English at the University of Chicago, and edited a weekly financial journal and a department of the Chicago *Daily Tribune. Getting On in the World* first appeared as a series of articles in the Chicago *Tribune* in 1871. It was his only "success manual," but it sold 70,000 copies. The success of *Getting On in the World* led him to give up teaching for a literary career. He settled in Boston and published many other works, among them *Literary Style and Other Essays* (1881) and *Wit and Humor* (1888).[15]

Wilbur Fisk Crafts, best known for his ministry and reform work, was born in 1850 in Fryeburg, Maine, the son of a father who was a minister and an antislavery and temperance reformer. Crafts graduated from Wesleyan University in 1869, from the School of Theology at Boston University in 1872, and until 1880 served as a Methodist minister at Trinity Church in Chicago. Thereafter, he moved to Brooklyn, New York, were he was pastor of Lee Avenue Congregational Church; in 1883, he became the pastor of First Union Presbyterian Church in New York City. Crafts was vice president of the National Temperance Society, established the American Sabbath Union and a clearinghouse for Christian reform, edited a reform paper called *Christian Statesman,* and was much in demand on the lecture circuit for his talks on "Practical Christian Sociology." A prolific writer of works such as *The Bible and the Sunday School* (1876) and *What the Temperance Century Has Made Certain* (1885), Crafts wrote the success manual *Successful Men of Today and What They Say of Success* (1883), which almost certainly outsold his other books. Adding a pseudo-scientific twist to the typical success manual formula, Crafts couched the normal admonitions and prescriptions in the context of a survey of prominent men that "documented" the importance of sound morals, humble origins, and sterling character as keys to success. By 1887, *Successful Men* had already sold over 38,000 copies and continued to be reprinted in the following years.[16]

Another success writer proved to be overly zealous in his own pursuit of success. William Dale Owen (1846–1906), author of *Success in Life, and How to Secure It: or Elements of Manhood and Their Culture* (1882), had careers in law, the ministry, and public service. He served as a representative from Indiana from 1885 to 1891 and as Indiana secretary of state from 1895 to 1899. It was his last career in business that did him in. In 1906, he was indicted in Boston for a "gigantic swindle" connected to a Mexican rubber plantation and real estate scam. While a codefendant was apprehended, Owen apparently disappeared and was reported to have died a year later in Europe.[17]

Finally, two very different kinds of businessmen are known to have written success manuals: Archer Brown and P. T. Barnum. Archer Brown (1851–1904), author of a success manual entitled *Top or Bottom—Which? A Study of Factors Which Most Contribute to the Success of Young Men* (1903), was known primarily as a New York iron and steel merchant. A principal in Rogers, Brown and Company, he was reputed to have handled one quarter of the raw iron output of the United States in the 1880s. But he began and ended his career as a writer and publicist. His first job was on the staff of the Cincinnati *Gazette*. He founded and ran the Cincinnati *Tribune* before joining William A. Rogers in the iron business. He wrote for a variety of magazines and papers on economic aspects of the iron trade and other miscellaneous topics and was a "prominent and energetic worker for the YMCA." At the age of fifty-three, a year before his death in 1904, he wrote *Top or Bottom—Which?* It was printed privately, apparently by his business partner. According to his biographer, this work "abounding in sensible advice to young men" passed through many editions and was translated into Japanese and Chinese.[18] The publisher prominently emphasized the fact that Brown was a businessman; a second subtitle on the title page described the book as "An Inquiry into the Causes of Success and Failure in Life from the Standpoint of a Business Man." But this success manual offered no more practical business know-how than any other success manual, nor was it any less moralistic than success manuals written by ministers and educators. Archer Brown stayed true to the success manual formula.

P. T. Barnum (1810–1891), the renowned circus man, proprietor of "Barnum's Great Asiatic Caravan, Museum and Menagerie," wrote a success manual entitled *Dollars and Sense, or How to Get On: The Whole Secret in a Nutshell* (1890), published by the subscription house Peoples Publishing Company. Barnum was well aware that books on the theme of success enjoyed wide popularity. His first book, *Struggles and Triumphs* (1854), was an autobiographical account fashioned on the "self-made man" theme. It sold over a half million copies, partly based on sales to the large crowds at Barnum's shows, and became a best-seller in a seventy-year period when only five nonfiction works became best-sellers.[19] True to the Barnum reputation, he enhanced sales by publishing and selling *Struggles and Triumphs* under several different titles, including *The Life of P. T. Barnum, the World-Renowned Showman, Written by Himself* and *How I Made Millions, or the Secret of Success.*[20] Though *Struggles and Triumphs* was not properly a success manual (it was an autobiography and published prior to the period in which the success manual genre appeared), the title seems to have anticipated both the titles and the message of the success manual and may well have been one of the prototypes that influenced the shaping of the success manual genre.

PROFILE OF A SUCCESS WRITER

By combining these vignettes with the scattered bits and pieces of biographical data that exist, a number of generalizations can be made about success writers. In brief, most were white, Anglo-Saxon, Protestant men born between roughly 1820 and 1860 who, like their readers, grew up in small towns or rural areas of New England or the Midwest and came mostly from families of modest means. Here similarities with their audience ended. The men who wrote success manuals left home to attend and graduate from college, many earning not only B.A. degrees but also graduate degrees, sometimes more than one, in areas such as divinity, law, medicine, and rhetoric.

Success writers came of age during the years 1835–1880. They witnessed the dramatic revolutions of the era and were in a position to be well-versed in the conflict and debates these changes engendered, from sectional conflict to the rise of industrialism, from the advent of Darwinism to the emergence of the "social question." Imbued with the moral, preindustrial, Jeffersonian worldview of their youth, success writers were nonetheless contemporaries of the great "captains of industry" like Astor, Vanderbilt, and Rockefeller, who were among the "self-made men" success manuals canonized. Insofar as most became ministers, teachers, college professors, newspaper and magazine editors and publicists, authors, and lecturers and often had multiple, overlapping careers in these fields, the writers of success manuals were in a special position to take the pulse of the nation and participate in shaping its ideas.

They brought not only the authority of "position" to their writing, but also the authority of age. They produced these works in their maturity, when they were in their forties, fifties, and sixties, perhaps reflecting a feeling on their part that they were seasoned men who had fatherly advice to give to the younger generation.

Those about whom we have more detailed information relocated several times during their careers, often moving from New England to spend some time in the Midwest. At the peak of their careers they were settled in important cities such as New York, Boston, Philadelphia, or Chicago, where they spent their remaining years. This geographic mobility afforded them familiarity and perhaps direct experience with conditions and sentiments in both rural and urban, East Coast and Midwestern parts of the country. This experience no doubt sensitized success writers to the concerns of the audience they wished to address. But their actions stood in contrast to their advice to readers, whom they advised to look for success close to home.

As college-educated men, writers of success manuals were part of a tiny elite. Looking at the year 1870, which is toward the end of the period in which this cohort of success writers were educated, only one in every sixty young men between the ages of eighteen and twenty-one was enrolled in higher education. Though the number of college degrees granted was rising rapidly, doubling in a thirty-year period, the totals were still relatively small: the decade 1871–1880 produced 113,131 graduates with bachelor degrees; between the years 1891–1900, 226,531 were graduated. In 1870, only one doctorate was awarded by American institutions. It was not until 1888 that 100 academic doctorates were awarded in a single year.[21]

But an elite education did not necessarily indicate an elite heritage or even a secure upper-middle-class family background. In fact, it is likely that more than a few of the men who wrote success manuals came from relatively humble origins and were themselves searching for their own route to upward mobility. Higher education afforded young men a distinct advantage in terms of both career mobility and social mobility. As Americans came to appreciate this fact, some families of very modest means and no capital to provide sons a start in life were willing to make extreme sacrifices in order to send a boy to college to improve his chances of success and assure him a place in the middle class.[22] Russell Conwell and Orison Swett Marden were striking examples of this faith in higher education as the route to upward mobility.

The professions most often pursued by those who wrote success manuals also tell us something about the men themselves and the web of aspirations and constraints characteristic of their careers. These professions—especially the ministry, journalism, and academia—were common choices of educated nineteenth-century men without capital who wished to advance themselves. They were vehicles for what Burton Bledstein termed the "vertical vision," in which practitioners sought the means to self-advancement. More than any other single occupation, the ministry was the stated profession of the success writers. The ministry that success writers entered had been largely transformed in the mid-nineteenth century by a generation of poor boys who escaped economically depressed New England farms via church-sponsored scholarships to college and divinity school. The new minister was ambitious and thought more in terms of a career than a "calling." Rather than a lifelong commitment to a single congregation, a new generation of ministers moved from congregation to congregation and concerned themselves with rising salary and status.[23]

The hope of upward social mobility also shaped the aspirations and the ideas of those drawn to academic life. The cultural hegemony and semi-patrician status of the college professor and a career in the new universities of the era appealed to some of the young men who sought influence and mobility from the lower and middle ranks of the middle class to its upper professional level.[24]

Indeed, in Gilded Age America the pulpits of large urban churches, professorships in the new universities, and the editor's chair of major magazines and newspapers offered their occupants generous salaries, status, and considerable influence. But their influence was tempered and their tenure measured by the monied powers behind the institutions they served. They were locked into rather elaborate institutional frameworks that set the tone and the parameters for what was preached, taught, and written. The newly wealthy captains of industry who were remaking the economic and political order also made their influence felt in important American cultural institutions: the church, the school, and the press. They became lay leaders of churches, trustees of universities, and partners or owners of newspaper or press services. Through all these channels they labored to advance their policies and principles, sometimes directly, more often with skillful indirection.[25]

Pierpont Morgan not only provided the $500,000 to build the Cathedral of St. John the Divine in New York City, he became an active layman in the Episcopal church. Religious leaders such as Baptist minister Frederick Gates, who wooed and won the trust and the benevolence of John D. Rockefeller, became mentors of more than the soul. Some ministers directed the investment of millions of dollars in public charities, becoming major investment bankers in their own right, buying and selling securities and properties. When great industrialists built churches and endowed universities, grateful ministers and college presidents scarcely needed direct orders from their benefactors to lead their institutions in ways that were consistent with the prevailing wisdom. After the bestowal of one of Rockefeller's fabulous gifts, the religious press and clergy described the oil trust as an organization begun and carried out by Christian men and "eminent Baptists who honor their religious obligations and contribute without stint to the noblest Christian and philanthropic objects. . . . All of them illustrate in their daily lives their reverence for living Christianity." When some people accused Rockefeller of stealing the money he gave to the church, the pastor of Euclid Avenue Baptist Church in Cleveland came to his defense, saying "he has laid it on the altar and thus sanctified it." [26]

In the university, the marriage of patronage and educational policymaking was explicit. Its impact was nowhere more obvious than in the rocky and sometimes brief careers of controversial university professors. Certain American intellectuals who took an interest in socialist ideas in their early careers learned where the controlling power of respectable opinion lay.[27] Economist Richard T. Ely was brought to public trial by the University of Wisconsin on charges of "siding with labor and socialism, of consorting with union organizers, and of threatening to boycott a printer doing university business for not adopting a union shop." [28] He was exonerated only by denying that he was a socialist, denying that he favored labor, and denying that he had counseled labor leaders or supported local attempts to organize. Further, Ely declared that had he held such views and engaged in such activities, he would have no right to teach in a university. Thereafter, his silence on controversial issues seems to have been the price of university employment. Henry Carter Adams learned the limitations of the influence he had hoped to wield as a professor at Cornell University. His enthusiasm for the Knights of Labor and his advocacy of a theory of public control of private property caused Cornell trustee and benefactor Russell Sage to order him fired. Only after publishing a restatement of his theory and backtracking on his views did he secure a permanent appointment at the University of Michigan. He never again wrote on the theory of public control of private property.[29]

These examples are not intended to suggest that there was no room for dissent from the dominant order or that independent voices were automatically and effectively muzzled. Critics of the new order such as Terence Powderly, William Jennings Bryan, Eugene Debs, Henry George, and Edward Bellamy not only made their mark, but helped to set the terms of the debate. Furthermore, there were undoubtedly small churches, newspapers, and schools in local communities across the country where independent-minded ministers, writers, and educators of more modest personal aspirations could be heard without bringing down the wrath of a powerful establishment upon their heads. But for men whose goal in life included individual upward mobility, the most certain route was the mainstream.

And for those watching for the cues of mainstream acceptability, events such as the spectacular but selective institutional largesse of the titans of industry and the disciplining of controversial university professors did not go unnoticed. Events like these helped define the mainstream of respectable, establishment opinion and through the mechanism of reward and punishment created a climate of hope and fear in the cultural and intellectual world that paralleled that in the crisis-ridden economic world.

For the men who wrote success manuals, it was probably the hoped-for rewards, an unexamined identification with those in power, and aspiration for at least some small share of the bounty that most inspired them. Certainly they were not the soul-searching dissidents and socialist intellectuals who had to be convinced, or coerced, to quiet their criticism and change their course. But even here—among the American intellectuals who first entertained and then disavowed socialist ideas—the explanation for their disaffection lies not only in the coercive measures of firings and university censorship but also in self-censorship motivated by the desire for professional acceptance and upward mobility within the establishment.[30]

Whatever the background of college-educated American men in the second half of the nineteenth century, they were unlikely to be immune to the commercial spirit of the age. Their choice of profession and most assuredly the decision by some of them to write success manuals reflected an interest in individual self-advancement as well as a commitment to enlighten and guide the public. By taking care to conduct themselves in ways that might earn the approval of the new arbiters of scholarly rectitude and Christian doctrine, such men were practicing what they preached in the success manuals. They were learning to internalize the rules of the new order in the hope of securing a place for themselves within it.

EARLY INFLUENCES AND BOOKS THAT MATTERED

The instinct of so many Gilded Age American men of the cloth, of letters, and of the press to cleave to a common mainstream ideology was shaped not only by the rewards and punishments they perceived in adult life. For men of the generation and profile who wrote success manuals, an impulse to internalize the cues of the dominant order was built into their earliest training and most certainly into their college educations. A century before success manuals reached their heyday, educational reformers began their mission to "educate the character" of Americans through a national network of alumni associations and student societies, a network connected not only to other elite colleges and newly established universities but to communities throughout the country, where college-trained ministers, teachers, and lecturers brought their ideas and their influence through moral reform and evangelism, common schools, the lyceum, and other mutual-improvement and educational societies.[31]

Believing that internal self-control was of central importance for securing both individual success and social order, Yale-educated Congregational clergyman and educator Timothy Dwight (1752–1817) and his followers devised new forms of discipline and pedagogy that represented a shift from shame to guilt, from external conformity to internal reform. The result ideally would be the individual who was self-motivated to do well and be good. In the nineteenth century, the special qualities that such an education imparted came to be known as "character." An individual "possessed character to the extent to which he could be counted on to act correctly and responsibly of his own accord in situations in which he would have been free to act otherwise." [32]

It seems certain that success writers were a product of this movement and furthermore that they reflected its influence in the success manuals they wrote. Not only did they present "character" as the most often stated "key to success," but the goal of character education—to teach individuals to internalize authority and self-control as a means to both individual success and social stability[33]—is one of the important subtexts of the success manual.

One way to look at the specific manifestations of "character education" and at other intellectual influences on men of the ilk who wrote success manuals is to identify some of the books that they most certainly would have been exposed to, especially those works likely to have provided models and actual material for the success manual genre.

A type of book that few success writers could have escaped was the college ethics text used in the senior seminar in moral philosophy. In the nineteenth century, the moral philosophy course was a hallowed institution in American college curriculums across the country. Required of all seniors, and often taught by the college's president, it was intended to be the high point of a young man's college education. The ethics texts used in these courses had titles such as *Elements of Moral Science* (Francis Wayland, 1835) and *Science of Moral Philosophy* (Asa Mahan, 1848). As a genre, they emerged in the 1830s, flourished through the 1860s, and continued to be reissued into the 1890s. They were written mostly by college presidents, many of them clergymen, who sought to instruct their students—and the nation—in what could be characterized as the "Science of What Ought to Be." Taken together, these works expressed the official ethic or public philosophy of nineteenth-century America—the moral values Americans believed they ought to desire.[34]

True to the goals of character education outlined by Timothy Dwight years before, virtue was not to be taught entirely for virtue's sake. In a democratic society, moral philosophy was to substitute for the customs, traditions, and coercive institutions in more traditional European societies; it was to provide and implement moral values while restraining and directing men. The ultimate goal was the formation of the individual who was self-regulating and inner-directed.[35] According to this view, the cultivation of sound (Christian) character was good for the individual but even better for the social order as a whole.

Many of the themes of moral philosophy texts reverberate through the pages of success manuals, most especially their insistence on the efficacy of individual virtue, their concern to delineate a morality that squared individual virtue with material progress, their attempt to accommodate the old to the new, to accept change without abandoning tradition, and their faith in willpower and character. So striking are the parallels of certain themes within the ethics texts and the success manuals that it might be fair to say that the success writers had taken up the torch of their mentors to become the moral philosophy "professors" for a new generation—the restless, growing, unschooled, American nation beyond the classroom walls and the college campuses. The tone of the success manual was more secular and more individualistic, but the desire to situate individual and national progress in a moral framework bore the imprint of the college moral philosophy textbook.

In fact, the ethics text may have been a prototype for the *form* of the success manual as well the inspiration for some of its content. The "composite" quality of these texts are certainly suggestive of the format as well as content of the later success manual. Given that moral philosophy courses and the texts used in them were a part of the education of most success writers and given that ethics texts continued to be published through the 1890s, it is likely that at least one such text was on the bookshelf of any of the men who wrote success manuals. And given the propensity of success writers to "borrow" from the works of other authors, it is equally likely that the moral philosophy texts provided a certain amount of "material inspiration" for the success manual.

Even success writers who did not have the benefit of a college education and exposure to college ethics seminars and texts were likely to have encountered "character education" in other forms during their youth. In the 1830s, there emerged an important and popular genre of advice literature designed especially for young men.[36] Typical were John Todd's *The Young Man: Hints Addressed to the Young Men of the United States* (1844), Henry Ward Beecher's *Lectures to Young Men* (1844), and T. S. Arthur's *Advice to*

Young Men on Their Duties and Conduct in Life (1849). The popularity of such works continued through the midcentury; new editions of certain works were still being issued in the 1860s. Though sales figures for the young men's guides were more modest than those of the later success manuals, circulation figures were high, especially for the antebellum period. Some titles were reputed to have sold tens of thousands of copies. The men who became success writers could not have missed at least a passing acquaintance with such books.

Like success manuals, these young men's guides read like an interminable sermon on the importance of the bourgeois habits of industry, temperance, honesty, health, and moderation. But their emphasis on moderation and self-control is particularly significant, distinguishing them from other kinds of advice literature. These were the works that were so filled with admonitions against masturbation, euphemized as "building castles in the air" or "flights of fancy."[37] According to their advice, self-control—and specifically sexual self-control—was necessary to achieve mastery in the outside world and success in professional life. What better way to encourage adolescent males to internalize the values of the dominant order than to somehow link those values with both the achievement of professional success and the attainment of a certain kind of sexual power and mastery. And what better way to address the fear and anxiety of young men starting out in life than to describe the task and the dangers before them in profoundly personal as well as professional terms?

Though associations having to do with success, manhood, and the undercurrent of male sexual symbolism can be seen more clearly in the postbellum success manual, these antebellum guide books for young men were no doubt part of the inspiration for these and other themes in the later genre. These young men's guides are more genuinely the antecedents of the Gilded Age success manual than are the more commonly cited antebellum mercantile and business handbooks. Even though the character-oriented guides for young men did not use the word "success" and did not focus on the wealth, fame, and power of great men to the same extent as the success manuals, they are like success manuals insofar as (1) they presented *being good* as the means to worldly success; (2) they defined *being good* not only in terms of the traditional economic virtues of honesty, industry, and frugality but in terms of self-discipline and self-control, symbolized in sexual metaphor; and (3) they concluded that *being good*—being a man of character—was at least part of the definition of success. Like the moral philosophy texts, these young men's guides were likely to have been both a part of the formative influences upon the men who wrote success manuals and a ready source of material to be incorporated into their own writing of success manuals published just a few years later in the century. Furthermore, to entrepreneurially minded authors and prospective authors, the sales and circulation of this earlier type of advice literature may have been taken as promising evidence of an extensive and perhaps not fully tapped market for a particular type of book.

Another apparently universal and beloved part of the educational experience of young men of the success writers' generation was reading the essays or, even better, hearing the lectures of Ralph Waldo Emerson. To say that Emerson was a favorite lecturer on college campuses and at young men's associations in the 1840s and 1850s scarcely does justice to the fervor his visits created. His lecture tours took him to small towns and large cities across the nation, where he inspired excited and life-transforming responses from his youthful, male audiences. G. Stanley Hall described reactions to Emerson's lectures at Williams College in the 1860s: "in my set a veritable Emersonian craze ran rampant . . . I felt that I had come into personal contact with the greatest living mind." [38] Emerson's one-day visit to Williams College was extended to an entire week upon popular demand, and when college officials refused to allow the chapel to be used for his lectures, students procured the largest hall in town and filled every seat. Another young man in the audience, James A. Garfield (who later would become President of the United States), remembered not being able to sleep that night and recalled Emerson's lecture series as "the beginning of his intellectual life." [39] Though there were no doubt many writers who influenced the young men of this generation, Emerson seems to have had a special magnetism and was clearly one of the important inspirations for the manhood theme in the success manual; his masculinized and sexualized language anticipates that characteristic of success writers. In his 1841 journal, Emerson calls for "initiative, spermatic, prophesying man-making words," and his early essays proclaim "an explicit rhetoric of man making." Especially in "The American Scholar," "The Divinity School Address," and "Self Reliance," Emerson insists on manly power as the essence of mental energy and rails against what society does to manhood. For example, he writes: "The state of society is one in which the members have suffered amputation from the trunk, and strut about so many walking monsters, — a good finger, a neck, a stomach, an elbow, but never a man. . . . The main enterprise of the world for splendor, for extent, is the upbuilding of a man." In other essays and addresses, he laments that "society everywhere is in conspiracy against the manhood of every one of its members," and says men have become "parlor soldiers," "city dolls," "a mob." A true man, he argued, should be a "firm column" who, as soon as he realizes his inborn power, "stands in the erect position" and "works miracles." [40]

It is little wonder that Emerson's lectures had such an impact on his youthful male audiences. Their reactions demonstrated that they understood Emerson's message. Recalling Emerson's lectures, Charles Woodbury observed, "With his coming, adolescence ended and virility began, he *belonged* to the young men."[41] Emerson's call for man-making words must have been compelling to young men contemplating careers as clergymen, educators, and editors—that is, to the kind of men who wrote success manuals. And it is not surprising that so many of Emerson's man-making words found their way into success manuals. The uncertainty about what it meant to "be a man" that haunted Emerson's antebellum America only intensified and broadened in the Gilded Age. In articulating his own dilemma, Emerson gave words to the dilemma of a whole stratum of American men;[42] he expressed certain unresolved tensions in their lives and in their culture and gave them a new and powerful way to see themselves and their mission. Most importantly, he gave them words that inspired "feelings of access to manly power."[43]

Finally, the men who wrote success manuals would have known something about the ideas and work of the English philosopher Herbert Spencer. Spencer's work was fully understood by few, and many, if not most, who did understand his ideas rejected them.[44] Nonetheless, Spencer was widely known among educated Americans from the 1860s to the turn of the century. Spencer was credited with a theory of social evolution that paralleled in some but not all respects Charles Darwin's theory of biological evolution. Spencer argued that in the world of human beings, as in the world of plants and animals, the impersonal forces of competition, the brutish yet natural struggle for existence, over centuries and centuries of human history determined which species would thrive and which would die. He coined the phrase "survival of the fittest," an alternative to Darwin's term "natural selection," to describe the result of this process. Spencer did not intend his theories as a description of contemporary social conflict or as a rationalization or justification for the "brutishness" of the age.[45] But certainly some readers and listeners interpreted his ideas exactly this way. Hence, Spencer and his ideas were very controversial. To say that success writers would have been exposed to the works of Herbert Spencer is not to say they were Spencerians or social Darwinists. There was much about Spencer's thought (and most certainly about social Darwinism) that would have been unpalatable to the success writers, most especially a determinism that seemed to deny the power of individual will to shape one's own destiny. But Spencer's vivid language portraying life as a brutal struggle for existence resonated with success writers' experience or view of the world in much the same way as did Emerson's "man-making words." Furthermore, the idea that only the fittest might survive in the battle of life—if separated from its fatalistic implications—might serve as a goad to redoubled efforts, rather than a reason to give up in despair. Even if one accepted the idea that certain men were somehow constitutionally "fit" to succeed while others were destined to fail, this too might be inspiration for a man to demonstrate by his own effort that he was among the "fit"—nature's "elect"—who were predestined to survive. In any event, the language of "the battle of life" in success manuals was no doubt inspired in part by the language, if not the conclusions, of Herbert Spencer and his popularizers.

LITERARY MEN IN A COMMERCIAL WORLD

Moral philosophy texts, guidebooks for young men, the essays of Ralph Waldo Emerson, and the theories of Herbert Spencer represent one type of influence on the men who wrote success manuals. But educated men who came of age in the third quarter of the nineteenth century and pursued the kinds of careers typical of success writers were also aware of the contemporary reading tastes of the general population. They would have taken a keen interest in commercial developments in the press and in the magazine and book-publishing industries. They could not have missed, for example, the boom in the subscription book industry that occurred just after the Civil War. They were likely to have known of the giant subscription sales success of P. T. Barnum's autobiography with the self-help theme, *Struggles and Triumphs* (1854). They may also have known that Harriet Beecher Stowe had a subscription "hit" that capitalized on the "self-help" motif. Her book about the careers of abolitionists and Civil War heroes, first entitled *Men of Our Times* (1868), was republished and sold exclusively by subscription in 1872 under the new, more success-oriented title *The Lives and Deeds of Our Self-Made Men*. They certainly knew the books of the Scottish writer Samuel Smiles—*Self-Help* (1860), *Character* (1871), *Thrift* (1875), and *Duty* (1880)—which were widely distributed by mail order as part of the so-called "cheap libraries."[46] Smiles would come to be the most often quoted authority, with and without attribution, in the American success manual genre.

In short, there was plenty of material from which to create a genre of success literature, much of which was a common part of the early reading experience of the type of men who wrote success manuals. Furthermore, there was plenty of evidence that the theme of success and the self-made man was a popular moneymaker in a burgeoning new book industry. Finally, there was little in the philosophical makeup or the social position of these men that would cause them to eschew personal material gain or hesitate in merging personal interest in a commercial publishing venture with the mission to preach moral rectitude through character education as the only true means to true success.

It is proper to frame the lives of the success writers in a way that helps us appreciate the fact that they would naturally have been attuned to the material possibilities for self-advancement. But it would be a mistake to portray them simply as opportunists—entrepreneurs of the written word—or merely as apologists or ideologues for the titans of the new industrial order. They were men caught up in the midst of change, no doubt themselves grappling with the ongoing debates about the meaning of the emerging new industrial order. They were in positions to know that the concerns of their peers and the anxieties of their audiences were real. And they were in professions, especially the ministry, that saw their role as addressing the worries of the public. They had direct experience that bridged worlds that were then so much in conflict—rural versus urban, manual versus mental work, haves versus have-nots, new versus old conceptions of manhood. And finally, as college-educated men, they bore the heavy responsibility of leadership, of preserving traditional cultural values and of helping maintain social stability. However trite and formulaic the success manuals may now appear, there is no reason to assume that their writers did not take seriously the ideas embodied in them, nor is it contradictory to suggest that success writers were personally motivated by the spirit of stewardship as well as the spirit of self-help.

3

Inspiration for the Battle of Life:
The Possibility of Success despite Difficulty

There is always a way to rise, my boy,
Always a way to advance;
Yet the road that leads to Mount Success
Does not pass by the way of chance,
But goes through the stations of Work and Strive,
Through the valley of Persevere;
And the man that succeeds while others fail,
Must be willing to pay most dear.
For there's always a way to fall, my boy,
Always a way to slide,
And the men you find at the foot of the hill
All sought for an easy ride.
So on and up, though the road be rough
And the storms come thick and fast;
There is room at the top for the man who tries,
And victory comes at last.
—Alexander Lewis, "Room at the Top,"
in *Manhood-Making: Studies in the*
Elemental Principles of Success

The writers of success manuals did not assume that they were preaching to the converted. In fact, they made the opposite assumption. In prefaces, dedications, introductions, and statements of purpose, success writers addressed themselves to those they described as the "anxious," the "discouraged," and the "disenchanted." They reached out to young men who they believed had lost hope or held the mistaken belief that only the rich and fortunate could succeed. Furthermore, success writers did not paint a glowing picture of the pursuit of success in their times. The "battle of life," as they described it, was a brutal affair in which many fell by the wayside — a sobering reality even for the intrepid, and paralyzingly frightful for the faint of heart. It was against a backdrop of danger and gloom that success writers presented themselves as missionaries of enlightenment and hope. They brought the good news that despite difficulties there was still "room at the top for those who really tried." They offered inspiration for the battle of life and confirmation about the legitimacy and exigency of the struggle.

SELF-DOUBT, ANXIETY, AND DESPAIR

The most jarring and revealing few pages of success manuals are those at the very beginning — the introductions, dedications, prefaces, statements of aim or purpose. The upbeat success-oriented titles of success manuals might lead us to expect these authors to preface their works with a celebration of opportunity and success. In fact, these beginnings contain a striking undercurrent of gloom and malaise that reemerges in certain chapters throughout the manuals. The gloom had to do with the presumed attitude and state of mind that the success writers believed they were addressing. The stated "object" of Orison Swett Marden's *Rising in the World* was to "arouse to honorable exertion youth who are drifting without aim, to awaken dormant ambitions in those who have grown discouraged in the struggle for success."[1] In the preface to *Hidden Treasures*, H. A. Lewis modestly asserted, "If this book shall serve to awaken dormant energies in ONE PERSON who might otherwise have failed, we shall feel abundantly repaid."[2] Success writers presented their books and their upbeat message as a solution to a problem, a remedy for an illness. They dedicated their books to bringing hope to the "despondent and faint-hearted," courage to the "faltering traveler," and inspiration to the "disenchanted."[3]

Success writers agreed on the problem: not enough young men were achieving success; even worse, some refused to try. William Thayer insisted that there were "millions of young men in our country who ought to possess a strong desire to win in the battle of life."[4] But what ought to be and what was often differed. Tilley worried that "great masses of men are too easily conquered by circumstances, instead of resolving at all hazard to conquer them,"[5] and Samuel Smiles decried what he called "the frequent tendency toward discontent, unhappiness, inaction and reverie, displaying itself in a premature contempt for real life, and disgust at the beaten tracks of men."[6] Alexander Lewis found it "fearful to think how many of our young people are drifting without aim in life,"[7] and William King conceded that many would not even "attempt a vigorous struggle."[8]

Success writers believed that the problem lay within the individual, specifically in a misconception about the possibilities that were within the grasp of even a poor boy.[9] Edward Bok dedicated a success manual entitled *Successward: A Young Man's Book for Young Men* to correcting the mistaken view that there was no room on the ladder of success for the man of modest means: "The average young man is apt to think that success is not for him. . . . 'The rich, the fortunate—they are the only people who can be successful,' is the way one young fellow recently expressed it to me, and he thought as many do. It is this wrong conception of success which this book aims to remove."[10] Tilley deplored young men's "lack of confidence in the possibilities at hand,"[11] and Smiles underscored the seriousness of the problem by lamenting, "Nothing can compensate for loss of hope in a man."[12]

Success writers noted evidence of hopelessness and worse; some saw indications of "failure of nerve." Marden wrote of the "sin of fretting" and recommended "cheerfulness" as an antidote to "break spells of melancholy."[13] John Dale, who reported that business growth was accompanied by a growth in nervous disease, devoted a chapter to "The Sin of Worry."[14] Entire chapters were devoted to the topic of depression; they had titles such as "Enthusiasm" and "Persistency." "Lack of enthusiasm" was the euphemism for depression; "persistency" suggested positive thinking and action therapy as an antidote for depression. These chapters noted suicides, "attacks of lethargy," "despondency arising from surroundings," and "moments of weakness, apparent or real dissatisfaction with [one's] own performance and destiny, [and] gloomy temper." Advisors encouraged readers to buck up: "Look on the bright side . . . hours of depression will come; but wait. It is always darkest, we are told, just before day, a brighter turn of affairs may come at any minute."[15]

Success writers thus concerned themselves with the attitudes and emotions of the new generation, especially regarding their prospects of getting on in life. They observed and lamented a growing sense of hopelessness and anxiety, uncertainty and despair, spiritual malaise and self-doubt, and sometimes even "indifference to life's prizes and purposes."[16]

Certainly success writers were not the only ones to take note of an apparent illness in the American spirit. Physicians and medical advisors observed a state of "nervous debility and irritability," which they described in the popular medical treatises of the day as "neurasthenia." Dr. George M. Beard addressed the question in his influential work *American Nervousness: Its Causes and Consequences* (1881). He concluded that the cause of the lack of nerve force could be found in the very character of modern American civilization—the speed, the change of a mechanical age, the pressure of competitive environment, the striving for "eminence or wealth," and the fear that this new civilization might be undone either by the eventual degeneracy of this new elite or by the violence of the clamoring, rampant city mobs below.[17] The medical treatment of neurasthenia involved retreat from the stresses and strains of modern life through "rest cures" and "exercise cures" intended to restructure the patient's perceptions and help him or her to adjust to modern civilization.[18]

Though success manuals echo some of the language of Beard and others in the medical profession who worried about American nervousness, Beard described neurasthenia as a phenomenon specific to a small class of people quite different from those who made up the market for success manuals. Beard believed that this nervous disease afflicted the ambitious and striving members of an urban, professional class of "brain-workers." As Alan Trachtenberg points out, Beard made "American nervousness" a badge of distinction, explicitly excluding the "muscle-workers" and the "lower orders."[19] The success manuals, on the other hand, were directed to a broad stratum of Americans, rural and small-town people of modest circumstances, struggling as much to keep their place in life as to advance it.[20] The anxieties of these people were more likely to be related to the fear of being left out and passed by than to the bourgeois stresses of "overcivilization." It is difficult to imagine that typical readers of success manuals would have sought medical treatment for their malaise. And if they did, their class position as well as their rural residence probably would have precluded Dr. Beard's diagnosis of neurasthenia and retreat from everyday life as a practical cure. Success manuals themselves may have been the closest thing to a tonic for despair and disenchantment to reach the marginalized rural sectors of the American population.

As transitional figures who themselves had moved from the hinterland to the metropolis, most success writers were in a position to know that the spiritual malaise of their audience was more likely to be explained by anxiety about how to make a living than by the pressures of urban life on the fast track. But by using the term "neurasthenia" and the metaphor of illness, success writers borrowed a new, "scientific" idiom to acknowledge and address the very real worries of a broad stratum of Americans whose anxieties were more fundamental than those of the urban bourgeoisie. The fact that success writers adopted the language of nervousness is one of many examples of their ability to synthesize and popularize strands of contemporary thought. In so doing they diluted and transformed the central ideas to conform to their own worldview and to the interests of the audience to which they sought to appeal.

Like Beard, success writers located the cause of distress in the transition and adjustment to modern civilization and the accelerated struggle for survival it engendered. And like Beard, they believed that these social conditions impacted on men's attitudes and consequently on their ability to act. But unlike Beard, they framed their explanation in a way that included the struggles of those at the bottom of the ladder as well as the anxieties of those at the top. And unlike Beard, the success writers prescribed a cure that allowed for no retreat and no time out, only action therapy. In the concept of "the battle of life," success writers found a metaphor that had broad applicability. It identified the problem and outlined the solution for every man regardless of his circumstances. In the world of the success manual, each man was called to prove his mettle and fight for victory or go down in defeat. "The battle" provided a way to see the world as a contest in which all men had an equal chance to win and each man—through individual effort—had the potential to determine the outcome.

THE BATTLE

Volume after volume and chapter after chapter warned readers that they lived in a new era unlike any humans had ever known—a "fast-moving age," an "age of specialization," an "electric age," an age in which life itself was an "ever-changing panorama."[21] William Mathews's characterization was typical:

> Never before in the world's history was competition in every calling and pursuit so fierce as now . . . in this latter half of the nineteenth century. Carlyle truly says, "the race of life has become intense; the runners are treading upon each other's heels; woe to him who stops to tie his shoestring!"[22]

Change was so rapid that it seemed to happen before one's eyes, as William King noted in 1894: "The sights of yesterday are old, the scenes of today are swiftly passing, and the picture of tomorrow will be new."[23] These manuals conveyed a sense of urgency and drama, gave witness to a great transition, and insisted on the specialness of the times. Reports that "men are falling by the hundreds in the thick of the fight"[24] only intensified the drama. One author claimed that 97 of every 100 business or merchant ventures failed; others detailed stories of "financial reverse" and warned of what some called "the great vicissitudes of life,"[25] or the "insecurities of business life."[26]

The newness of the age, the speed of change, the intensification of competition all called for a new approach for the man who expected to survive. Readers were warned that the man who did not assert himself "must expect not only to be outstripped, but knocked, crushed, and trampled underfoot in the rush and roar of the nineteenth century";[27] authors charged that "the times are sifting the candidates more rigorously than ever before."[28] In an entire chapter devoted to "rivalries," Tilley claimed that competition was legion in every walk of life, in the street, the workshop, the senate, the marketplace, and on Wall Street. If competition was everywhere and all could compete, he argued, then everyone was an adversary or opponent: "[Life is] a struggle in which we go forth armed and equipped to contend with our fellows. No matter how friendly the competition is, it is competition. If we go up others must give place to us and go down." "There is no escape from it," he insisted. "The great fact confronts one at the outset of his career. From the cradle to the grave, indeed, the strife continues."[29]

The language of the success manuals consistently and strikingly used the images and metaphors of conflict, danger, rivalry, and uncertainty. Success writers braced readers for "these days of fierce competition," for the "long and desperate struggle," for the "stormy ocean," or for the "raging sea of life."[30] But by far the most common metaphor for life in these times was the image of armed conflict, "the battle." Military heroes and the great wars of history were part of the stock-in-trade of success writers. The individual most often referred to through anecdote and analogy was Napoleon Bonaparte, symbol of both military might and the successful upstart. William Mathews, for example, took several pages to provide a detailed account of two Napoleonic campaigns in which "reserve forces" were decisive for victory. He concluded the discussion by likening these forays to the battle that aspiring individuals face in daily life:

> Life is warfare: it, too, has its decisive moments, when success or failure, victory or defeat, must hinge upon our reserve power. At the bar, in the senate, in the pulpit, in the fields of business, in every sphere of human activity, he only organizes victory and commands success behind whose van and corps of battle is heard the steady tramp of the army of the reserve.[31]

Samuel Smiles reversed the business/battle analogy; he credited the military victor with "business know-how." He praised Napoleon's opponent, the Duke of Wellington, for his great attention to detail and his ability as a "routinist," concluding, "His business faculty was his genius of common sense; and it is not perhaps saying too much to aver that it was because he was a first-rate man of business that he never lost a battle."[32] Success in a hostile world seemed to demand mobilization in a military way. Even the editor of the *Ladies' Home Journal*, Edward Bok, was anxious to identify himself as "a Napoleon of the mart." In a success manual he authored, Bok wrote of himself: "He thinks he knows what a fight for success means to a young fellow, and he writes with the smoke of battle around him and from the very thick of the fight."[33] Such striking language makes it difficult to re-member that the combat Bok experienced took place in the editorial office of the *Ladies' Home Journal*.

Weaponry provided an important metaphor for the means to success. Owen claimed that men must "be soldier-like, and rest on their arms ready to spring up and fire on the instant."[34] H. Risborough Sharman suggested that the schoolboy in learning his lessons of obedience and diligence was only "'polishing the weapons' of his later success."[35] Likewise, Jerome Paine Bates, in *The Imperial Highway*, describes an American scientist for whom "concentration of mind and power" was the "secret of his work." The scientist confessed: "I have but one idea, but I have learned that if I wish ever to make a breach in the wall, I must play my guns continually upon one point." "Such gunnery," Bates added, "is usually successful."[36]

It is difficult to ignore the phallic symbolism of these and other refer-ences, and this aspect of their meaning is explored later, in chapter 7. Suffice it to say here that the battle metaphor and the emphasis on weaponry made clear that it was a man's world; the phallic references helped to equate sym-bolically success and manliness.

Finally, these admonitions to gird and arm oneself for combat suggested not only the necessity and the urgency of battle; they suggest also the righ-teousness of battle. One of the clearest expressions of this theme was in the frequent mixing of the symbols of warfare and Christianity. These lines, for example, appeared in one success manual under the title "The Battle Cry of Success," dedicated as a "hymn to you young men":

> Thou my Helmet, Falchion, Leader,
> Lord and Savior, Interceder,
> Both my left hand and my right,
> Fill with javelins of Light
> And with ten archangels' might![37]

Here was the same kind of missionary zeal for righteous battle as was ap-parent also in the popularity of the hymn "Onward Christian Soldiers," in the founding of a benevolent society named the Salvation Army, and in the rhetoric of expansionist American foreign policy.[38] Here was a way of understanding the world in which force, hierarchy, and individualism could be glorified and legitimized while fear and uncertainty could be overcome.

"The battle" was thus an important symbol that found expression not only in the success manual but in a wide variety of cultural forms in late-nineteenth-century America. Memoirs of the Civil War were among the most popular of all subscription books, and the war remained a reference point in political and cultural life for nearly two generations.[39] The most widely known philosopher of the period, social Darwinist Herbert Spencer, provided a "scientific" language that popularizers readily appropriated to describe life as a "struggle for existence" in which "only the fittest might survive."[40] By the 1890s, Napoleon had become the most important hero in American magazines, while military music and parades flourished as never before.[41] Amateur boxing and professional prizefighting gained acceptance and popularity among the middle and upper classes as well as the working classes, while a physical fitness craze swept the urban bourgeoisie. Finally, in 1898 the nation answered the call for "strenuous manhood" and "muscular Christianity" by taking up arms against Spain in a war of territorial conquest in Cuba and the Philippines.[42]

The various manifestations of the admonition to "get tough" in late-nineteenth-century America have most often been interpreted as a compensatory response of the urban bourgeoisie to their increasingly soft, affluent, and sedentary culture. As frontiers were conquered, peacetime prevailed, and white-collar occupations proliferated, men of the managerial and professional classes encountered few opportunities to test their manhood by the exhibition of courage, physical strength, and prowess. The call to battle was a call for revitalization, to resist effeminacy and weakness bred by prosperity and to stave off the feared decline and fall of an overdeveloped civilization.[43] Gilded Age Americans—especially members of a bourgeoisie that felt themselves under siege—sought to revitalize their culture. They toughened themselves and their children through military drills and manly sport; they took a militant stand toward social dissidence through harsh penal codes and industrial labor policy; and they sought moral regeneration as well as an overseas empire through military adventure.[44]

But in trying to understand the importance and the appeal of the battle metaphor in the more specific context of the success manual, we must explore the meaning of such imagery for the have-nots as well as for the already affluent urban bourgeoisie. Elliot Gorn's study of bare-knuckle prizefighting is suggestive. Especially for the struggling lower classes, Gorn argues, combat might have been seen as a "rite of violence" that both reflected the brutality of life and provided a way to comprehend it. Prizefighting gloried in the fact that brutishness was part of man's fate; every man's victory implied another's loss.[45] Success manuals became popular in an era of brutal economic conflict and uncertainty, an era where, by success writers' own account, the man who did not assert himself would be "knocked, crushed, and trampled underfoot in the rush and roar of the nineteenth century" and where 97 out of every 100 business ventures failed.[46] For success manual readers—aspiring people of modest means who were economically vulnerable—combat may have symbolically represented harsh realities that they either perceived or experienced directly. Describing life as a brutal struggle for survival was one way for success manual writers to acknowledge rather than deny that times were indeed difficult and perhaps thereby gain credibility with readers who also found it so.

The battle metaphor contained within it both the diagnosis and the cure for the ailments of the age. The battle not only acknowledged that times were tough, it was a bracing call to action. A world of fierce and unrelenting battle justified, even demanded, a new, more aggressive approach in the struggle for success. In a do-or-die, sink-or-swim world of winners or losers, combat was more than valorous and manly, it was imperative—a struggle for survival.

Finally, the battle metaphor made it possible to see the conflict and difficulties of the age in strictly individual terms. The struggle was always one man against another; the outcome depended entirely on the personal attributes, abilities, effort, and determination of the individual. The image of one-on-one combat reduced complex problems to a simple and easily understood formula; it precluded other kinds of explanations that might take into account larger social, economic, and political forces. It provided a way to see the individual as powerful; it placed him in charge of his own destiny. In such a view of the world, wealth, privilege, and position held no sway; forces outside the individual man—monopoly, class conflict, boom-and-bust economies—had no meaning. Despite the Spencerian language used to describe "the struggle," the world of the success manual was not the pessimistic, predetermined world of the social Darwinists. Far from being a pawn of larger, impersonal, cosmic forces, the individual in the world of the success manual was the sole motive force. The battle of life might be brutal, but insofar as the individual had the power to determine the outcome, the battle symbolized hope and opportunity for the ordinary man. The battle metaphor contained both sides of a bipolar world—victory as well as defeat, opportunity as well as anxiety. Ultimately it was this optimistic, individualistic side of the battle of life that success writers promoted as an antidote for the ills of the age. And the remedy they prescribed was a self-help cure.

ROOM AT THE TOP

Nothing better captured the optimistic side of the success manual's worldview than the maxim, "There is always room at the top." A favorite cliché that appeared in chapter titles and throughout the texts,[47] it conveyed the more beneficent side of a brutal social order. "Room at the top" reminded readers that despite conflict, uncertainty, and even widespread failure, this new age boasted unprecedented growth, prosperity, and progress. Success writers employed a variety of metaphors to symbolize the upward struggle: pyramids, ladders, stairs, mountains. But whatever the metaphor, the meaning was constant. "Room at the top" stood for the promise of opportunity and reward for the ordinary man of great determination.

"Room at the top" also expressed a view of the social order that was at once hierarchical and mobile, stratified and fluid. The same acceleration that brought conflict and distress brought expanded opportunities. Although the competition was severe, the race was open to all. The authors of success manuals defended their age in these terms. They argued that because the path was rugged and many travelers fell by the wayside, there existed a great demand for men who could reach the top and assume positions of prominence. Owen, for example, discussed frankly the difficulties and offered encouragement in the task of seeking a place in the world:

> It is urged, there are no vacant places. True, there is a great press of people downstairs, but there is plenty of room upstairs. There are more first-class places than there are first-class men to fill them. The world is a rigid world, but in the long run it is an eminently just one. It never needed *men* worse than today. It is seeking for worthy men to bestow its honors on.[48]

Similarly, when Tilley described the various professions as pyramids, he observed that there was "always room at the top, though the bottom be crowded with commoners." Because the demand for capable men outstripped the supply, he argued, the really first-class men could "command a premium in any market."[49] All agreed that it was a seller's market for the strivers of the current generation.

> The avenues to the best success are being cleared and made wider so that thousands can achieve greatness where only scores could win in the last generation. The chances for riches are many times greater now for the poor people than even a decade ago; but the increase is by the hundred-fold in each ten years. . . . There never has been and there never could have been a period in the life of the world so full of potent opportunity for the young as that now coming.[50]

Opportunity was one thing; but what one did with it was quite another. Success writers were quick to remind readers that the "door of success says 'push' on it."[51] Individual effort was the motor force in this system—the requisite power to make the promise of the new age realizable: "People too often seem to believe that the Almighty will *make* them all they ought to be, and they have nothing to do but desire it. They should be taught that they have to fight the battle, and heaven helps those who help themselves, and no others."[52] Self-reliance, after all, was the preeminent virtue of the self-made man, and success writers never tired of discussing the importance of self-help, praising the man of independence and ridiculing those who "leaned on others for support."[53] Self-help wisdom was condensed into oft-repeated maxims, some of which still have a familiar ring: "Where there's a will there's a way," "A pound of pluck is worth a ton of luck," "Self-made or never made," and, particularly appropriate for the age of industry, "Better to wear out than to rust out."[54] Poetry, too, might cheer readers on to manly self-reliance. These verses, entitled "Rely on Yourself," appeared in more than one success manual:

> In battle or business whatever the game—
> In law, or in love, it is ever the same;
> In the struggle for power, or scramble for pelf,
> Let this be your motto, "Rely on yourself."
> For whether the prize be a ribbon or throne,
> The victor is he who can go it alone.[55]

Self-reliance and the competitive individualism it represented were part of the antidote for the difficulties of the age. No one promised that all could have success for the asking, and no one posited a society of equals. But the man who relied on himself had a chance. The success manuals promised him the "opportunity to compete for the prizes"[56] and assured him that "each may run the race unhindered by any, and encouraged by all."[57] The assertion of the principle of equal opportunity repeatedly led to a defense and glorification of the competitive ethic. There was presumably "room at the top" and equal position at the starting line, but there was no getting around the fact that man was pitted against man all along the way. This reality brought success writers back to the metaphor of battle time and time again in increasingly intensified forms, exemplified in the following discussion of a prizefight.

Let no one suppose that this rivalry among men has not its rightful place. "A prize fight," says Dr. Potter, "is probably the most disgusting spectacle on earth, but it has in it just one moment which very nearly approaches the sublime, and that is when the combatants shake hands with each other and exchange that salutation, as old as the classic arena,—'May the best man win!' It is the equitable thing that the best man should win. Let no man be afraid to say to his fellow, 'I am your rival in this race, and I mean to beat you if I can.'"[58]

Only the battle could encompass a world characterized by danger, hostility, and failure on one hand and opportunity and reward on the other. Furthermore, only in such a competitive new social order could the pursuit of individual self-interest be justified as behavior necessary to survive.

4

Success or Failure—Which? The Exigency of Success and the Efficacy of the New Industrial Order

☛

Young man, two ways are open before you in life. One points to degradation and want. The other to usefulness and wealth. In the old Grecian races one only, by any possible means, could gain the prize, but in the momentous race of human life there is no limiting of the prize to one. No one is debarred from competing; all may succeed, provided the right methods are followed. Life is not a lottery. Its prizes are not distributed by chance.—Harry A. Lewis, *Hidden Treasures, or Why Some Succeed While Others Fail*

The idea that there was "room at the top" for the man who really tried may have been compelling to Gilded Age Americans, particularly to those likely to have read success manuals, but it was hardly the only view of what was in store for the man of modest means in the new age of industry. The optimistic individualism expressed in success manuals competed with the harsh prognoses of critics of the new industrial order. In fact, the population that the subscription book trade targeted as the best market for success manuals was the same population from which the rural protest movements of the late nineteenth century drew their strength.[1] Three successive economic depressions brought falling farm prices, foreclosures on farm and home mortgages, waves of unemployment, and swelling membership in organizations such as the Farmers' Alliance, the Knights of Labor, the Populists, and the Socialist Party. Lecturers from these organizations fanned out across the country, bringing a radical critique of the American political and economic system to people scattered at great distances from each other and far removed from the urban industrial centers.[2] Nor were people in small towns and rural areas immune from news of the growth of industrial unionism and the violent clashes between labor and capital. Especially events such as the great railroad strike of 1877 were widely reported and debated in the popular press. Prompted by a 10 percent wage cut for railroad workers, a strike that began in Baltimore spread to Pittsburgh, Chicago, St. Louis, Kansas City, and San Francisco, generating sympathy strikes and community support along the way. Only a combination of local police, militia, and federal troops ended the conflict. The drama and scope of this strike and later the Haymarket bombing in 1886, the Homestead steel strike in 1892, the success of the Populist party in 1892, and the Pullman strike and Coxey's march on Washington in 1894 all intensified a sense of crisis. Prosperous and established citizens feared mob violence, people of modest circumstances and their sympathizers feared that individual opportunity for the ordinary man was a thing of the past, and contemporary intellectuals, sensitive to the social unrest around them, speculated about the possibility of a European-style revolution in America.[3]

The intensity of the debate about the efficacy and the future of the new order could also be seen in a more subtle indicator—in the types of books that became best-sellers in the Gilded Age, that is, books whose total sales were equal to at least 1 percent of the U.S. population during the decade they were published.[4] In the years between 1870 and 1910 only six works of nonfiction became best-sellers. Two were success manuals focused on the individual quest for success, self-improvement, and well-being: *The Royal Path of Life, or Aims and Aids to Success and Happiness* (1879) by Thomas L. Haines and Levi W. Yaggy, and Frank Channing Haddock's *The Power of Will: A Practical Companion Book for Unfoldment of the Powers of Mind* (1907). Both sold by subscription, which meant that the price of these books ranged between two and five dollars.[5] Two other best-sellers of the period were handbooks for two radical political movements. Henry George's *Progress and Poverty: An Inquiry into the Causes of Industrial Depression and Increase of Want with Increase of Wealth the Remedy* (1879) held that economic rent was robbery and called for public ownership of property; it was the bible of the single tax movement and "land and labor clubs." William H. Harvey's *Coin's Financial School* (1894) was the main treatise on bimetallism, the movement supported by the Populists and others in favor of a silver standard for currency as the panacea for the country's economic woes. All four of these best-sellers are estimated to have sold from 800,000 to more than a million copies.[6] The most popular work of fiction offering a critical view of the new order was Edward Bellamy's *Looking Backward: 2000–1887* (1888), which sold 200,000 copies in the first three years of publication. *Progress and Poverty, Coin's Financial School,* and *Looking Backward* were all available in paperback at a price ranging from ten to seventy-five cents.[7] George, Harvey, and Bellamy, each in different ways, addressed themselves to the so-called "Social Question," the concern that as great fortunes were amassed by the few, the nation would become divided between haves and have-nots and that the resulting conflict between capital and labor would deteriorate into class warfare. These and other critics of the new order envisioned a variety of solutions, ranging from legislative reform to a radical redistribution of wealth to utopian visions of a new society. But what these critical works had in common that made them so different from the success manuals was their belief that the new industrial order had generated ills that the lone individual was helpless to redress or overcome. They put forward social solutions to problems they saw in the new industrial order; success writers insisted that solutions lay within each individual.

The authors of success manuals did not assume that their own optimistic individualism was the only view or even the dominant view of life in their times in the last quarter of the nineteenth century. They wrote with a keen awareness of contemporary critics and reformers and in fact took an active part in the ongoing debate about the efficacy and legitimacy of the new industrial order.[8] They did not always identify their opponents directly, but success writers nonetheless plunged into the fray, attacking ideas they deemed heretical to their faith in individual opportunity and insisting on their own special view of the world. The intensity and character of their defense of the new industrial order suggests that they believed that their audience was aware of and susceptible to the ideas and proposals of radicals and reformers. Success writers fought fire with fire. They appropriated the socialist theory that the world was divided by class but gave it their own interpretation: the two great classes were not capital and labor, but rather the successful and the failures, the industrious and the lazy, the honest and the spendthrift. They countered the claim that "capital had bound labor" by insisting that there was "bread and success under the American flag" for every boy who was willing to work for it. They lampooned all efforts to reform society en masse. Finally, success writers reassured readers about the sanctity of success and money-getting. They were critical of the excesses of the new industrial order and the abuses of what some termed the "few greedy capitalists," but they insisted that self-help and the pursuit of individual self-interest was neither sacrilege nor crass materialism, but a duty to God, country, and mankind. As one writer put it, "God demands success." Even the pursuit of great wealth—if gotten by tried and true means—was not only a legitimate goal but a blessed endeavor.

In short, success writers refuted and dismissed attacks on the efficacy of the new industrial order and reiterated their own more optimistic view of a world that orbited around the virtuous individual who had the power to determine his own fate. The problems of the world could be reduced to a simple question that each man must answer for himself: "Success or failure—which?" Success writers challenged each man to demonstrate through his actions a faith in the promise that even in this new and sometimes hostile age, each man still had the power to determine his own success or failure. Implicitly, and perhaps unwittingly, they called readers to pledge allegiance to a new American industrial order, and to a belief in its ultimate beneficence and legitimacy.[9]

THE WORLD HAS EVER BEEN SHARPLY
DIVIDED INTO TWO CLASSES

Success writer James Cole's view of the world as "sharply divided into two classes"[10] was a typical one; success writers routinely presented the world in terms of polar opposites. They saw no middle ground; every situation required a choice between two radically divergent alternatives. The "royal path" led to "honor, success, and happiness," while the other was fraught with gloom and "ruined hopes."[11] Success writers could not have been more explicit: "you are either a success or a failure; or you are neither one—nor the other, which is almost as bad as being a failure."[12]

The maxim that best captures this bipolar view of the world was "sink or swim," attributed to the American president success writers quoted most, James Garfield. Success writers used the "sink or swim" analogy more frequently than any other single remark or anecdote. In *Rising in the World*, Orison Swett Marden offered one of the more literal renderings:

> Poverty is uncomfortable, as I can testify, but nine times out of ten the best thing that can happen to a young man is to be tossed over-board and compelled to sink or swim for himself. In all my acquaintance I have never known a man to be drowned who was worth saving.[13]

Like the metaphor of the battle of life, "sink or swim," expressed a view of how the world operated and challenged the individual to "choose" one of two outcomes: victory or defeat, success or failure, do or die. In short, it was a view of the world that stressed the exigency of success over failure as a matter of survival in a dog-eat-dog world.[14]

Success writers made the same sharp distinctions among men. In a success manual entitled *Top or Bottom—Which?*, Archer Brown claimed that there were only "two kinds of men in the world: those who sail and those who drift; those who choose the ports to which they will go, and skillfully and boldly shape their course across the seas with the wind or against it, and those who let the winds and tides carry them where they will. . . . The men who sail . . . do not wait on fortune or favorable currents; they depend on themselves and expect no help from circumstances. Success of the real kind is always in the man who wins it, not in conditions."[15] Others put it more succinctly: the world was divided between the "pushers" and the "pushed";[16] a man was either to rule or to be ruled; "he must conquer or be conquered."[17]

Success writers frequently characterized the two types of men as belonging to one or another "class." In some cases they used the term "class" simply as a category: that class of men "tremulous as the aspen, enthusiastic in their callings," as opposed to the "slow coaches that job on at a lazy pace . . . who need the whip, not the rein."[18] But on other occasions, success writers employed the term "class" in ways that paralleled and appropriated the language of the socialist critics of the new industrial order. They adopted the paradigm of a class-divided society and then redefined it in ways that harmonized with their own moral, individualistic view of the world. "The world has ever been sharply divided into two classes, the few who succeed and the many who fail," declared James Cole.[19] In *Dollars and Sense, or How to Get On*, P. T. Barnum described "the world as viewed by the two different classes that inhabit it"; there were "those who look on the dark side and those who look on the bright side."[20] Likewise, in *Self-Help*, Samuel Smiles observed: "The world has always been divided into two classes,—those who have saved and those who have spent, the thrifty and the extravagant."[21]

These observations both invoked and denied the idea that society was polarized into two fixed classes. The paradigm of class division provided a framework in which success writers advanced their own view of a class-divided society where class itself was ultimately based on man's place in the secular moral order rather than on place in the socioeconomic order. Personal virtue and faith in individual opportunity not only made for success, but distinguished the successful from the failures in life. The virtues that determined a man's class were not "some special gift or opportunity vouchsafed to one and withheld from another" but rather a matter of personal effort of which presumably all were capable.[22] Thrift, industry, initiative, and self-reliance were attributes any man could cultivate. Henry Clay, quoted in *Hidden Treasures*, assured readers that there was "no failure in this country for those whose personal habits are good, and who follow some honest calling industriously, unselfishly, and purely.""If one desires to succeed, he must pay the price—WORK."[23] The man who wanted to do only the very easy things failed to realize that he thereby enrolled himself "among the classes least in demand."[24]

Hard work and good habits quite literally stood between those who were successful and those who were not. The "so-called petty vices" such as "chewing, smoking and snuffing filthy tobacco" brought tens of thousands of families to poverty, claimed one writer. He calculated that if the estimated dollar a week some families spent on tobacco were saved and deposited every six months at 7 percent compound interest, for example, it would in fifty years amount to $22,423, and at the end of eighty years there would be a "snug fortune" of $181,773. "But for these vices," he concluded, "they might soon be well-to-do capitalists."[25] In this and myriad other ways, men determined their own class; the successful had themselves to thank, while the failures had only themselves to blame.[26]

Success writers dismissed not only the lazy, spendthrift *poor* but also the lazy, spendthrift *rich*. They mounted an attack on privilege and inherited wealth of all kinds and heaped contempt on *all* of the "drones in the hive of human industry," whether clothed in "purple and fine linen" or "decorated with rags."[27] One success writer described "the gentleman" as anyone who had nothing to do and was outside the workhouse. The man who relied on his ancestry, he said, was like a potato: "the only good that belongs to him is underground." And he warned that young men cursed with the wealth of their fathers were destined to lead lives of "emasculated idleness and laziness": "Their parents toiled and grew strong; built up their forms of iron and bone; but denying all this to their sons, they turned them upon the world boneless—simple gristle, and soft at that."[28] Contrary to popular belief, success writers argued, ease, dependence, and having "a start in the world" frequently led to "poverty and obscurity."[29] Tortoise-and-hare-type anecdotes illustrated how those who started in poverty and obscurity might turn the tables on those of privilege. For example, Samuel Smiles wrote of the industrious workman who purchased his former master's estate and then chided him about his neglect of business, which had resulted in his loss of the property.[30] Success writers' attack on inherited wealth and privilege was more than an attack on old wealth. It was an implicit critique of the excesses of the newly wealthy "captains of industry" and an attempt to assert moral parameters of successful wealth-getting. Furthermore, it was a way of honoring American democratic tradition in a post-Jeffersonian era—a way to hate privilege and the excesses of great wealth without hating capitalists.

If the failures in life might include *all* of those who refused to cultivate the virtues needed for success, the rich as well as the poor, then the definition of the successful might include both the strivers of modest means as well the already wealthy self-made men. Success writers reasoned that the hardworking, self-reliant laborer was really just a "lesser capitalist,"[31] belonging to the same class as the industrialist who himself might be thought of as simply a "workman" on a grander scale. The two great classes were not capital and labor or rich and poor, but those who were virtuous and those who were not—the successes versus the failures, the strivers versus those who sat idly by. The industrious, honest, and frugal—be they capitalist or worker—had no quarrel with each other; they were simply at different places on the same continuum, on different rungs of the same ladder of success. It was up to the man himself not only to take that first step up but to determine his place on the ladder. The success manuals provided a strikingly clear statement of how upward mobility, or at least the ethos of upward mobility, might help insure social harmony; individual opportunity was the antidote to class conflict.

The success manual thus offered readers an alternative perspective on the idea that the world was coming to be divided between rich and poor, haves and have-nots. The success writers accepted the view that the world was divided by class, but they changed the terms of the debate and the parties to the conflict. They offered an interpretation of the economic distress and social upheaval of Gilded Age America that focused not on the conflict between rich and poor or capital and labor, but on the battle between virtue and vice, between success and failure. If two classes existed, they were the frugal, hardworking men of all ranks who stood above the lazy and spendthrift complainers who depended on others for support, be they paupers or aristocrats.

This moralistic, individualistic rendering of class and class conflict in Gilded Age America was one way to reassure readers that, despite reports to the contrary, the ordinary man could still find a place for himself in a fast-moving, competitive, new industrial order. Some success writers, however, took on the critics, naysayers, and reformers more directly, insisting as did Russell Conwell that "capital [had] not bound labor"[32] but rather had set an example for labor to emulate.

CAPITAL HAS NOT BOUND LABOR

In perhaps the single most famous piece in all success literature, "Acres of Diamonds,"[33] Russell Conwell railed against the "kind of orators that come to talk about the oppressive rich" and "call capitalists wicked and labor enslaved."[34] "This is a lie," he insisted and urged his readers to take a more conciliatory approach: "Let the man who loves his flag and believes in American principles endeavor with all his soul to bring the capitalists and the laboring man together until they stand side by side, arm in arm, and work for the common good of humanity. He is an enemy to his country who sets capital against labor or labor against capital."[35] Conwell claimed that if such ideas were to be countered "we must meet declamation and argument with argument. Capital has not bound labor. No man need be a slave under the stars and stripes."[36] In Conwell's view, "Any working man who would not be a capitalist and an employer is un-American if he is not a fool; and never was there known a more favorable age for the poor mechanic than is now seen in America." [37]

In their energetic rebuttal of the socialist critics of the new dominant order, success writers reveal important assumptions about their readers. They assumed readers were aware of the debate, familiar with the critics of the new order, and perhaps even susceptible to their calls for reform or even radical change. Success writers took it upon themselves to dismiss radical reformers and to show that America was a country unsullied by rank or caste.[38] They offered the rise of the self-made man and the lives of successful capitalists as proof that "the barriers [had] not yet been erected which declare to aspiring talent, 'Thus far and no farther.'" [39] According to these authors, "our famous men" were the "great workmen of society" who rose from humble origins, overcame great difficulties, and upon taking positions of prominence, used their wealth for the good of mankind. Not only did the "captains of industry" give freely to numerous charities and other worthy causes, their enterprises alone made magnificent contributions to society: "Millionaires do well indeed to combine their capital to make possible the construction of railroads, cable, steamships, and great manufacturing plants. They thus give employment to millions who need the pay and they add much to the general good of humanity." [40] Though some contemporary observers at the turn of the century claimed that the good old days when a poor boy could work his way up were past,[41] success writers assured readers that the lines of promotion were open.[42] "The chief glory of America," explained Chamberlain in *Makers of Millions*, "is, that it is a country in which genius and industry find their speediest and surest reward. Fame and fortune are here open to all who are willing to work for them. Neither class distinction nor social prejudices, neither differences of birth, religion, nor ideas can prevent the man of true merit from winning the just reward of his labors in this favored land." [43] In a similar vein, Conwell wrote: "There is bread and success for every youth under the American flag, who has energy and ability to *seize his opportunity*. It matters not whether the boy is born in a log-cabin or in a mansion, if he is dominated by resolute purpose, and upholds himself, neither men nor demons can keep him down." [44]

But success writers did more than celebrate the land of individual opportunity; they alerted readers to the failings and defective reasoning of those who did not share the faith in self-help and the American dream. Mathews explained that those who looked to the government or some workingman's association to reform society were simply "reluctant to admit" that "ill success" was their own fault. In his view, "No amount of legislation can make the spendthrift a rich man," or make the "idle industrious, the thriftless provident, or the drunken sober."[45] Once property was acquired, the law might protect it, but no law could help in the acquiring, warned Dale in *The Way to Win*: "The most legislation can do is to make every man equal before the law, and leave him to make what he can of himself."[46] It was the individual, not the mass, that counted, as H. Risborough Sharman explained in *The Power of the Will, or Success*:

> That portion of the press which seeks to promote the elevation of the masses would do well to insist on the fact that, as the unit is, so is the mass composed of such units; and that, without waiting for teachers, or preachers, or philanthropists, or legislators, or anybody else, there is always *one* of those units with whom the work of reformation may be at once and effectually begun. It is the man himself. We shall approach the millennium in proportion as we multiply such units, who men *and* women, weary of waiting for regeneration *en masse*, or for some new law, or for some additional benevolence, or for anything of a material and outward kind, set about the work by themselves, in themselves and for themselves, *individually*.[47]

Success writers warned that those who failed to embrace the doctrine of individual self-help as the only true means to true success were not only lazy but dangerous. Owen denounced "the men who make incendiary speeches in that valuable organization, 'The Workingmen's Union,' and lead mobs to fire cities and depredate on capital. They put their blind, insensate muscle against the progress of today, that demands muscle mixed with brains."[48] Conwell lampooned labor unions because they "reduce the five dollar man to a two dollar and fifty cent man to raise the imbecile who isn't worthy of fifty cents to two dollars and fifty cents."[49] And Dale dismissed what he called "all cheap schemes to make the lot of men equal" as the "veriest of quackeries."[50] In *Dollars and Sense*, P. T. Barnum gave "the socialist" a satirical treatment:

> The poor spendthrift vagabond said to a rich man: "I have discovered that there is money enough in the world for all of us if it were equally divided; this must be done, and we shall all be happy together." "But," was the response, "if everybody was like you, it would be spent in two months, and what would you do then?" "Oh! Divide again; and keep dividing, of course!"[51]

On occasion, success writers acknowledged with dismay the existence of the very social problems that fueled critics' dire predictions; they cited incidents that offended their sense of fair play[52] or noted troubling extremes of wealth and poverty that they took pains to rationalize. Conwell, for example, conceded that there were a few "selfish" capitalists who encroached on the rights of the "lesser capitalist who only owns his labor."[53] In so doing, he gave expression to the critical voices among even the defenders of the new order, who believed that free enterprise did not mean a free hand, that moral self-constraint was required. But generally when success writers noted the unsavory aspects of the new order, they were quick to explain them away as exceptions to the rule, as temporary conditions, or as necessary evils which themselves offered important object lessons.[54] Tilley wrote of a woman who, upon observing the "cottagers" of Newport pass by in their elegant carriages, felt like dragging them out and making them walk like herself, and remarks: "Nothing could be more absurd. A little common sense would show that wealth honestly obtained, has as good a right to its pleasures as mediocrity has to its own." Common sense might have inspired this woman to say, "I'll presently ride myself if I can."[55] If some had to be poor, value might be found there, too. Mathews, wrote that "social order is maintained by want," warning, "let every man in the community have as a rule, a few dollars more than he wants, and anarchy would soon follow."[56] Success writers urged their readers not to "indulge in useless and unmanly complaints" or "believe the world is doomed."[57] "The good old days weren't so good,"[58] they argued, and a quick look around should convince people that they lived in "a marvelous age of industrial progress."[59] For those who would "have us believe that the former days were better than these," Tilley suggested that steamships and railroads be outlawed, and gas lamps, water pipes, and steam heaters be removed from their homes.[60] If problems existed — even fantastic rates of business failure, poverty, inequities[61] — readers might console themselves and buoy their spirits with the reminder that "no surroundings, however unfavorable, can keep a true man from true success."[62]

As a last resort, the demise of those who simply failed to appreciate the advantages around them might serve as an example to the persistently unfaithful. John Farwell, in the introduction to Dale's *The Secret of Success*, argued that the key to America's national greatness was in the ability to form the characters of our sons, an accomplishment he found all the more remarkable in light of what he called the "wretched material" we had to work with, the "moral and political refuse" of Europe.[63] To Farwell, the ultimate punishment was not too severe for those who steadfastly refused to have their character so formed. He offered the execution of the "Chicago Anarchists" of the 1886 Haymarket riot and bombing as an object lesson: "The significance of that tragic event lay in the determination to make these men an example to all those who refused to adopt the lofty standards of American citizenship."[64]

The extremity of Farwell's statement gives testimony to both the fact and the intensity of a political debate—a debate in which the writers of success literature took part. The success manuals' self-help advice was more than an approach to "getting on in the world." Success writers offered readers a rebuttal of contemporary radical critiques and gave assurance of the efficacy and exigency of the new industrial order. "Self-help" as an ideology was an insistence on a view of the world as an arena in which—despite fast-paced change, intense competition, and the growth of large-scale industrial enterprise—the individual still had the ultimate power to determine his place. Furthermore, the ideology of self-help as articulated in the success manual represented a faith in the belief that individual upward mobility could eradicate the strife between haves and have-nots and foster an ethos of class harmony.

But success writers seemed to understand that readers who accepted the exigency of self-help might still have doubts about the orthodoxy of self-seeking. Since questions about the legitimacy of the pursuit of wealth were rooted in religious considerations, reassurance and clarification could come from only one source. Success writers asserted their answer boldly when they declared: "God demands success."

GOD DEMANDS SUCCESS

Success writers justified wealth-getting and defended the wealthy in both moral and religious terms. Tilley advised, "never for a moment allow yourself to believe that there is any necessary antagonism between success and downright integrity of character,—uprightness of heart and life." [65] "It is no sin to be rich," assured the Rev. Thain Davidson, or to "wish to be rich or to try to be rich." The mistake lay "in being too eager after riches." [66] The "love of money," not money itself, was the "root of all evil." [67] For money was a "power for good in the hands of the wise." It could "alleviate suffering," aid "the needy and unfortunate; disseminate truth and intelligence," and "make the world brighter, happier, holier." [68] "Those rich men inspired by the right spirit spurned idleness" and accepted the responsibility attached to the possession of wealth and property. [69] To such men, wealth was not "absolute ownership" but a trust. [70]

A small remnant of mankind carries all the rest on its shoulders. For every man of means, of influence, of power to help, there are nine (perhaps ninety-nine would be nearer the mark) to lean on him. The business he has built up employs scores or hundreds, who in turn support dependent families. The brain work he does affords capital which hundreds who do not use their brains live upon.[71]

These assurances may seem strange in a period named the Gilded Age—famous for its unbridled materialism. But the pursuit of wealth went against the grain of the religious beliefs of many Protestants, steeped as they were in Biblical warnings of the incompatibility of wealth and piety.[72] Success writers found religious and moral grounds to overcome these ideological obstacles in the doctrine of self-help. They insisted that there were good ways and bad ways to get rich. Cole complained of "an almost insane desire abroad among men to get riches not by the old-fashioned and slow steps of industry and economy, but by the quick road of speculation." Furthermore, one did not have to be a "skinflint" or a "gambler" to make a fortune; most American businessmen, he claimed, were honest and honorable.[73] Lest any of the unvirtuous turn up in the ranks of the well-to-do, readers might take consolation in Dale's claim that only honestly acquired wealth could give true enjoyment and that the corrupt wealthy usually lost their fortunes.[74]

Success writers asserted that it was a waste of breath "to cry out against the universal craving and struggle for the good things of this world,—for which money is a synonym."[75] Wrote Mathews: "The dangers of poverty are tenfold worse than the dangers of riches." It was wealth "above all other things" that gave "character, standing and respectability in this country."[76] Conwell, more than any other success writer, was famous for forthright justifications of wealth. A professional in the Bible-pounding school of oratory, Conwell's style comes across even in print: "I say you ought to be rich; you have no right to be poor. . . . Money is power; money has power, and for a man to say, 'I do not want money,' is to say, 'I do not wish to do any good to my fellow man.'"[77] Conwell thus neatly united self-interest with duty to mankind in an ideology of stewardship. The possession of wealth was a trust, a responsibility that must be faithfully discharged.[78]

Success writers couched their closing argument for the exigency of the pursuit of success in scripture and in the ultimate justification that God demands success.[79] "God designed that men should be rich,"[80] assured William King; the Bible was a "business manual,"[81] wrote William Makepeace Thayer; and Smiles asked, "Seest thou a man diligent in business? He shall stand before Kings."[82] The favorite biblical illustration of God's endorsement of the success ethic was the Parable of the Talents from the book of Matthew.[83] In the story, a man departing from his country leaves his goods to his three servants. To the first, he leaves five talents; to the second, he leaves two; and to the third, one. The first two servants invest their talents while the third buries his in the ground. On the master's return, the first two receive his praise for they have doubled their talents: "Thou good and faithful servant: Thou has been faithful over a few things, I will make thee ruler over many." The third servant, however, does not fare so well. The master chastises him as a "wicked," "slothful," and "unprofitable" servant. His one talent is handed over to the servant who has ten, and he is cast into "outer darkness." [84]

Although the religious meaning of the parable has to do with "spiritual investment" [85]—enriching God's kingdom, not man's—the strictly spiritual meaning was lost in the success manual. Success writers used the parable to illustrate the importance of improving one's lot and to make the point that heaven helps in proportion to how much one helps oneself. [86] As Mathews put it, "For unto everyone that hath, shall be given, and he shall have abundance: but from him that hath not, shall be taken away even that which he hath." [87] The parable provided a scriptural celebration of attributes deemed necessary for success and offered reassurance about the godliness of wealth-getting. But as a story whose hero is a "good and faithful servant," the parable of the talents has another meaning, one that is at best ambiguous when offered as inspiration for the aspiring self-made man. It offered a prescription for the "good worker" idealized from the point of view of the employer: an employee whose honesty, industry, and initiative multiplied the employer's wealth. The ambiguity of the image of the "good and faithful servant" captures a paradox that pervades the success manual genre. On the one hand, as we have seen, success writers preached self-reliance and self-help and presented a view of the world in which the individual was all-powerful to determine his own fate, to snatch victory from the jaws of defeat, to choose success over failure. On the other hand, success writers preached loyalty, duty, discipline, and sometimes even blind faith in the ultimate beneficence of the established order. For example, in *The Way to Win*, John T. Dale reported that Stephen Girard hired a man for one dollar a day to perform a nonsense task. He was to move a pile of stones from one street to another and back all week long. At the end of the week, the man allegedly received Girard's commendation for doing a "useless job unquestioningly." [88] Similarly, Elbert Hubbard praised the man who "quietly takes the missive, without asking any idiotic questions," as one who "never [got] laid off nor had to go on strike for higher wages." "Civilization," continued Hubbard, was "one long, anxious search for just such individuals." [89]

Such advice is at first difficult to square with the image of the self-reliant man battling his way up "Mount Success." But if one imagines a preindustrial, Jeffersonian world of small proprietors, in which working for others was regarded as a temporary stage, an apprenticeship, on the way to becoming an independent enterpriser, the two images seem less incongruent. This was the world, however idealized, that constituted the success writers' primary reference point. The self-employed shopkeepers, merchants, tradesmen, and farmers that predominated in earlier generations, could presumably employ and profit from their own application of the Franklinesque, economic virtues. Furthermore, the diligent clerk or journeyman might reasonably expect that his lowly position was but a stepping stone to proprietorship. But in a new world in which permanent dependence on wage labor or salaried employment was fast becoming the rule for most men, the virtues of self-discipline, industry, initiative, loyalty, and self-sacrifice had very different implications. It was these two very different understandings of work and how men would earn their livings that the success manuals tried awkwardly to bridge.[90] The fact that a genre of success literature that idolized the self-made man might also be read as a call for self-discipline in the workplace was most likely the unintended consequence of success writers' attempt to apply the values and perspectives of an older, preindustrial era to a radically changed, modern industrial society.[91]

The tension between an older, more familiar world of work and the new was revealed even more clearly in the plethora of advice about selecting an occupation, or what one success writer described as "choosing a calling," to which we now turn.

5

Choosing a Calling: Old and New in the World of Work

The question, "What shall I do?", is a very important one, and demands much
careful consideration. Multitudes inherit their occupation as they do their
disposition, from their parents, and so the child follows the business of the father
simply because the father was in it before him. While this course has very many
advantages, it is not always the best. You may perhaps be able to do better things.
If so, why should you do only what your forefathers have done? Life is full of
opportunities. They are fairly hurled upon us. Look about you. This is an age of
specialties,—in agriculture, in mechanics, in science, in art, in literature.
You cannot do all, but you can do one thing well. You can surely find, then,
the place and work for which are you adapted, and, having found it, stick. Life is
far too short to be spent in roaming.—James Cole, "Selecting an Occupation,"
in King, *Portraits and Principles*

The young man who was convinced that he had a chance in life—and was
steeled with the realization that he alone could determine that chance—
next had to consider exactly how to make his way and what vocation to pursue. Every success manual included chapters addressed to this topic with
titles such as "The Right Vocation," "What Career?," "Selecting an Occupation," "Choice of Profession," and "Choosing a Calling." Nowhere was
the success manual's advice more filled with contradiction and paradox than
when it came to advising young men about how to choose and prepare
for their life's work. These chapters both revealed and denied fundamental change in the structure and nature of work characteristic of Gilded Age
America. In so doing, they expressed much of the tension and ambivalence
associated with the transition from an older, more familiar world to a new
and uncertain way of living and making a living.

"Choosing a Calling"—not only a chapter title but a common expression in success manuals—captured the poles of this tension. Insofar as the Puritan notion of a calling evoked a presumably stable and pious albeit idealized past, it suggested that which was comfortably familiar and accepted in rural and small-town America: a view of work characterized by long-standing patterns of father-to-son occupational continuity and self-employment in farming, the trades, and local commerce. On the other hand, the more modern concept of choosing rather than inheriting one's life work opened the doors to a world of new possibilities. With the proliferation of new kinds of work in manufacturing, transportation, finance, distribution and sales, science and engineering, the trend toward an increasingly mobile and urbanized labor force, and the decline of older occupational patterns, more and more young men of the late nineteenth century left home in search of work with which they and their fathers had no experience and very little familiarity.

Success writers helped to bridge the gap between these two different worlds of work when, by likening the selection of an occupation to a "calling," a Godly summons, they suggested that young men setting forth to find their fortunes were not roaming,[1] drifting, or rejecting the values of the parental household, but rather were making a "choice determined by the prayerful and thoughtful exercise of judgment, that the man and the task may be fitted the one to the other."[2] This last phrase, "that the man and the task may be fitted the one to the other," was essential to the meaning that success writers gave to the concept of choosing a calling. This was the built-in mechanism that helped bridge another gap in the transition from one era to another—the gap between the ideal of boundless opportunity for self-employment and success and the new reality for many young men of permanent dependence on unskilled wage labor or dead-end salaried employment in a corporate hierarchy. In the success manual, the invitation to choose a calling did not mean that a man could achieve success in whatever calling he chose. It came with the admonition to select that vocation to which one was best suited, however grand or humble it might be.

It was this compromised idea of "choosing a calling"—buttressed by the doctrine of the "dignity of all labor"—that helped cushion the transition to a world of work in the new industrial order in which hierarchy and inequality were both pervasive and sanctioned. At the same time, success writers' celebration of an idealized past and their antipathy for many aspects of the new world of work constituted an implicit critique of the new industrial order they often seemed to defend.

OPPORTUNITIES WHERE YOU ARE

Although success writers urged readers to be willing to break with the past and to explore new opportunities and possibilities, their advice also revealed a distinct bias for that which was familiar, close to home, and accessible to all. They recommended that young men take advantage of the circumstances and talents most immediately at hand, stick to the opportunities available in rural and small-town life, and depend upon the "school of experience" as the best preparation for success. There was no more popular or forceful statement of the admonition to seek "opportunities where you are" than Russell Herman Conwell's popular sermon "Acres of Diamonds."[3]

The sermon began with the story of a Persian by the name of Al Hafed, the owner of a large farm near the River Indus. One day a Buddhist priest visited Al Hafed, sat by his fire, and told of how the world was made—the hills, the valleys, and the minerals within them. When the priest spoke of diamonds, how they were formed and of their great value, the farmer began to covet. "Al Hafed . . . went to his bed that night a poor man—not that he had lost anything, but poor because he was discontented and discontented because he thought he was poor." Upon awakening, he sought out the priest to ask where he might find diamonds. The priest replied, "If you will find a river that runs over white sand between high mountains, in those sands you will always see diamonds." "Do you really believe that there is such a river?" asked Al Hafed. "Plenty of them, plenty of them," answered the priest. "All you have to do is just go and find them, then you have them." Al Hafed sold his farm and went in search of diamonds, but when the poor man had traveled the world over, his money spent, he stood in rags on the shore of Barcelona; he cast himself into an incoming tidal wave and "sank beneath its foaming crest, never to rise in this life again." Meanwhile, the priest paid a visit to Al Hafed's successor on the farm. He saw there a flash of light from the mantel. Rushing to it, he exclaimed: "Here is a diamond—here is a diamond! Has Al Hafed returned?" "No, no," replied the new owner. "Al Hafed has not returned and that is not a diamond; that is nothing but a stone; we found it right out here in our garden." But the priest was right, and in the white sands of the farmer's garden, where his camels drank from a pool of the River Indus "were discovered the diamond mines of Galconda, the most magnificent diamond mines in all the history of mankind."[4]

Thus, Conwell outlined the first lesson needed in choosing a calling. He taught that if man would be content with cultivating those opportunities before his very eyes, success would follow: "Had Al Hafed remained at home and dug in his own cellar or in his own garden, instead of wretchedness, starvation, poverty and death in a strange land, he would have had 'acres of diamonds'—for every acre, yes, every shovelful of that old farm afterwards revealed the gems which since have decorated the crowns of monarchs."[5]

Conwell's lectures were filled with stories of great opportunities discovered by ordinary men, and he had a facility to adapt his talks to the particular audience at hand, integrating anecdotes about people from the locale in which he was lecturing, making each example more personal and immediate. The story of Al Hafed may have seemed remote to Conwell's audience, but it is hard to imagine that anyone was uncertain as to the message of the lecture when he concluded the ancient parable with a modern-day analogy like this one:

> I was once lecturing in North Carolina, and the cashier of the bank sat directly behind a lady who wore a very large hat. I said to the audience, "Your wealth is too near to you; you are looking right over it." He whispered to his friend, "Well, then, my wealth is in that hat." A little later, as he wrote me, I said, "Wherever there is a human need there is a greater fortune than a mine can furnish." He caught my thought, and he drew up his plan for a better hat pin than was in the hat before him and the pin is now being manufactured. He was offered fifty-two thousand dollars for his patent. That man made his fortune before he got out of that hall.[6]

Other success writers echoed Conwell's sentiments. Most events were opportunities that could be "used or neglected."[7] It clearly took a man of initiative to seize "common occasions and make them great." As Marden urged, "What you call 'no chance' may be your 'only chance.' Don't wait for your place to be made for you, make it yourself."[8] Furthermore, readers were advised to cultivate not only opportunity around them, but also that which was within: "Not how much talent have I, but how much will to use the talent that I have, is the main question,"[9] "It is not a question of what someone else can do or become, which every youth should ask himself, but what can I do?"[10] Those who wished, like Al Hafed, to find "acres of diamonds" were advised: "Do what you can with what you have where you are today."[11]

"Acres of Diamonds" had another special meaning in the success manual. The admonition to cultivate opportunities close at hand translated easily into a celebration and defense of rural and small-town life and a warning about the iniquity and false promise of the city. Success writers insisted that the best chances for success were in the country, that rural values and a rural upbringing offered the best preparation for success. They enumerated the failures among those who sought success in the big cities and cataloged the corrupting influence of urban life. William James Tilley's chapter entitled "Country Boys" began with two anonymous quotes: "God made the country, and man made the town" and "The country home is the support of the nation." He acknowledged the "glittering" "attractions of the city" but warned of the "hardships, danger and miseries" that were "out of sight." "City boys," he claimed, were "less likely to succeed, and more likely to go to jail," and he argued that "cheaper living and less risk of disaster," more opportunity (especially in the South and West) and less competition made the chances of wealth for the poor boy as great in the country as in the city.[12]

In *The Way to Win*, in a chapter entitled "Words to Farmers," John Dale also encouraged young men to stay on the farm rather than risk life in the city, where young men were "tempted to go into that dangerous class who have ambitious longings but no hope; luxurious tastes, without means to gratify them, and keen intellects, but no legitimate field for their activity." In advice intended to show how to make farm life more attractive to sons, Dale evoked romanticized notions of the pleasures of agrarian life while insisting that farming offered "far better reward than the envied salaried positions . . . that the city holds out." "Efficiency and frugality," he argued, could turn a farm into a successful business.[13] In *Rising in the World*, Marden was both bold and lyrical in his juxtaposition of city and country:

> The muscle and sinew, the nerve, the stamina, the staying powers, the courage, the fortitude, the grit, the grip and pluck of the world, have ever come mostly from the country. The tendency of city life is to deteriorate the physical and the moral man. There is more refinement, but less vigor, more culture, but less stamina; more grace, but less hardihood; more sentiment but less sense; more books but less knowledge; more learning, but less wisdom; more information but less practical ability; more of the ethereal but less of the substantial; more gristle, but less backbone; more newspaper reading, but poorer memories; more society, but less sincerity.[14]

The celebration of country life and the vilification of the city were hardly new themes in the popular culture of nineteenth-century America.[15] But in the success manual the juxtaposition of rural virtue and city vice had special poignancy and meaning. These works were marketed to people in the last decades of the nineteenth century who witnessed firsthand what Henry Nash Smith called the "failure of the Agrarian Utopia."[16] Waves of drought and pestilence, worldwide depression of farm prices, high interest rates, tight money supply, and arbitrary rates for the storage and transportation of crops all combined to produce a decline in farm incomes and a rise in farm failures, foreclosures, and farm tenancy. By 1900, more than 35 percent of all American farmers had become tenant farmers, and the number was increasing. Many farms technically listed as cultivated by their owners were so heavily mortgaged that the lawful owner was hardly his own master.[17] In *Main-Traveled Roads* (1899), Hamlin Garland repudiated the idealization of rural life with his stark personal account of the poverty and desperation of farmers caught in a web of debt and drudgery. Alan Trachtenberg has described the countryside in Gilded Age America as an impoverished zone, a market colony whose function was to "remain a backwater, to remain dependent," a cheap source of food, labor, and certain raw materials for the distant industrial metropolis. As waves of new hopefuls moved west to start farms, many others abandoned the countryside to seek employment in the cities. It is estimated that 5 to 8 million people migrated from northern farms to larger towns and cities between 1860 and 1890. In the same years, the proportion of Americans residing in municipalities of more than 2,500 people nearly doubled, rising to 30 percent, and the number of towns with 10,000 or more residents increased from 100 to 200.[18]

However dramatic the process and the pace of urbanization in Gilded Age America, in order to understand the appeal of the success manuals' juxtaposition of city and country, it is important to also look at what the other sides of these statistics say. The fact remains that as late as 1890, America remained predominately a rural nation, with 70 percent of the population residing on farms or in towns and villages of less than 2,500 people. If country folk were marginalized by the emergence of a new industrial metropolis, it was the marginalization of a very large majority of the American population, a fact that no doubt heightened the sense of crisis in the hinterland.

But the story of rural and small-town America in the last decades of the nineteenth century was not one only of hard work, poverty, and defeat. The rise as well as the fall of fortunes was a visible aspect of rural life. In the wheat country, for example, the farmer (or local businessman-turned-farmer) who could capitalize sufficiently to add acreage and purchase the new mechanical reapers and steam-driven tractors might not only prosper but hire on as laborer or sharecropper a less fortunate neighbor who had lost his farm to foreclosure. The drama of success and failure was played out within a local community where anxious fears of failure mingled with equally anxious hopes for success. Much anticipated developments such as the extension of railroad trunk lines to remote townships represented both opportunity and danger. Local farmers now had rail access to distant markets for their crops and the availability of more consumer goods for themselves and their families. But by being linked to the larger economic world, they were also made more subject to its whims and temptations. The hopes for profits in commercial farming could be dashed by a capricious increase in railroad freight rates or a rise in interest rates. The potential for higher profits through higher capitalization tempted farmers further into debt.[19] At the same time, the mass production, advertisement, and distribution of wondrous new consumer goods set new standards of domestic comfort, engendering "needs" that could scarcely be satisfied by most farm incomes. Mail-order catalogs and drummers made these goods visible and potentially available even to those in remote townships and homesteads beyond even the most distant railhead. Some in rural and small-town America were in a position to take advantage of new opportunities brought by linking the hinterland to the metropolis, others were not; and some were put out of business by that which they hoped would be their salvation.[20]

Success writers' celebration of farm life at the moment when it seemed so precarious may in part reflect the nostalgia of urban writers for a rural past that appeared to be slipping further away. But for the millions of rural and small-town families who came up with two to five dollars for the price of a success manual, the victory of the country boy might be seen instead as an affirmation of a way of life and as a source of hope, inspiration, and reassurance for the future of their children. When success writers insisted that the best opportunities were still in the countryside, they offered an antidote for the anxieties of readers who lacked the means or the courage to leave and reassurance for parents who were skeptical of the city or wished to keep their children home on the farm. Subscription book publishing companies that marketed success manuals targeted this rural and small-town audience and advised their traveling book agents to pass by the homes of the wealthy and the well-educated and visit instead the modest homes of farmers and mechanics, who they said were "good pay and ambitious for their children." Those who were anxious about how they would succeed—not those who were already successful—would become the best buyers of success manuals. Success writers knew their audience and aimed to please. They appealed to both the hopes and the fears of their readership and made a virtue out of what certainly was for some a necessity. In the pages of the success manual, the country boy—far from being outstripped in the race of life—was the one who had virtue, character, and stamina, that is, the best potential to succeed. It was he, they claimed, who was best positioned to exploit opportunities that lay at his very doorstep if only he took the initiative to seek them. "Acres of Diamonds" and the demise of the foolish Al Hafed offered not only an inspirational parable for those far from the city lights but condemnation of the haste and greed of a new age that compelled some young men to desert the life and the values of their rural homesteads.

But success writers did not entirely dismiss those who had been lured to the city. They themselves fell into this category—most had been born and raised in small towns and rural areas and migrated to the city to seek their fortunes. Rather, they projected rural virtue as the saving grace of the otherwise wicked cities. The benefits of rural upbringing, the virtues cultivated in country living, would not only fortify the man who was transplanted to the city but would be the city's salvation. As Conwell explained in *The New Day*, what little character and principle saved the city from utter ruin was brought there by that part of the population that was reared at least to youth on a farm.[21] Thus success writers had it both ways; they could defend rural life and rural values without narrowing their audience to those who resided in the villages and towns of the American hinterland.

A similar kind of defense of the old while making allowance for the new is evident in the success writers' equivocating position on the value of formal education. As with their advice about *where* to seek one's calling, success manual advice about *how* to prepare for one's life work focused on seeking "opportunities where you are." For most readers that would mean only one thing—forgoing higher education and enrolling instead in "the school of life." In 1870, only one in every sixty young men between the ages of eighteen and twenty-one was enrolled in an institution of higher education. By 1900, the proportion had grown to one in every twenty-five, a dramatic increase but hardly making higher education the norm.[22] Even high schools were not commonplace until the twentieth century. Those that existed in the nineteenth century were most likely to be located in populous commercial areas. They admitted students by competitive exam and functioned primarily as preparation for the children of middle-class families bound for college or professional schools.[23] For farm families and others of little means, sending a son away to high school or professional school meant not only the cost of room and board and perhaps tuition, but more important the sacrifice of years of labor or wages that teenaged sons would otherwise contribute to the family.[24] Higher education was simply beyond the reach of a large majority of young men in the late nineteenth century, especially that part of the population targeted for the vigorous marketing of success manuals, those of modest means residing in rural and small-town America.

Thus, success writers charted a cautious path when it came to offering advice about the efficacy of formal schooling. They acknowledged the possible usefulness of higher education, but true to their larger view of the world, they were reluctant to describe any asset that was not available to all as a critical factor in the search for success. They advised readers that nothing could duplicate the value of working one's way up from the bottom in a particular field of endeavor, learning each step of the process without the benefit of formal education.[25] They celebrated the achievements of self-schooled men and lampooned the effete collegian, who they suggested lacked physical stamina and knowledge of the practical aspects of life. Samuel Smiles explained that the college man, preoccupied with books, missed out on the "school of experience"; given a choice between relying exclusively on books or experience, experience was always the best.[26] In his view, "the energy of individual life and example acting through society," provided the best education. Not books, but "action, conduct, self-culture, self-control—all that tends to discipline a man truly, and fit him for the proper performance of the duties and business of life" were the key. Smiles advocated work rather than reading, action rather than study, and life rather than literature.[27] Some even suggested that a college education was a liability: "It is a sad sight to see thousands of students graduated every year from our grand institutions, whose object is to make stalwart, independent, self-supporting men, turned out into the world saplings instead of stalwart oaks, 'memory-glands' instead of brainy men, helpless instead of self-supporting, sickly instead of robust, weak instead of strong, leaning instead of erect. So many promising youths, and never a finished man!"[28] Such ridicule of the college man may have been an expression of sour grapes for the benefit of those who would never have the opportunity to attend college.

Success writers were careful not to entirely dismiss the value of higher education. To do so would be to disavow their own credentials and degrees, narrow their audience unnecessarily, and deny too blatantly what to many was an increasingly obvious fact—the growing relevance of formal education and specialized training for vocational success in a new industrial order. The new careers of an industrializing society in finance, science, technology, and management called for increasingly specialized training, while the requirements for and the availability of higher education in older professions like medicine and law also expanded. Between 1876 and 1900, the number of professional schools in law, medicine, pharmacy, dentistry, veterinary science, and theology nearly doubled; the number of medical students rose from 11,000 in 1878 to 24,000 in 1899; the number of law students grew from 3,000 to 12,000 in the same period. Though scientific, technical and engineering schools were listed separately, when the new technical and engineering colleges are added to professional schools, the growth of professional education was even more dramatic.[29]

Furthermore, there was growing evidence that more and more Americans who succeeded in life had the benefit of a college education. Before the Civil War, one in every three persons in the *Dictionary of American Biography* had attended college. By the turn of the century, one half to three quarters of those listed had attended college.[30] Even among the Gilded Age business elite—ostensibly models of the self-made man—more than a third attended college or had professional training, and most did not take their first regular job until about age eighteen.[31] These facts were downplayed in success manuals and in the popular press that promoted the idea of the self-made man. But the importance of higher education was not entirely lost on parents who had aspirations for their sons. Even as early as the middle years of the nineteenth century, some parents were acting on the realization that education was a critical element distinguishing those who made it into the new middle class of white-collar business, professional, and technical careers from those who were mired in unskilled jobs that had little future. Higher education meant an extended childhood—a longer period of dependence on family resources. Boys from families of the "middling sort" depended on the extra labor and sacrifices of parents and sisters to finance their education and afford them the delayed entrance into the workforce that higher education required.[32] However, many youth lacked the family resources that might have put college, professional school, or even high school within their reach.

Thus, success writers accorded equivocating or at best guarded recognition to the value of college or professional education.[33] Dale went further than most in claiming that, given men of "equal natural ability and force of character," the college graduate had the advantage.[34] Those who did endorse higher education joined with business leaders of the day who called for a practical approach to instruction.[35] They distinguished between what they called a "common sense" college education—a reformed program of math, science, and modern language—as opposed to the traditional classical curriculum.[36] Owen urged, "Let poets and preachers, artists and astronomers, lawyers and physicians, professors and philosophers bestow more time on material matters and less on ethereal; . . . and let our schools and colleges remember to make men—stalwart, invincible *men*—who are neither to be tripped up by the tricks of fortune nor trodden down by the heel of rivalry."[37] An ephemeral education, it seemed, threatened the very fabric of American manhood. In *Rising in the World*, Marden warned readers of the withering consequences of an improper education:

> A liberal education is a true regeneration. When a man is once liberally educated, he will generally remain a man, not shrink to a manikin, nor dwindle to a brute. But if he is not properly educated, if he has merely been crammed and stuffed through college, if he has merely a broken-down memory from trying to hold crammed facts enough to pass the examination, he will continue to shrink and shrivel and dwindle, often

below his original proportions, for he will lose both his confidence and self-respect, as his crammed facts, which never become a part of himself, evaporate from his distended memory.[38]

When success writers insisted on the primacy of self-help and the "school of experience," they both recalled an older era of the yeoman tradition and denied the realities of the new industrial order. If higher education was an asset in the search for success and this asset was available only to the few, then the ridicule of college training and college-trained men might both minimize its significance while diverting attention away from the unsettling fact that opportunities for youth without special advantage were diminishing and that self-help was not enough. Only by dismissing all forms of privilege as a hindrance rather than a help in the struggle for success could success writers posit a world of equal opportunity. Their equivocating not only revealed an ambivalence about the value of formal education, it also allowed room for exceptions and modifications to be made in the self-help ethic of common sense versus book learning, to accommodate the growth and importance of professions in which education was increasingly necessary and more widely available. The equivocation, vacillation, and contradiction typical in success manuals were not simply examples of carelessness on the part of writers and editors; they were integral aspects of these advice books and served a purpose. The sometimes tortured logic and contradictory statements in the books helped to bridge contradictions in the real world and created instead a consistent portrait of a world in which each man, no matter how humble, no matter who or where he was, could find something in his particular background and experience that provided the material from which great success might be carved.

THE RIGHT VOCATION

There were two striking features of success manual advice about the "right vocation." The first was its firm mooring in a world of rural, preindustrial work, a world that by most other accounts was rapidly slipping away. The second and related feature was the remarkable absence of practical information and advice about occupations and career options. The world of work that success writers described for readers was more the Jeffersonian world of farmers, artisans, shopkeepers, and merchants than the modern world of industrialists, engineers, scientists, technicians, accountants, bookkeepers, copyists, managers, or factory workers. It was more a world that honored independent proprietorship and disdained salaried employment or wage labor; it was a world that took as a given the need to combine brawn and brain to earn one's daily bread. Success writers defended the producer ethic and the dignity of all labor and condemned what they saw as the rejection or disregard for time-honored patterns and values in the way that men made their living. Furthermore, success manual advice about the "right vocation" once again offered a defense of the rural versus the city while celebrating all that was old and familiar in the world of work versus that which was new and uncertain.

In 1873, William Mathews complained about the American trend to leave agricultural, mechanical, and manual labor in preference to occupations that called for "living by their wits." "The sons of our farmers, shoemakers, blacksmiths and carpenters no sooner become their own masters than they straightaway throw down the scythe, the awl, and the hammer, and rush to the city to engage in the nobler work of weighing sugar, selling tape, hawking books, soliciting insurance or posting ledgers."[39] Likewise, Cole noted the "growing disposition among young men to despise manual labor and seek for a genteel living." "In some homes," he claimed, the young were taught "the folly that only professional, mercantile or office work is respectable." Cole was disturbed that some thought it beneath their dignity "to hold a plow, or drive a plane, or run a lathe or loom, or work in a kitchen or preside at a washtub for a living."[40] Owen observed as early as 1878 that "society has come to such a pass that if [a man works] at a trade he is pronounced a failure."[41] Such "contempt of labor"[42] resulted in what Lewis considered an absurd situation: "Witness society as it bows with smile and honor to the eight-dollar clerk, while frowning on the eighteen-dollar laborer. This is wrong; work is work, and all work is honorable."[43]

Success writers railed against very real changes in mid- and late-nineteenth-century work life that threatened the values and the opportunities of rural and small-town Americans. Clerkships in merchant establishments and other businesses were extremely attractive to country boys. Thousands were drawn to the larger towns and cities across the country, hoping for a start in business that might eventually result in partnership or proprietorship. But clerkships were difficult to secure for the boy with no special connections, and it was increasingly unlikely that a clerkship would represent the hoped-for step toward bigger and better things. As large-scale industrial concerns with sophisticated hierarchies of management became the new norm, prospects dimmed for the young man looking to a clerkship as the route toward entrepreneurship.[44] Just as in manufacturing, when the factory replaced the artisan shop and the journeyman became a permanent "hand" rather than a master craftsman, the idea of a clerk apprenticeship as a stepping stone to independent proprietorship would give way to the demands of businesses for large regular corps of *permanent*, salaried white-collar workers.[45] And the idea of a permanent clerkship was hardly the ideal in a literature that made heroes out of the American self-made man. Success writers warned readers not to be enamored with prospects that did not offer at least the potential of self-employment. "It is a low grade of content [*sic*] which finds its full satisfaction in being a hired man all through life."[46] Only the man of "little will" was advised to take a position with a "salary or stipend"—the strong-willed man sought a "sphere where his efforts will meet with appropriate reward."[47] In a chapter entitled "The Victorious Mechanic," the victory was not to become a successful mechanic, but to work past this position to become self-employed and ultimately to employ others.[48] And success writers bridled at the seductive vogue of what they saw as "soft" or "genteel" work. "Don't choose [a career] because it is considered the 'proper thing' or a 'genteel' business," advised Marden. "The mania for a 'genteel' occupation, for a 'soft job' which eliminates drudgery, thorns, hardship, and all disagreeable things, and one which can be learned with very little effort, ruins many a youth."[49] Dale had similar advice: "Do not make the mistake of those deluded creatures who despise honest labor and seek some genteel employment, and finally drift into that large class who live by their wits, and their petty meanness and deception."[50] Not only did success writers question the efficacy of the clerkship as a route to success, they expressed contempt for and suspicion of the manicured clerk in the gracious and refined environs of a large city business establishment— a sentiment that may well have resounded in the minds of hardworking farmers, tradesmen, and mechanics of America's backroads worried about how to keep their sons at home. Here as elsewhere, success writers both defended the ultimate beneficence of the new order while expressing great discomfort with particular aspects of the changes it wrought.

Certain other types of work were dismissed by their total absence from the pages of success manuals. Chapters on "the right vocation" or "choosing a calling" rarely included discussion or even mention of the truly modern occupations of an industrial age, such as the myriad of new white-collar jobs—clerical, technical, professional, and managerial positions in the fields of communication, transportation, engineering, science and technology, and finance. Awareness of just how dramatically the occupational structure of the country was being transformed, and especially the knowledge of work in new and specialized technical fields and large-scale enterprise was not widespread and was slow to come to many Americans.[51]

It is possible that the men who wrote success manuals knew little about the new trends and occupations. But even if they were familiar with the transformation of work, there would have been little motivation to enlighten readers as to these changes. Constituting a formula literature whose hero was the self-made man, success manuals were dedicated more to providing inspiration than information. Put another way, if the fact that success writers overlooked the truly modern jobs of the new industrial society was not out of ignorance, it might have been out of deference to their readership—"sensitivity" to their market—the before-mentioned aversion to recommending that which might be out of reach to most readers and out of line with their view of the industrial order. The new white-collar professions were neither familiar nor readily available to the typical success manual reader; such career opportunities existed primarily in the cities, and most required increasingly specialized and advanced formal education or professional training.

Yet success writers did not suppose that all readers would follow in their fathers' footsteps in the family trade or on the family farm. They highlighted certain vocations in which a man might participate in a new world without giving up everything of value in the old. The occupations that they most consistently discussed with approval were the older "professions." Some success manuals, for example, devoted a chapter each to the lawyer, the minister, the statesman, the doctor, the educator, the writer, and the inventor.[52] These selections may have been in part self-referential, given that most success writers were ministers, educators, and writers. But the focus on these professions was also a way to present a recognizable world of work that linked preindustrial work values with success in the new industrial order. Most of these professions would have been familiar to even the most provincial reader, and most represented fields—law, medicine, education, religion, mechanical or scientific invention—that would not only survive, but would grow in importance in the new industrial order. Furthermore, these were vocations that seemed to honor values of the earlier era. All presumably could be practiced in the country as well as the city. All represented useful, respectable work. All embodied some of the qualities of self-employment, entrepreneurship, or at least a measure of self-determination. Success writers' focus on the work of the doctor, the statesman, the lawyer, the writer, the educator, the clergyman, and the inventor deflected attention away from the disturbing fact that in an age characterized by the decline of farming and artisan production and the rise of wage and salaried labor, it was precisely those qualities that these particular older professions retained that were increasingly absent from the newer occupations and from the society in general.

But to present these older professions as the preserve of traditional preindustrial work values required success writers to overlook changes within each of these occupations that mirrored the more general transformation of work brought by the emergence and consolidation of the new industrial order. The work of the "inventor" provides a clear and striking example. Whether describing Franklin, Watt, or Edison, success writers cast the inventor in the mold of the self-made man: industrious, self-reliant, and persevering, the lone inventor, motivated by his own inspiration, single-mindedly pursued and developed his "idea" without the benefit of formal education or any special "start" in life. His mode of labor exemplified the most valued aspects of the work patterns of an earlier era, while the fruits of his labor were the essential innovations of a new age of industry. In short, the inventor described in the pages of success manuals was not the scientist or engineer who by the turn-of-the-century was becoming a part of the hired staff of industrial concerns. Rather he was a figure cloaked in the mantle of an earlier era, whose special contribution to the age of industry bridged old and new worlds of work.

The popular reputation and career of the most famous of all American inventors, Thomas Edison, illustrates this phenomenon. The contemporary periodical press as well as the success manual presented Edison in the mode of the self-made man. They emphasized his natural genius and his instinct for entrepreneurship, which enabled him to produce something of use (meaning marketable) for the new industrial society.[53] As Alan Trachtenberg described it, the public Edison "seemed to hold together the old and the new, the world of the tinker and the world of modern industry. . . . He made the new America of cities and complicated machinery seem to evolve in an orderly fashion from the old America of country towns and youthful high jinx on country railroads."[54] But many of the facts of Edison's career give quite another picture. His most famous inventions—the phonograph, the improved telephone, the incandescent lamp, and the basic elements of a central power-generating system—were not the products of a lone, inspired, self-educated genius. They were developed in an industrial research laboratory that Edison established in Menlo Park, New Jersey, between 1876 and 1881. Far from being mired in a preindustrial world, Edison pioneered new, collaborative approaches to scientific research. He hired university-trained scientists and mathematicians for his research staff. Menlo Park and the later laboratories that Edison established were testing grounds for the industrial research organization that would be developed within private industries such as General Electric and American Telephone and Telegraph Company by the turn of the century.[55] Edison was a scientist with a sophisticated understanding of the relationship between specialized knowledge and the evolution of industrial capitalism. He realized and capitalized on the commercial implications of his scientific work. When he had perfected a lightbulb that could glow consistently, he created a company, acquired the financial backing of J. P. Morgan, and in 1882 opened the first central power plant in New York.[56]

In the success manual, the portrayal of the inventor as self-made man may have made inspirational reading for youth looking for guidance about selecting a career. But this idealized formulation disguised the fact that more and more of the new occupations of an industrial age would be either unattainable to many readers because they required specialized education or capital, or undesirable because the work itself was stripped of skill, autonomy, and opportunity for self-advancement.

On the surface, at least, law, the ministry, statesmanship, and medicine were professions that seemed to effectively bridge the two worlds. They had both long-standing familiarity in the preindustrial world and carried cherished aspects of preindustrial work into the new industrial age. The country doctor or lawyer might well be a self-employed practitioner. The minister, professor, or statesman presumably enjoyed a significant degree of autonomy in the discharge of his duties. At the same time, as Conwell explained in a chapter entitled "The Old Professions," law, medicine, and the ministry were growing and understaffed fields.[57] It is one of the paradoxes of the success manual that a self-help literature that downplayed the importance of higher education featured occupations that are normally thought of as requiring a level of formal education that would be beyond the reach of all but a few. But the focus on these professions is not as contradictory as it first seems. In some fields, requirements for extensive professional training were relatively new and not uniformly observed across the country. For example, even as late as 1900, in Pennsylvania and New Jersey the prerequisite for entrance into medical school was only a common school education (usually through sixth grade), while New York and Illinois required graduation from a four-year high school.[58] It was not until 1899 that most medical school programs constituted four years of study; in 1875, most required two years and none required four years.[59] No doubt many went into practice in a variety of professions with considerably less formal education. One thinks in horror of McTeague, the character in Frank Norris's novel of the same name, who practiced dentistry in San Francisco at the turn of the century and whose training consisted of having watched the itinerant dentist who visited the mining camps where his father worked.

Law was another profession for which a young man might prepare without necessarily engaging in extensive and prolonged training. This was true especially in the middle decades of the nineteenth century—the formative years for many of the men who wrote success manuals. Standards for admission to the bar varied greatly from state to state; in 1860, few lawyers had liberal arts college diplomas, and some states required no more than "good moral character and a fee" for admission to the bar.[60] The ministry provided another route to upward mobility and a professional career even for some young men with little means. Since the early years of the nineteenth century, a certain number of poor New England farm boys had prepared for the ministry with the support of scholarships and professional charity.[61] Thus, for the youth of Gilded Age America who would not stay home on the farm or in the shop, the older professions at least symbolized honorable pursuits in which a certain number might reasonably expect to meet with a degree of success.

These fields, however, were not immune to the kind of change that transformed other kinds of work in the last decades of the nineteenth century. As the trend toward corporatization, rationalization, centralization, and standardization spread through the business world, it also reshaped social and cultural institutions. Ministers, college professors, writers, and newspaper editors came under the sway of increasingly vigilant patrons, boards of trustees, and owners. The image of the country lawyer would be replaced by the reality of the corporate attorney—part of a large team, each with a separate legal specialty. Professions of medicine, law, dentistry, veterinary science, pharmacy, and engineering became more institutionalized, requiring more stringent standards of education and licensing; a literary and publishing establishment became a powerful agent in determining what was to be published and marketed.[62]

But these changes in the professions and the more general transformation of work were neither well understood nor widely perceived in late-nineteenth-century America. For most contemporary observers—probably success manual writers as well as readers—the facts and the implications of the "incorporation of America" were indistinct if not indiscernible.[63] On the back roads, where country and small-town youth sought a focus for their career aspirations, the old-time professions retained a special appeal; they showed a way to be successful in the new industrial order without either rejecting the values of an older age or confronting those of the new.

MENTAL VERSUS MUSCULAR POWER

However suitable professions such as the ministry, law, and medicine may have been in symbolically joining an earlier era to the new, they also went against the grain of older patterns in one particularly important way. The work of most professionals was singularly devoid of the physical labor and activity that built strength and bodily vigor. And by every success writer's account, physical stamina, if not muscular might, was essential in winning victory in the battle of life. In a country in which man's conquest of nature was an important part of its history and mythology, muscular might and physical prowess had a particularly important place in the identity of its citizens, especially its male citizens. But the primacy of physical man was threatened more by the transformation of work engendered by industrialization than by the closing of the frontier. Making a living for most men in preindustrial America called for the application of both mental and manual skill and ability. Farmers, tradesmen, artisans, mechanics, sailors, builders, storekeepers, coachmen, timbermen, and miners required physical strength and stamina along with knowledge, experience, judgment, planning, and decision making.

In the modern industrial workplace, the unity of head and hand became a casualty of the transformation of the work process.[64] Mechanization and the division of labor resulted not only in the splintering of a single production process into a myriad of isolated, unskilled tasks, but also in the splitting of manual and mental labor into fundamentally different kinds of occupations, to which different social standings were attached. The "rationalization" of work meant the de-skilling of shop floor production and production workers and the concentration of knowledge and control in the hands of industrial managers and professional, college-trained engineers.[65] But the separation and differentiation of manual and nonmanual labor occurred not only in the factory. As early as the 1870s the distinction could be observed in the small shops of city tradesmen, such as shoemakers, tinsmiths, and tailors, where all of the functions of production and sales had traditionally occupied the same space and the same people. Increasingly, workrooms where the messy business of production took place were physically separated from salesrooms where employees, distinguished by their clean and presentable dress, met the public and engaged in nonmanual retail work or clerical work. "White collar" status became one of the distinguishing marks of the new urban middle class.[66]

Success writers both acknowledged and denied these changes in the structure of employment and in the nature of work. The idea of a world in which the work of head and hand might be permanently separated was especially troubling to these writers. They noted the growing importance of "intellect" and "thought" for men who would succeed in life, but they warned against the development of either intellectual or physical attributes at the expense of the other. In *Success in Life, and How to Secure It: or Elements of Manhood and Their Culture* (1882), William Owen made the case for "skilled intellect":

Fifty years ago men were paid for strength of muscle. That was the gala-day for the giants. Now, muscle is at a discount, while skilled intellect and dexterous fingers are in demand. Engines and machines for field and shop, and for all sorts of business, glut the market. Thus is toil shortened and surplus human flesh discarded. The man who does not now bring mechanical genius to his assistance must suffer loss. No man can expect with mortar and pestle to make headway against a modern flouring mill. Thought is the only thing that can win, and every pursuit is calling for men of mind.[67]

But when the "brain is cultivated at the expense of the members," Smiles warned in *Self-Help*, the body is bound to suffer: "Hence, in this age of progress, we find so many stomachs weak as blotting-paper,—hearts indicating 'fatty degeneration,'—unused, pithless hands, calveless legs and limp bodies, without any elastic spring in them."[68] "A well-balanced and perfectly furnished man would have body, brain, heart and will," concluded Jerome Bates in *The Imperial Highway*; "taken together they make up the whole man."[69] Smiles concurred in the need for a well-balanced development: "Cultivate the physical exclusively and you have an athlete or a savage; the moral only and you have an enthusiast or a maniac; the intellectual only, and you have a diseased oddity—it may be a monster. It is only by wisely training all three together that the complete man is formed."[70]

Even though the professions, most especially the clergy, were careers where the intellectual and moral aspects of work might overshadow the physical aspects, success writers not only accepted but advocated the professions as suitable career choices. Two tactics made their advocacy of professional careers more palatable and more consistent with a view of the world that called for the unity of brain and brawn. First, by employing the important nineteenth-century words "grit" and "pluck," success writers found a way to write about physical vigor and strength *independent from* actual physical labor or physical activity. Entire chapters were devoted to "pluck" and "grit," qualities that denoted courage, boldness, decisiveness, and aggressiveness. These virtues symbolized a physical as well as a mental state. The word "pluck" meant quite literally "guts," and its use derives from the tradition that the heart and liver were the seat of heroism.[71] It was often used in the maxim, "A pound of pluck is worth a ton of luck."[72] "Grit," explained Marden, "is a permanent, solid quality, which enters into the very structure, the very tissues of the constitution. A weak man, a wavering, irresolute man, may be 'spunky' upon occasion, he may be 'plucky' in an emergency, but pure 'grit' is a part of the very character of strong men alone."[73] "Grit" had connotations of bodily vigor and physical power. As one writer observed: "In the long and desperate struggle, the man who wins is he with firmest nerve, the strongest muscle, the best blood; for out of these come the 'grit' which is bound to conquer or die."[74] Pluck and grit made up that fundamental toughness that would carry the man through—whatever the endeavor and whatever the circumstances.

Secondly, success writers—along with many other late-nineteenth-century, middle-class Americans—found in the concept and the movement known as "physical culture" a way to rejoin muscular and mental power in professions that some might otherwise consider too genteel or effete.[75] They showed how the professional man who had developed his intellectual capacity to the exclusion of the physical might escape the fate of those who withered to mere "memory-glands." The answer lay in the cultivation of his muscular power through "healthful exercise" and "manly sport."[76] "Daily exercise in the open air," claimed Mathews, was the "true stimulant, more potent and healthful than champagne or cognac." "There is no calling in which men do not need that sturdy vigor, that bodily strength and agility, without which all mental culture is but a preparation for disappointment and mortification."[77] Physical culture was the foundation of all real intellectual ability. Success writers spelled out this claim in chapters with titles such as "Power of Endurance,"[78] "Health and Happiness,"[79] "Bodily Vigor,"[80] and "Physical Culture."[81]

The theory behind physical culture began with the basic assumption that the body was the "home of the mind."[82] "Brain power," wrote Thayer, "has a strong ally in muscular vigor."[83] Tilley concurred, noting that "the greatness of our great men is quite as much a bodily affair as a mental one."[84] Given this close relationship between mental and muscular power, the would-be professional men in particular needed to be taught that the "great prizes of life fall to those of stalwart, robust physiques."[85] Even in nonmanual labors, physical weakness was something that could not be disguised—it showed in every step, word, and letter, as success writers took great pains to illustrate:

The success even of professional men depends in no slight degree on their organic stamina and cultivated physical strength. Thus, a well-developed thorax is considered almost as indispensable to the successful lawyer or politician as a well-cultivated intellect. The thorough aeration of the blood, by free exposure to a large breathing surface in the lungs, is necessary to maintain the full vital power on which the vigorous working of the brain in so large a measure depends. The lawyer has to climb the heights of his profession through close and heated courts, and the political leader has to bear the fatigue and excitement of long and anxious debates in a crowded House. Hence, the lawyer in full practice, and the parliamentary leader in full work, are called upon to display powers of physical endurance and activity even more extraordinary than those of the intellect.[86]

Mathews spared no words in his ridicule of the clergy on this score. Instead of "remaining the pale, ghostly-looking, over-read, over-fed, intellectually *blasé* spectres" that they so often were, he advised that "they should spend part of their time in getting up animal power to back up their attenuated intellectual power."[87] Marden claimed that "Muscular Christianity" was "the demand of the hour,"[88] and Owen found it exemplified in the careers of the "two most popular preachers in Boston"—men of "entirely exceptional physique—hard to be matched anywhere in the world for size and strength. They exercised the charm which can only come from complete manhood—the equipoise of thought and intent with voice and might."[89] Crafts had a similar idea in mind when he recommended that every boy, rich or poor, learn a trade, some manual labor in which he might learn the habits of industry. He wrote: "If physical education were thus combined with mental and moral culture, we should not have so many sickly ministers, editors and teachers, whose weak bodies stagger under the work which is put on them by their strong minds."[90]

Rhetorically, at least, the call for physical culture along with the concepts of pluck and grit enabled success writers to "put humpty-dumpty back together again"—physical man and mental man might be reunited, at least in certain professional and white-collar careers. But the celebration of physical culture for a professional class did not entirely disguise the fact that in many modern workplaces, physical man and intellectual man were irreparably split into different jobs with different status, power, and income. Many of the unskilled positions that would become the majority of jobs in the new industrial hierarchy offered neither valued aspects of a preindustrial work culture such as skill and autonomy nor real opportunity for advancement. Once again, success writers' discomfort with such developments, and even their attempts to minimize their significance, reveal the subtle dialectic of a text that simultaneously critiqued and extolled the new industrial order. They did not go out of their way to acknowledge the extent of the growth of unskilled wage-labor and dead-end jobs, but they admitted, indeed insisted, that all callings and all places in life were not equal, just as all men were not equal. As William Owen explained, men were like "vessels of differing capacities," a truth that each young man was to consider thoughtfully as he sought his life's work.

VESSELS OF DIFFERING CAPACITIES

Success writers argued that the key to selecting the right vocation had much to do with "choosing a calling to which [one's] abilities are fitted."[91] In the words of William Owen:

> Men, like vessels, are brought onto the sea of life, differing in construction and capacity. All cannot carry the same burden, nor ride safely through the same storm. Some are very humble, feeling that they must be contented, like fishing smacks, to sail in shallow water. Others are like ships of a thousand tons, fitted to carry commerce of nations; while here and there is one that is undoubtedly designed for a flagship.[92]

Though Owen claimed that it was a "law of our nature that every man can excel in his vocation, and a steadfast principle in business that every man can succeed in his calling,"[93] the claim held only if the man had indeed found that mission for which his talents precisely fit him,[94] be it a flagship or a fishing smack. In this light, to find the right vocation was to implicitly accept as innate—"brought onto the sea of life"—inequalities among men. The concept of a calling had always contained the notion of fixed stations, that God chose specific individuals to fill the various positions and to perform the various tasks in life, be they humble or grand. Success writers picked up this theme and took it a step further with the idea of *choosing* a calling. No longer was it necessary to call on the authority of God to mete out inequality in the world. Rather, the inevitability of hierarchy and inequality might be recognized and internalized by each individual,[95] who would then seek his mission accordingly. In one sense at least, choosing the *right* calling meant knowing one's place.

Deciding upon an occupation, success writers explained, required "following [one's] bent,"[96] finding a "nitch" which "focuses the largest amount of [one's] experience and taste,"[97] and selecting that which agrees with one's "natural aptitude" and "physical constitution."[98] According to Marden, "It is right that one should make a choice as to his life-work, because all men are not alike and all callings of life are not alike. There are men and there are places, but all men are not intended for the same place, neither are all places to be filled by the same kind of man." In a chapter entitled "Round Boys in Square Holes," Marden advised parents to let their children discover their own aptitudes. The chapter included anecdotes in which famous people were discouraged as youngsters from pursuing interests in areas where they later revealed great genius. The inventor of the steam engine, James Watt, for example, was punished as a boy for playing with steam in the teapot.[99]

But following one's own bent did not by any means guarantee that the young man would discover hidden genius or an exalted calling; it might instead lead to the realization that he was best suited for some humble task. It was a "law of nature" that men differed in "natural endowments, fitness and aptness for particular pursuits."[100] In seeking the "right vocation," therefore, a young man had to be prepared to consider a whole range of possibilities, including the possibility that he had as much "natural aptitude" for digging ditches as for practicing law. Cole elaborated in a chapter entitled, "Selecting an Occupation":

> For what is he naturally fitted? By this is not meant simply what one desires to do, but what can he do? For what has he an aptitude? Wishes, longings, impulses, however good, are not always the indications of genius, nor are they invariably a forecast of an adaptation for a special pursuit in life. If mere wishes could make men great, or rich, there would be not a poor or an insignificant person on earth. While, therefore, it is always advisable to aspire after the higher, one should not undertake what to him is impossible, nor should he fret out his days aping after the so-called great ones of the earth. Be yourself. You have your own special place and work. Find it, fill it. Do your work well. The World is in need of faithful, loyal workers. If your position is humble and lowly, strive for a higher place. Larger positions await you as soon as you are prepared to fill them.[101]

Cole and other success writers portrayed a world in which differences between men and place were the natural order of things, and they urged readers to accommodate themselves to this fact. Some were born to lead and command and others to follow and obey, explained Tilley, and he saw no point in resisting that truth. The struggle against this "inevitable inequality" was useless, he wrote, because "men, like water, are perpetually finding their level."[102] Owen observed that "men differ in mind as they do in body and no power can ever make them equals."[103] "[I]t must be the lot of the great mass of men to perform the drudgery and toil of life," Dale remarked, "for this must also be done, and men are wanted who will do it faithfully."[104]

This seemingly dismal reality might have been cause for some to despair, but success writers took quite a different tack. They assured readers that the existence of difference in place did not mean that the way to success was blocked for the humble. Bok assured his readers that "some of us must live for the few, as others again must live for the many, just as some are born to occupy important positions while others are intended for humbler places. *But both lives are successful.*"[105] In Owen's words, "Each is capable of the greatest prominence in his sphere. . . . Small men working in their sphere are just as great as the mightiest working in their's. It is only when they change positions that the difference becomes offensive." [106] Though Owen clearly wished to minimize the significance of such "differences" between the "small" and the "mighty," he—like Tilley, Bok, and many others—asserted the legitimacy of a world of hierarchy and inequality in which *wealth, power, and fame* could come only to the few. At the same time, they insisted that *success* was within the reach of the many. They could make this promise only by extricating "success" from its association with wealth, power, and fame, and allying it instead with that which was positive but less tangible. Success writers partially bridged the chasm between success-for-the-few versus success-for-the-many with the concept of the "dignity of all labor." Just as the "class" of the successful could include the hard-working poor as well as the self-made rich, so also might all "workers," great or small, be seen as bound together by virtue of the dignity of their labor in a way that transcended distinctions in occupation or rank and conferred success on both: "Work is not a curse. It is not a mark of degradation, not servitude, but an insignia of royalty. . . . Whatever your position in life is, be assured, first of all that all honest work, whether of hand or brain, is noble. It is the worker who dignifies the task, and not the task that ennobles the worker." [107] In a chapter entitled "Relation of Work to Rank," one author thanked God "for a nation of *workmen*, a nation where the professional man and the merchant, as well as the day laborer, by something attempted, something done, have earned a night's repose." [108]

The concept of the dignity of all labor had a variety of possible meanings in nineteenth-century America, and success writers exploited the ambiguity in the interest of advancing their own particular view of how to succeed in a new and uncertain world. The success manual's celebration of the dignity of all labor evoked a reassuring past in two important ways. First, it suggested that the idealized, preindustrial notion of success was typical in the culture of the American yeoman prior to the industrial revolution, a definition that stressed competency and respect in one's calling.[109] Second, the dignity of labor recalled the free labor ideology that united northerners (labor and capital) against the South in the Republican Party in the antebellum and Civil War years.[110] But in the Gilded Age the uneasy consensus symbolized by republican virtue and free labor ideology broke down, and bitter conflict between labor and capital took its place. There were 37,000 recorded strikes involving 7 million workers between 1881 and 1905.[111] A government study showed that state troops were called out nearly 500 times to subdue labor unrest in the years between 1875 and 1910, and by the 1890s they were being supplemented with federal troops.[112]

In the last quarter of the nineteenth century, powerful and wealthy industrialists still spouted the old republican platitudes, but to working-class radicals such as the Knights of Labor, the dignity of labor no longer stood for class harmony. The "nobility of toil" became a rallying cry to unite the "producing classes" against the growing concentration of wealth and power in the hands of bankers, speculators, and industrialists who had no regard for the interests and rights of labor.[113] When success writers evoked the doctrine of the dignity of all labor, they appropriated the rhetoric of contemporary critics of the new industrial order and employed it to downplay the significance of the widening gap between the haves and the have-nots. In the success manual, the "dignity of all labor" was a doctrine of accommodation and consolation. It called on readers to resign themselves to the fact that, as Dale wrote, "all will not be called to high places."[114] Samuel Smiles concluded a long chronicle of the rise of certain self-made men with the following disclaimer and advice:

> Self-culture may not, however, end in eminence, such as we have briefly described in the numerous illustrious instances of self-raised individuals above cited. The great majority of men in all times, however enlightened, must necessarily be engaged in the ordinary avocations of industry; and no degree of culture which can be conferred upon the community will ever enable them—even were it desirable, which it is not—to get rid of the daily work of society, which must be done. But this, we think, may also be accomplished. *We can elevate the condition of labor by allying it to noble thoughts, which confer a grace upon the lowliest as well as the highest rank.*[115]

Smiles articulated perfectly the harmonizing and narcotizing possibilities of the doctrine of the dignity of all labor. And, ironically, in a work entitled *The Way to Win*, John Dale became philosophical about the virtuous finding contentment with their place in life. In a chapter entitled "Be Content," he observed:

> We live in an age of unrest. The great mass of mankind are eagerly striving after something which they have not, instead of enjoying and making the most of that which they have . . . The poor are longing to be rich, and the rich desire to add still more to their wealth; and so discontent seems to pervade every condition of society. . . . Be content, though your path in life leads only to simple everyday duties. . . . Be content, though you are not gifted with genius to win the honors of this world.[116]

Finally, for those in lowly ranks who would not be consoled by the prospect of elevating their condition with "noble thought," success writers evoked the old authority of Divine Providence and the obligation of duty. The definition of success according to Dale was "the highest order of usefulness in whatever condition it may have pleased Providence to place us." If one was so unlucky as to have been placed in a difficult place, Dale suggested that one might be "sustained through toil by the consciousness that you are doing your duty." [117] God gave each work to do, advised Cole: "Do not disappoint him and shame yourself by asking for easier tasks, but do the work at your hand and do it well." [118] In *Onward to Fame and Fortune*, Thayer counseled: "Having found out what you have to do—whether to lead an army or to sweep a crossing, to keep a hotel or drive a hack, to harangue senates or address juries, or prescribe medicine—do it with all your might, because it is your duty, your enjoyment, or the very necessity of your being." [119]

It is one of the great paradoxes of the success manual, that a literature dedicated to offering advice and inspiration about how to find "Fame and Fortune," "Success in Life," or "The Way to Win" also made the case for accepting one's lot in life, and not asking too much. Just as paradoxical is the fact that while their anecdotes and examples often associated success with the few—those who were great and wealthy—their advice about choosing a calling defined success broadly to embrace the many: every calling, even the most humble, could be dignified and ennobled by the man himself and what he brought to it. But these paradoxes were important in creating consistency of another kind; the success manual consistently offered something for everyone, and when defining success, they consistently cast the net wide. They offered hope and inspiration for those who might reach the pinnacle of wealth, fame, and fortune, while simultaneously providing reassurance, dignity, and self-respect for those whose "success" might be of a more modest nature. Given this expansive definition of the successful, it was clear that every man,—every man of true character, at least—could indeed discover a calling in which he might find success in life. By the same token, it was also clear that "acres of diamonds" would remain for most, no more than an enticing figure of speech.

6

Character Is Capital:
The Moral Definition of a New Middle Class

Above all things in the World, character has supreme value. A man can never be
more than what his character—intellectually, morally, spiritually—makes him.
A man can never do more, or better, than deliver, or embody, that which is
characteristic of himself. . . . Nothing valuable can come out of man that is not in
him—embodied in his character.—John T. Dale, *The Way to Win,*
Showing How to Succeed in Life

Whether a man's calling was lofty or humble, there was still the question
of exactly what it would take to succeed in it. The writers of success manuals had no difficulty with this question. They could sum it up in a single
word, a key word that recurred more frequently than any other in the entire
genre. *Character*, they claimed, was the key to success. Character—and all
of the carefully cultivated, personal virtues it symbolized—was the foundation of the self-made man and the common denominator of all who were
truly successful.

The importance and expedience of character was hardly a new theme
in nineteenth-century America. A whole range of didactic literature that
flourished fifty years before the advent of Gilded Age success manuals exhorted young men to be virtuous in order that they might succeed. Antebellum and midcentury common school primers, advice books for young
men, and the moral philosophy texts used in the capstone senior seminars
in American colleges, for example, all exemplified "character education," an
attempt to mold the kind of individual who would be motivated to do well
and be virtuous.[1] By the late nineteenth century, the idea that character was
the route to individual advancement and social progress was met with some
skepticism. In some quarters at least, such a moralistic philosophy seemed

impossibly naive if not totally obsolete. In the popular juvenile fiction of Horatio Alger, for example, the success of the typical urban boy-hero was often due as much or more to the cynical gambits of the smooth-talking "confidence man" as to personal integrity and sterling character.[2] Such heroes may have been the harbingers of the transition from a nineteenth-century focus on character to a twentieth-century emphasis on personality and the salesmen ethic of a consumer society, where ability to persuade would become more important than the authentic self implicit in the concept of character.[3]

But the fact remains that even as late as the turn of the century, millions of Americans in small towns and rural areas across the country were spending as much as a week's salary to purchase books that claimed that character was the key to success. At least in this market, the idea that individual virtue might still be the key to success was alive and well. What is distinctive about the idea of character as it appears in Gilded Age success manuals is not only its persistence well into the twentieth century but, more importantly, the way success writers adapted the concept of character to meet the challenges of modern circumstances. In voices both strident and defensive, success writers claimed that individual virtue, far from moribund in the competitive new age of industry, was what young men who hoped to succeed needed most. The character ethic of these works implied a critique of the haste, greed, materialism, and intemperance of the new industrial order, but it was a critique framed in the lingua franca of that age: CHARACTER, they claimed, was CAPITAL.

The assertion that character was capital was an equation that joined an older age with the new—it merged the best of both worlds. Success writers dusted off the personal assets that really mattered and laid them out for all to see and use. Far from obsolete, they claimed, virtues such as honesty, industry, frugality, sobriety, punctuality, modesty, tact, loyalty, diligence, determination, initiative, and politeness constituted the stuff most needed to succeed in a modern age. Success writers' evocation of "character" as key in the search for success was more than a mere indulgence in nostalgia. With the claim that character was capital, they linked the moral worldview and the cherished values of an idealized past to both material success and a consoling sense of place in what by their own accounts was a frenzied, unpredictable, and alienating new industrial age. Success writers offered their readers CHARACTER as a powerful and propitious tool of action and as a badge of spiritual membership in the large and amorphous mainstream known as the American middle class. Middle-class virtue provided a way for readers of success manuals to distinguish themselves from those deemed indulgent and excessive at both ends of the social scale: the overzealous, ostentatious capitalists on the one hand and the unrestrained, unacculturated, immigrant underclass on the other.

RICH WITHOUT MONEY

In the success manual, "character" was "the poor man's capital."[4] In the words of Samuel Smiles,

> The crown and glory of life is character. It is the noblest possession of man, constituting a rank in itself, and an estate in the general goodwill; dignifying every station, and exalting every position in society. . . . Though a man have comparatively little culture, slender ability, and but small wealth, yet if his character be of sterling worth, he will always command an influence, whether it be in the workshop, the counting house, the mart, or the senate.[5]

Orison Swett Marden dedicated *Rising in the World* to "those with neither friendship nor capital other than a determination to get on in the world."[6] In *Masters of the Situation*, William James Tilley argued that a resolute character and the power of rigid application were "as good as capital—sometimes better."[7] "Your character is your best capital and fortune," claimed John T. Dale in *The Way to Win*.[8] Success manuals provided a number of variations on this theme. In *Success in Life*, William Owen wrote of virtue as capital,[9] Dale likened integrity to capital,[10] and in *Hidden Treasures*, H. A. Lewis claimed: "The best capital with which a young man can start in life, nine times out of ten, is robust health, good morals, fair ability and an iron will, strengthened by a disposition to work at some honest vocation."[11] Success writers were explicit in their substitution of character for capital of the pecuniary sort, and they urged the earnest but humble to join the fray. "To have nothing," claimed Marden, "was not poverty,"[12] for even the poorest boy could cultivate character. "Millions" he assured, looked "trifling beside character":[13]

> The grandest fortunes ever accumulated or possessed on earth were and are the fruit of endeavor that had no capital to begin with save energy, intellect and the will. From Croesus down to Rockefeller the story is the same, not only in the getting of wealth, but also in the acquirement of eminence; those men have won the most who relied most upon themselves.[14]

The power and meaning of the declaration that character was capital depended on several implicit, prior understandings of the term "capital."

Success writers made certain assumptions about their audience. First, they assumed that readers were familiar with the conventional definition of capital as cash, land, or other potentially productive property. Second, they assumed that readers viewed the possession of capital as important, maybe even essential to the achievement of success. Third, they assumed that readers were *not* securely in the possession of significant capital of the conventional variety. An appreciation of the importance of capital may have been particularly acute to those who made up the typical success manual audience, people in rural and small-town America where owner-operated farms and local trades and businesses, rather than wage labor, were the norm, and where the rise or fall of the fortunes of one's neighbors was a highly visible aspect of life. For families who owned and operated their own farms, for example, the capital to purchase new farm machinery and expand acreage often made the difference between those who survived and even thrived as commercial farmers versus those who lost their farms to foreclosure.[15]

When success writers asserted that *character* was capital they simultaneously acknowledged and denied the importance of capital in the modern era. They confirmed the idea that young men needed some special start in life, but they rebutted the idea that a special start need be in the form of wealth, property, or place. Success writers offered *character* as a nonpecuniary substitute for capital; even a poor boy might succeed in life by cultivating character. The individual virtues that made character constituted a kind of inner capital on which a man could trade. The youth of little means created his own capital, his own start in life, by becoming a man of character. Success writers thus provided a cheery alternative to what otherwise might have seemed like dreary prospects for those of modest means. At the same time, they offered a rebuttal to those who believed that opportunity for the poor boy was a thing of the past. If *character* was capital, success was theoretically possible for the many and not just the few. Insofar as even those who owned nothing tangible could possess this means to success, they might indeed become "rich without money."

THE USE OF ADVERSITY AND THE
SPECTACLE OF TRIUMPHANT MEDIOCRITY

A man could be born to capital of the conventional sort, but character was a type of capital reserved for those who could earn it. In the world of the success manual, character was a special asset available only to those lucky enough to have been born into poverty or difficulty. These were the circumstances that called men to rely on themselves, rise to the challenge and overcome obstacles in the battle of life; in short, these were the circumstances that built character.

Success writers spelled out the special fortunes of those who lacked wealth, privilege, or position in chapters with titles such as "The Advantages of Difficulty," "The Use of Adversity," "Success under Difficulty," "The School of Difficulty," and "The Use of Obstacles."[16] In Mathews view, it was "not helps, but obstacles, not facilities, but difficulties" that made men,[17] and Thayer insisted, "A smooth sea never made a skillful navigator, as a smooth road never leads to success."[18] "Is Poverty a Hinderance?" asked Charles Kent rhetorically in a chapter title. "Boys born in poverty have the best chance for success, for the best of all reasons. They are compelled to rely upon themselves—upon their own individual efforts—while the sons of the rich rely upon the wealth of their fathers, and have no incentive to industry and economy—no dire necessity which throws them solely upon their own resources."[19] "Poverty," wrote Marden, was that "priceless spur, that develops the stamina of manhood, and calls the race out of barbarism."[20]

In each case, these advisors urged readers to accept difficulty as an opportunity to shape their own success. Not only was poverty no reason to complain or to be discouraged, it was an ennobled state with vast possibilities. Those without difficulties were demeaned, while failure was exalted as the springboard for a mighty return. Tilley likened the businessman to the great hunter and the military man: "He who wins without danger triumphs without fame."[21] Dale asked readers: "Would you wish to live without a trial? . . . Then you would wish to die but half a man."[22] Marden included a chapter entitled "The Victory in Defeat," in which failure was the "first step to something better." "He who never failed," Marden wrote, "has never half-succeeded."[23] These advisors discounted untried success: the man who had "tried, failed, and tried again" was worth more than he who succeeded with ease.[24]

The most fitting analogy for the quest for success was the parable of the tortoise and the hare. Success writers delighted in telling anecdotes in which the slow plodder overtook the man of wealth or genius. "People of moderate mental calibre and medium capacity" were most likely to succeed, argued Dale, in a chapter bluntly entitled "Consolation for the Dull." He gave examples of famous people who, thought to be dull as youths, compensated with persistence; he included Sir Isaac Newton, Sir Walter Scott, Jean-Baptiste Molière, and Ulysses Grant.[25] Smiles insisted that the difference between one man and another had to do with energy, not talent. Success depended on perseverance, as he explained in a story of the dull boy who became chief magistrate of his native town: "Yet, slow though he was this dunce had a sort of dull energy of purpose in him which grew with his muscles and his manhood; and strange to say, when he at length came to take part in the practical business of life, he was found heading most of his school companions, and eventually left the greater number of them far behind."[26] "Depend upon it," wrote Dale in a chapter entitled "The Worker the Winner," "it is the worker who wins the prizes of the world, and not, as many imagine, the lucky man or the great genius."[27]

Character forged in the battle of life made it possible to turn to one's own advantage the very conditions that had seemed the source of so much distress and discouragement. Poverty, difficulty, low birth, or modest talent were opportunities in disguise, for it was only in overcoming these obstacles that a man built the character necessary to succeed. This was the explanation for what success writers lauded as the "spectacle of triumphant mediocrity,"[28] the ability of those of modest resources to "outstrip genius"[29] and pass by privilege in the race of life.

When success writers claimed that character was capital, they took the idea that opportunity for the poor boy was curtailed in the new industrial order and stood it on its head. In the scenarios they created, poverty was a "priceless spur," the worker was the winner, and the mediocre triumphed. These conclusions did more than add a happy ending. They rationalized economic hard times by making a virtue out of poverty and the hard work that for many was a grim necessity; they detracted attention away from the fact that capital (of the conventional variety) was increasingly concentrated in the hands of few; and they blurred the growing distinction and conflict between the haves and have-nots in Gilded Age America.

OLD-FASHIONED VIRTUE IN THE
AGE OF ENTERPRISE

Success writers used the bulk of their ample volumes to flesh out the exhortation to cultivate character. Chapter after chapter named, cataloged, and illustrated through examples and anecdotes the old-time virtues a young man should cultivate and the vices he should avoid in order to secure success in life. A glance at chapter titles in the table of contents of almost any success manual reveals a chaotic array of virtues, values, and ideals more commonly associated with the petit bourgeois ideology and an agrarian and artisan past than with the modern age of monopoly capitalism, virtues such as perseverance, self-reliance, decisiveness, courage, punctuality, energy, industry, modesty, duty, self-respect, courtesy, accuracy, common sense, honesty, tact, principle, habit, and loyalty.

The fact that so much of success manual advice evokes an earlier era can be explained in part by the fact that some of the material was first published a generation or more earlier. As noted previously, success manuals were often synthetic works, compilations (without credit) of articles and essays from periodical literature and earlier success and advice manuals. Some success writers candidly and graciously acknowledged their plagiarism as a kind of gentlemanly "borrowing" from their "betters" of an earlier generation, "picking posies from other men's flowers," all in the interest of repeating those truths that bear repeating. The persistence of old-time virtue in the success manual no doubt also reflected authors' nostalgia for an idealized past, perhaps the past of their own rural childhoods—the memories and myths of a gentler world now eclipsed by the "battle of life" that success writers so vividly described in the same works.

But plagiarism and nostalgia do not entirely explain success writers' focus on the virtues of an earlier era; nor do they explain the significance or the appeal of "character" as a central theme in a success literature that enjoyed enormous popularity well into the twentieth century. Whatever the inclinations and motivations of success writers, the agrarian and artisan values of Jeffersonian America took on new meaning when presented as prescriptions for success in the changing context of the new industrial order. It is possible to discern certain patterns, themes, and "lessons" in the success manuals' inventory of virtue. By examining these lessons against the new setting of Gilded Age America, a fuller understanding of the significance of old-fashioned virtue in the age of enterprise comes into focus. These "lessons for success" can be summarized as follows.

First, success manual readers learned that it was a good idea to work hard, to save, and to lead a sober, responsible life. In other words, they were exhorted to cultivate the tried and true economic virtues of preindustrial America. Foremost among these were industry and self-reliance, about which much has already been said. These ideas, the very high value placed on hard work and independence, were at the core of such self-help literature. But the success manuals' elaboration of the virtues associated with earning a living went further. They addressed entire chapters to themes that recalled Benjamin Franklin and Cotton Mather, themes such as honesty, frugality, diligence, and duty. To these the manuals added decisiveness, perseverance, aim, economy, tact, concentration, application, energy, method, accuracy, common sense, thoroughness, enthusiasm, nerve, courage, and motive. Put another way, the careful success manual reader learned that it was important to be a good worker.

Every success writer blamed what he saw as an epidemic of business failures on the absence of such virtues. In a chapter entitled "Failure and How to Avoid It," William Makepeace Thayer claimed that 97 out of 100 businesses and merchant enterprises failed, and offered the explanation that those "lacking in tact, economy, judgement and persistence would not have prospered in any pursuit."[30] Smiles observed that those who failed were apt to blame others rather than attributing failure to themselves and to their own lack of attention, application, accuracy, method, punctuality, and dispatch in their business.[31]

The overall message was this: be stoic and self-reliant, work hard, earn, and save. Honesty and diligent, uncomplaining industry combined with frugality and modesty would bring success. The Puritan work ethic and the prescriptions of *Poor Richard's Almanac* were alive and well in Gilded Age America. But there was a difference—not so much in advice as in context. Cotton Mather, Benjamin Franklin, and Thomas Jefferson envisioned a world of individual entrepreneurship: self-employed farmers, tradesmen, and merchants. The application of these economic virtues was a means to acquire and improve one's own property. Wage labor was viewed as a temporary state on the way to independent proprietorship. But in the late nineteenth century, when self-employment was in decline and more and more Americans would be wage laborers or salaried workers for their entire lives, the old economic virtues had new implications. In the factories, workshops, mines, and railroads of Gilded Age America, for example, the "good worker," through his industry, diligence, sobriety, honesty, and frugality might enhance the proprietor's profits yet find himself rewarded with exhaustion, poor health, and an impoverished existence. Another aspect of the new industrial reality that was at odds with a Jeffersonian vision of America was the concentration of more and more of the most valuable and productive property in the hands of fewer and fewer wealthy individuals and corporations. Generally, success manual advice seemed designed to blunt the pain of some of the more distressing changes of the modern age in part by either denying or disguising their implications. When success writers claimed that "character was capital," they revised the Lockean vision. They offered "character" and "individual virtue" as the best means to guarantee individual and national well-being, as alternatives to widespread property ownership and enlightened self-interest. They softened the blow of the failure of Jefferson's agrarian democracy while providing the rationale to maintain faith in self and in the efficacy of the new social order.

Second, the careful reader learned not to be a *greedy* capitalist. Success manuals taught that in business, good guys won. Furthermore, they won in the old-fashioned way—not only by employing honesty, frugality, and hard work but by an ethic of decency, fair-mindedness, conservative investment, and patient contentment with modest returns. Success writers warned that the undoing of so many once successful men flowed from a greedy haste to get rich, a desire to shorten the tried and true paths to success, a craving for a genteel life.[32] Tilley warned against making money an idol.[33] Smiles criticized those who were "over-speculative" and intensely selfish in their haste to be rich.[34] Hewitt claimed that there was nothing inherently wrong with having as a motive the acquisition of wealth if the dangers of wrong methods could be avoided. He outlined a business ethic that disallowed all of the following: "misrepresentation on the part of the seller," "grinding the faces of necessitous workmen" by paying "starvation wages," "speculating with borrowed capital," "trading in futures which is nothing but gambling," and "taking advantage of bankruptcy laws . . . to evade the payment of . . . just debts."[35]

These authors deplored extravagant living, arguing that it led inevitably to debt and that it undermined character. Mathews explained: "In this country, especially since the late war, there has been a growing tendency in all classes of society to overspend. In every town and village there is a fearful ambition abroad for being 'genteel.' One half of our families are engaged in a perpetual and desperate struggle to keep up appearances,—to pass for that which they are not."[36] Mathews went on to trace the life that led to indebtedness:

> Marrying early, the young lawyer, merchant, or mechanic is not content to begin life in the simple style in which his father began, increasing his comforts as his earnings increase; but he must live from the very start as the veterans of his calling live after years of toil and economy. The rents he pays, the furniture and ornaments of his house, the luxuries of his table, the number of his servants, the clothes of himself and his family, his expenditure for opera-tickets, concerts, lectures, hackney coaches,—not to include the cost of what Charles Lamb would call his "virtuous vices," such as smoking, etc., or dinners at Delmonico's are all far above his means.[37]

Here and elsewhere, success writers cataloged aspects of the new social order that violated the dominant, yet increasingly vulnerable values of rural and small-town America. These advisors interpreted such crass, spendthrift, pretentious ways as anomalous, and doomed for failure. But the very fact that they felt called upon to attack these practices is evidence of the growing tension between older yeoman ideals and the business ethic of the Gilded Age. This defense of older values and attack on the new also suggest a tension between haves and have-nots. The fact that extravagance and genteel living were actually noted as causes of failure may have provided a self-righteous sense of satisfaction for those for whom such ease and luxury were not possible. Not only were those of modest means free from such vices, albeit by necessity, this doctrine offered the opportunity to elevate those traditional virtues of a simple but secure and respectable life above the ways of those who might otherwise be considered "superiors." The success manual offered readers a view of the world in which morality, justice, and respectability were primary and stood opposed to the more irreverent and crass side to the competitive new order. They provided a critique of the excesses of the new order by framing the legitimate range of behaviors in a moral matrix. Paradoxically, this aspect of success manual ideology paralleled that of the Knights of Labor, who, despite their radicalism, were not necessarily anticapitalist or antiemployer. They attacked those capitalists who did not share their vision of republican virtue, morality, and fair play.[38]

Third, success manuals taught that democracy was the best policy. Success writers rejected ideas that were tinged with airs of privilege and pretension, and they redefined concepts such as "gentleman" and "politeness" in terms of the presumed honesty, kindness, and generosity of "ordinary folk." "Snobbishness doesn't pay and never will," wrote Kent. "This dropping on one's knees to aristocracy, and falling back on one's dignity to ordinary people, is an exhibition of the absolute want of genuine politeness."[39] In a chapter entitled "Who Is the Gentleman," Dale wrote: "Before you can find a gentleman, you must first find a man; for the gentleman is a pattern of manliness."[40] He defined the term as literally a "*gentle* man," stressing honesty, generosity, and bravery—"all those sterling qualities of mind and heart."[41] King spelled out oft-repeated distinctions when he wrote of "true politeness" versus "superficial veneer":

> There is a vast difference between "society customs" and genuine good manners. The former is a bold but fruitless attempt to counterfeit a noble virtue, while the latter is the natural expression of a heart filled with honest intentions. True politeness must be born of sincerity. It must be the response of the heart, otherwise it makes no lasting impression, for no amount of "posture" and "surface polish" can be substituted for honesty and truthfulness. . . . Good manners are developed through a spirit imbued with unselfishness, kindness, justness, and generosity.[42]

These sentiments in part reflected existing mainstream American values, especially in the countryside. As with the concern with fair play, success writers' concern with democracy and "true politeness" expressed ideas that also had great appeal to populist-oriented protest movements such as the Knights of Labor, the Farmers' Alliance, and the People's Party. But in the success manual, the advocacy of democratic manners was more than rejection of aristocratic pretensions and class snobbishness. And it was also more than an attempt to temper the excesses of the new industrial order.

Success writers laid the groundwork of tolerance and generosity of spirit that would be needed in a broadly defined middle class that would include like-minded individuals of vastly different economic means.

Fourth, readers were advised that moderation and respectability should govern their personal habits and demeanor, which included everything from the company they kept and the way they dressed to manners and church attendance. Success writers cautioned readers against vices such as drinking, smoking, gambling, and immoderate amusements and praised the simple pleasures of home, family, and church. Much of the success writers' advice on decorum and personal behavior seems calculated to identify themselves and their readers as white, native-born Protestants and to distinguish themselves from immigrants, Catholics, and others who were deemed intemperant and oblivious or hostile to a kind of mainstream, small-town, middle-class culture. For example, Conwell advised: "Strong drink of all kinds, highly seasoned food, late hours in entertainment weaken all the forces needed for the best achievement and need to be turned down or avoided with a will of steel."[43] A chapter by Tilley, entitled "Pitfalls," warned against liquor, tobacco, gambling, "bad habits," and "evil associates."[44] Lewis added pool and billiards to the list of vices,[45] while Dale recommended literature, art, athletics, parlor games, and good company and opposed the "artificial pleasures" of horse racing, baseball, prizefighting, sensational theater, cards, and dancing.[46] In *The Imperial Highway*, Jerome Paine Bates observed that "the *slave* is often happier than the master who is nearer undone by license, than his vassal by toil,"[47] and success writers generally evoked high ideals to encourage readers to resist the temptation of these and other vices. Warning about "liquor drinking," Dale advised readers to "take sides against this evil, and be a champion for purity, sobriety and a high manhood."[48] In a chapter entitled "Sowing His Wild Oats," Bok denied that "sowing wild oats" built manhood. Good men, Bok insisted, did not "call a young man a 'ninny' when he leads an upright life; they call him a manly fellow, and take him into their hearts and their homes."[49]

In matters of dress Bok and others advised "cleanliness, modesty, and neatness"; a young man should dress in a manner that was neither "flashy" nor "shabby." Bok had nothing but contempt for those who were guided by any but the most simple and modest tastes: "The marvelous combinations we see in young men's clothes, of extreme long coats, of light clothes and large patterns in suiting, of razor pointed shoes, of pink shirts, white collars and blue cravats . . . worn by extremists in dress or by those of mediocre taste whose exhibition of those tastes always keeps them in the lower stations of life."[50]

Though all of this advice suggests the old-fashioned values of a presumably moral and unmaterialistic past, these guides did not advocate virtue for virtue's sake. Honesty, explained Smiles, was good business policy; generosity would be repaid.[51] Success writers made it clear that a program of modest respectability was part of the formula for success. They clued readers in to the fact that in a society that lacked rigid class distinctions, personal conduct and manners were important ways of distinguishing oneself.[52]

> The cultivation of manner, — though in excess it is foppish and foolish, — is highly necessary in a person who has occasion to negotiate with others in matters of business. . . . for the want of it has not unfrequently [*sic*] been found in a great measure to neutralize the results of much industry, integrity, and honesty of character.[53]

Good manners might pay off in a more direct way, too, as in the story Mathews told of a young man who was rewarded with an inheritance for the courtesy he showed in aiding two elderly spinsters.[54]

Nowhere was the expedience of a virtuous and respectable life made more apparent than in discussions of church-going. Religious life was of great importance to success writers, many of whom were, after all, ministers, but they often justified its importance in terms of the advances religious affiliation might bring to one's career. In *Manhood-Making*, Alexander Lewis quoted one wealthy businessman who claimed that church attendance had provided him opportunities for upward mobility: "By going to church we got acquainted with church people and that changed all our associates. Up to this time our acquaintances were factory employees, most of whom were uneducated people."[55] Another claimed that most of the wealthy men of both country and city led religious lives, and suggested that the character such men exhibited won the confidence of others and consequently brought business success.[56] The same notion was borne out in the experience of a young man about whom Dale wrote. Upon leaving home, he followed his mother's advice to attend prayer meetings. He reported the results as follows: "These habits gave me the confidence of my employers and I was rapidly advanced over others in positions of trust and responsibility."[57] And in *Success in Life*, William Owen declared: "The country over, the hired hand that is kept the whole year round, at good wages, is the one that reads the newspapers, dresses up, and goes to church."[58]

In summary, the exhaustive list of virtues and vices that crowded the tables of contents in success manuals can be distilled into four precepts: be a good worker; do not become a greedy capitalist; make democracy your policy in social relations; and make modesty, purity, and respectability your guide in personal conduct. The promise that success writers made to the man who followed these precepts could be read two ways. The first interpretation was that virtue would be rewarded, not just in some abstract spiritual way, but materially. Personal virtue was the foundation of the prosperity of the nation's successful businessmen, and the same virtues could be expected to bring the same result for young men starting out today. Character was an intangible form of capital, the application of which could bring the real thing. The second interpretation was that virtue was its own reward. Those who followed the precepts made themselves men of character and in so doing earned the right to claim a place of respect and honor in the community, irrespective of their wealth or family connections.

The second proposition—that virtue was its own reward—had implications for class identity, specifically for defining a new middle class and de-emphasizing the importance of class and muting class conflict. In their endless cataloging of virtues and vices, in their anecdotes, examples, and advice about what to do and how to behave, they systematized a set of virtues into a prescription for middle-class respectability and a definition of a new middle class. It was a self-ascribed status that could be achieved only by the individual and yet once achieved, it could be held in common with a presumably broad American mainstream, the decent, God-fearing, law-abiding citizens who had faith in American progress, and implicitly in the new industrial order that made this progress possible. Membership in the American middle class put a man in a community of believers without sacrificing either individual prerogative or individual accountability. The *idea* of the middle class was the ideological homeland of the self-made man; it promised spiritual membership in a class characterized more by a common way of seeing the world than by common economic interests. Even those who would never be successful in the traditional sense could earn middle-class status and respectability if they were willing to be virtuous and conform themselves to a particular way of seeing and living in the world. The achievement and maintenance of middle-class identity or status may have been more than a minor consolation for those whose lives did not replicate the fabled rags-to-riches story. In *Power and Civility*, Norbert Elias has suggested that at least among those of the upper classes in society, the "craving for prestige and the fear of its loss, the struggle against the obliteration of social distinction" and the "desire for more money and economic advantages" were "wound as a double and invisible chain about the individual."[59] The same may apply to those of the middling sort in nineteenth-century America. The lack of clearly delineated class positions in America—the general permeability of class lines—not only encouraged men to aspire to higher places, but also kept them scrambling to keep from slipping backwards into a lower class.[60] It put a premium on finding ways to distinguish one's self from those below. To Americans in precarious economic straits in a period of profound economic and social uncertainty, middle-class status provided a way to identify with the successful in the new industrial order and distinguish one's self from the failures. The extraordinary popularity of success manuals can be explained partly by the fact that these authors effectively addressed both the economic and social anxieties experienced by many Americans in this period. The idea of a vast, all-embracing middle class, seemed to offer at least a temporary place of safety and solace between two equally perilous states: success and failure. Even the purchase and display of one of these large, impressively bound success manuals could be seen as a reassuring demonstration of the kind of middle-class cultural consumption that some advisors hoped might represent both a commitment to middle-class values and a middle ground between the haves and have-nots.[61]

Samuel Smiles was explicit about the relationship between individual virtue and middle-class status. His work was the single most important model and source for the American success manual; taken together, his four books—*Self-Help* (1860), *Character* (1872), *Thrift* (1875), and *Duty* (1881)—sold over one million copies in the United States. In his view, a new and virtuous middle class symbolized the achievement of both individual advancement and class harmony. Quoting admiringly from an address delivered by a Mr. Bright to an assembly of workingmen at Rochdale in 1847, Smiles wrote:

> What is it that has made, that has in fact created, the middle class in this country, but the virtues to which I have alluded? [industry, frugality, temperance and honesty] . . . How is it that the hundreds of thousands of men, now existing in this our country, of the middle class, are educated, comfortable, and enjoying an amount of happiness and independence to which our forefathers were wholly unaccustomed? Why, by the practice of those very virtues. . . . I maintain that there has never been in any former age as much of these virtues as is now to be found amongst the great middle class of our community. When I speak of middle class, I mean that class which is between the privileged class, the richest, and the very poorest. . . . [P]ay no attention whatever to public writers or speakers who say that this class or that class, that this law or that law, that this government, or that, can do all these things for them. The working classes improve by practice of virtue and self-reliance.[62]

Forty years later, in *The Way to Win*, John T. Dale echoed Smiles's sentiments: "We need to go back to the gospel of old-fashioned honesty, industry and frugality, which Franklin so admirably set forth in his day, and then the perplexing question of labor and capital would be solved. The laborer would then very soon merge into the capitalist, and the day of the deadly feuds and envious complaining would soon pass forever away."[63] In the world of the success manual, the middle class, or at least the *idea* of the middle class, was a balm for class antagonism. In the success manual and elsewhere in American history, class awareness among the middle class was expressed in part by the denial of the significance of class.[64]

Character, shared virtue, and respectability might join, at least in spirit, the capitalists and the laborer, the self-made millionaire and the hardworking, self-reliant worker of even the humblest rank. Yet precisely because capital and labor did exist, these time-honored virtues took on new meaning. In the new and proliferating factories, mills, and workshops of Gilded Age America, employers recruited and trained waves of new workers, immigrants from the countryside and from abroad. In this setting, the virtues of industry, sobriety, respectability, diligence, frugality, punctuality, and duty, could be translated into a disciplined, productive, and profitable workforce—the coveted prize of many a frustrated employer. In the workplace, entrepreneurs and their foremen applied the proverbial carrot and stick—the carrot of favoritism and incentive pay and the stick of fines, corporal punishment, and firing—in what sometimes turned out to be vain attempts to enforce the work discipline personified by the ethic of self-help and success.[65] The message of the success manual might be viewed as a kind of ideological carrot and stick. Success writers offered the hope of individual advancement and the guarantee of respectability and middle-class identity to those who accommodated themselves to the new industrial order. They threatened the humiliation of unredeemable failure and placelessness for those who refused to buy into their ideology of success. The rewards and punishments of the success ethic were less immediate and less obvious than those employed by foremen on the shop floor. To reap these rewards, young men would have to discern and internalize the rules of the new industrial order, substitute self-discipline for work discipline, and replace outside authority by the authority within. Character was virtue internalized.[66]

From the point of view of the typical success manual reader—the man of little means, uncertain about how to make his way or find his place in the new order of things—the assertion that character was capital must have been welcome and reassuring news. The idea that virtue would be rewarded offered at least the hope, if not always the reality, that the man of little tangible wealth could prosper and perhaps even become a great capitalist.[67] Alternatively, the idea that virtue was its own reward offered consolation for those who might not be fortunate enough to achieve prosperity. Character conferred respectability and the possibility of middle-class identity to a wide range of Americans, including those who would strive in vain for the income and tangible comforts of real middle-class economic status.

To those who had already achieved success as owners of mills, factories, and workshops, the idea that character was capital had a different meaning. One success writer stated this logic candidly in a chapter entitled "Self-Mastery": "As vice makes poor workmen, and as poor workmen reduce and often destroy all profits, business interests require, even if there were no moral considerations, that you should be virtuous in order to succeed!"[68] This was no doubt what employers had in mind when they gave copies of a success manual entitled *Worth and Wealth* (1883) to employees in lieu of Christmas presents or bonuses.[69] Character may have indeed been capital, but in the new industrial order of late-nineteenth-century America, *whose* capital it was clearly depended on circumstances.

7

Manhood Is Everything: The Masculinization and Democratization of Success

ℐ

"God is after a man. Wealth is nothing, fame is nothing. Manhood is everything."
— Orison Swett Marden, *Rising in the World, or Architects of Fate*

In a "dog-eat-dog" world, character needed buttressing by a motive force — some power akin to the engine of the industrial age. Furthermore, character alone was not powerful enough to unite the poor-but-honest with the great capitalists in a common definition of success. Success writers found the unifying concept in the notion of "manhood," reinforced by what they described as the most manly of all traits, "will-power." These advisors masculinized "success" by defining manhood and manliness as the ultimate necessity for individual achievement. Success, they agreed, was the reward not simply of those of character but of those who combined character with manliness. They democratized success when they insisted that true manhood, like character, was a goal within the reach of the poor as well as the rich, the humble as well as the great.

A focus on manliness and manhood was not unique to success manuals. Historians of nineteenth-century America have noted the manhood theme in many aspects of the popular culture of the period — including medical advice literature, fraternal initiation rituals, and the popularity of bare-knuckle prizefighting — and in the writing and oratory published in American books and magazines, from the tales of Davy Crockett to the essays of Ralph Waldo Emerson, from the beginning of the western genre with Owen Wister's *The Virginian* to Theodore Roosevelt's call for a "muscular Christianity."[1] The preoccupation with manhood in the second half of the nineteenth century in part reflected the fact that ideas about what it meant to be a man were in flux. Changes in the relations of work, home, and family brought about by industrialization and urbanization narrowed and redefined men's roles as well as women's.[2] Traditional male identities as providers, protectors, and patriarchs were either diminished or transformed.[3] The dominant male ideal that emerged in the Gilded Age was increasingly one-dimensional and focused on entrepreneurship and money-making. The much celebrated "Napoleons of the Mart" and "captains of industry" were fast becoming new American heroes.[4]

But there was a problem with the entrepreneurial model of manhood; for most it was as unattainable as it was compelling. Tough economic times, the trend toward business concentration and large-scale enterprise, and the monopolistic practices of those who got there first all conspired against independent proprietorship. Even the American farmer—proud symbol of economic independence who thought of himself as a small-scale entrepreneur—was chastened by the impact of falling farm prices, high interest rates, and farm foreclosures. It was wage and salaried employment, not entrepreneurship, that would account for the way more and more Americans would make their livings. Furthermore, the conditions of the new industrial workplace generated a competing model of manhood among workers. Labor's notion of manhood was based on solidarity rather than individuality, and it posed a direct challenge to the entrepreneurial ideal of manliness and to the entrepreneur himself. This ideal of manhood was characterized by a fraternal recognition of group or class interest, especially as expressed at the workplace by a mutualistic "one for all and all for one" ethic and by a code of behavior that called for a "manly bearing" toward the boss. It was this idea of manhood that Eugene Debs had in mind when he described the American Railway Union's successful strike of the Great Northern Railroad in 1894. He attributed the victory to the unity of the workers who, as he put it, "stood up as one man and asserted their manhood."[5]

Success writers eschewed this militant model of manhood and celebrated the lives and the achievements of the great American captains of industry. Yet ultimately they defined both manhood and success in ways that had no necessary association with wealth, fame, or power. Success writers offered a notion of manliness that built upon the contemporary crisis about male identity, but went beyond it. Within the pages of the success manual "manhood" took on special meaning; "manhood" became an indispensable aspect of the American ideology of success. The ways in which success writers defined and equated manhood and success had far-reaching implications for how men might see themselves, how they might view their chances for success, and how they might regard the new industrial order that was the backdrop against which they would play out their own struggles with success and failure. Finally, the linkage of manhood and success had implications for how womanhood and the feminine would be defined. Indeed, the equation of manhood and success was built in part on the equation of the feminine with failure.

WANTED — A MAN

The words "manhood," "manliness," and "manly" recurred with frequency in success manuals. Authors rhapsodized about "manly qualities," "manly vigor," "manly character," "manly self-assertion," and that "layer of metal that makes manhood."[6] Success writers sometimes capitalized or italicized the letters of the word "man" or "manhood" for even further emphasis. The importance of manhood was evident even in the titles of certain success manuals, such as William Owen's *Success in Life, and How to Secure It: or Elements of Manhood and Their Culture* and Reverend Alexander Lewis's *Manhood-Making: Studies in the Elemental Principles of Success*.

In the world of the success manual, manhood meant far more than male adulthood. True manhood, like true success, was "self-made." Manhood, like character, was forged in the battle of life. In order to succeed in life, success writers urged readers to develop the "grandest possible manhood," the "stamina of manhood," or a "magnificent manhood."[7] According to these manuals, "manhood" was a quality everywhere in demand in a fast-moving, ever-changing, new age. Marden's *Rising in the World* began with the following announcement: "The world has a standing advertisement over the door of every profession; every occupation; every calling: 'Wanted—A Man.'"[8] In *Masters of the Situation*, William James Tilley wrote that the "real object of all training and all education should be to develop the best type of manhood."[9] Marden recounted the story of President James Garfield who, when asked in his youth what he planned to be, reportedly said: "First of all, I must make myself a man; if I do not succeed in that, I can succeed in nothing."[10] Owen wrote: "It is the man who makes the business, and if any undertaking has no *man* behind it, of how frail a texture it is! Broidered [*sic*] gold and lace cannot compensate for such a lack." And Tilley concluded: "The world is looking for men, and the success of all business enterprise depends on the character of those who manage them."[11]

What exactly did it take to be a man? Sterling character and personal virtue were always central in the success manuals' definition of manhood, just as they were in the advice to young men of the antebellum period. In some cases, success writers presented the terms "manhood" and "character" as practically interchangeable.[12] When Marden advised readers about selecting a vocation, he suggested a "clean, useful, honorable occupation," remarking, "You may not make quite so much money, but you will be more of a man, and manhood is above all riches, overtops all titles, and character is greater than any career."[13] Bates embellished this thesis in a chapter entitled, "Business Traits, Qualities and Habits":

> The highest object of life we take to be to form a manly character, and to work out the best development possible, of body and spirit—of mind, conscience, heart and soul. Accordingly, that is not the most successful life in which man gets the most pleasure, the most money, the most power of place, honor or fame; but that in which a man gets the most manhood, and performs the greatest amount of useful work and human duty. Money is power after a sort, it is true, but intelligence, public spirit and moral virtue are powers, too, and far nobler ones.[14]

Dale exhorted readers to have the "manliness to plead for the right," insisting that the "most manly men" were the most "godly," while Edward Hale announced in *What Career?*: "The central truth is proclaimed, that manliness is a moral quality,—that it belongs to spirit and the empire of spirit."[15]

But success writers agreed that in the rush and roar of the late nineteenth century, character alone did not make the man. The battle of life required that virtue be reinforced with some special power, some source of strength and energy suited to rugged times. In the individualistic world of the success manual, this power could come only from within. Thus the final element in the formula for success and the crowning glory of manhood was the power of individual will. Success writers described *will* as that "mysterious form of mental energy which makes the difference between the great and the insignificant."[16] Aggressiveness, determination, perseverance, decisiveness, self-assertion, and self-motivation were the hallmarks of the strong-willed man. Success writers presented "will" as a driving power within the man himself—a corollary to the machine power of the industrial age. According to Mathews, "will" was the "driving wheel" and the "spring of motive Power."[17] In a chapter entitled "The Will and the Way," Marden confided: "Were I called upon to express in a word the secret of so many failures among those who started out in life with high hopes, I should say unhesitatingly, they lacked will-power. They could not half will. What is a man without a will? He is like an engine without steam, a mere sport of chance, to be tossed about hither and thither, always at the mercy of those who have wills."[18] Smiles claimed that "energy of will" was the "central power of character in a man,—in a word, it [was] the *Man* himself. It [gave] impulse to every action, and soul to every effort." In short, he wrote, "it is *will*,—force of purpose,—that enables a man to do or be whatever he sets his mind on being or doing."[19] These advisors attributed an incalculable power to "will." In Tilley's words, "Nothing [is] impossible to a man who can will. This is the only law of success."[20] And Harry Lewis insisted, "Whether a man is conditioned high or low; in the city or on the farm: 'If he will; he will.' "[21] One writer admitted that willpower could not perform miracles, yet he assured readers that all history proved that it was "almost omnipotent."[22] And another concurred, claiming that "there are few circumstances over which a strong will has no control."[23] One writer suggested "banishing from the dictionary" the word "impossible," and another said of the man who sought success, "He must become a pugilist, knocking the 'I' out of 'If's.' "[24] Success manuals immortalized a number of still-familiar maxims, such as "Where there's a will there's a way," "Wishes fail, but wills prevail," "Strong men have wills; weak ones wishes," and "They can—who *think* they can."[25] The last is reminiscent of the children's story about the little locomotive who made it up a steep hill by saying "I think I can, I think I can," a story that may have originated in the American popular culture of this period.[26]

But much of the rhetoric about willpower had a more aggressive tone, evoking a do-or-die struggle of man against man. A "vacillating man," observed Mathews, "no matter what his abilities, is invariably pushed aside in the race of life by the man of determined will."[27] The conditions of modern life called for a new forcefulness. Marden wrote that "in this electronic age, where everything is pusher or pushed, he who would succeed must hold his ground and push hard."[28] In a chapter entitled "The Man of Push," George R. Hewitt proclaimed: "Push paves the way. . . . Today the thoroughfares of life are crowded; if a man would win a place in the ranks of professional or mercantile life, he must push for it. Push brings men of mediocrity to the front, and enables them to stay there. . . . Push is the passport to success."[29] True men, then, were a special breed of the male species, much in demand in a challenging new age. Successful men combined virtue and force, character and willpower.

WHERE THERE'S A WILL THERE'S A WAY

Success writers presented the power of will as not only the most aggressive element in the formula for success but as the most specifically masculine. It was especially in describing the power of will that success was not only masculinized but sexualized. In language rich in sexual innuendo, success writers linked symbolically the drive to achieve in the economic sphere with male libido and conquest in combat. In its milder forms, the qualities needed to succeed in business were likened to those needed to succeed in romantic or marital relations: "Know your business in all its details. Marry it. Take it with you wherever you go . . . devotion will tell on the profit side of the ledger."[30] Mathews advised, "No man ever need fear refusal from any lady, if he only gives his heart to getting her; and the same is true of success."[31] According to Marden, "A bank never becomes very successful . . . until it gets a president who takes it to bed with him."[32] But more extraordinary was the symbolic language in accounts of successful combat in the battle of life. Success writers portrayed what might be called a "phallocentric"[33] world of battle, which celebrated self-made men for their virility, their "potent spirits" and "erect and constant character."[34] William Owen recounted Henry Clay's confrontation with coworkers in his early career as a Richmond store clerk in just such language: Young Clay, mocked by the "city boys," finally counterattacked with repartee "like a scorpion's sting."

> That night he slept better than he had for weeks, and from that day forward he carried his sword unsheathed. He soon came to be recognized as the leader of the company. . . . While he was too generous to make war upon those who persecuted him in the days of his weakness, he was too much of a general to pause at the parrying of a thrust. He never stopped until he had disarmed his enemy.[35]

In explaining the virtue of decisiveness, Owen wrote that "men must be soldier like, and rest on their arms ready to spring up and fire on the instant. . . . It is a curious condition of mind that this requires. It is like sleeping with your pistol under your pillow, and the pistol on full cock; a moment lost, and all may be lost."[36] By combining phallic symbolism and military metaphor—these quotes likened both sexual prowess and combat readiness to the qualities needed to achieve success in the world of business and industry. Taken literally, they describe an intensely competitive and individualistic world fraught with danger, a world in which a "moment lost, and all may be lost," a dilemma in which one either conquers the competitor or risks being conquered by him.

The battle of life called not only for overt force but for a kind of secret readiness—"reserve" and "self-possession" that again had subtle and not-so-subtle sexual overtones. "Self-control is only courage under another form," advised William Makepeace Thayer in *Onward to Fame and Fortune*,[37] while Tilley mixed images of military might and industrial power in his description of the power of "reserve":

> Reticence and reserve seems to have an influence like that of the sides of a cannon, giving an added impetus to one's purpose and sending one straight to the mark. The great motive power which drives the engine is unseen, and held fast within the strong ribs of the boiler—when once seen, the steam has wasted its force and is useless. That brilliant electric flash but shows that a mysterious power has disappeared.[38]

Jerome Bates counseled:

[K]eep cool, have your resources well in hand, and reserve your strength until the proper time arrives to exert it. There is hardly any trait of character or faculty of intellect more valuable than the power of self-possession, or presence of mind. The man who is always "going off" unexpectedly, like an old rusty firearm, who is easily fluttered and discomposed at the appearance of some unforeseen emergency; who has no control over himself or his powers, is just the one who is always in trouble and never successful or happy.[39]

"Going off unexpectedly" could be understood not only as an analogy for failure in coping with the "unforeseen emergencies" in the outside world of business but also as a veiled reference to premature ejaculation. Furthermore, the phallic reference to an "old rusty firearm," an eminently untrustworthy device, suggests that a man's sexuality was potentially dangerous. In order to achieve success, writers advised readers to control themselves and their sexuality—the valuable yet dangerous faculty.

The belief that reining in sexuality was a necessary precondition for achieving success in business was not unique to the success manuals. Medical and sexual advice literature articulated what Ben Barker-Benfield called a "spermatic economy."[40] This doctrine held that sperm was the vital force of energy in the well-balanced economy of the male body. The imprudent loss of sperm could mean the loss of will and order, incapacitating a man for both marriage and business. The same consideration is reflected in the fact that in the nineteenth century, when success depended on capital accumulation (saving not spending), the vernacular for male orgasm was "spend."[41] Success writers couched much of their advice about how to succeed in terms of the accumulation, reserve, and expenditure of "fluid" resources. Mathews warned readers to "guard jealously against the little leaks in expenditures," explaining that "men fail of success from early exhaustion, from a lack of accumulated force, whether physical, mental or spiritual, which only can qualify them to meet any unexpected draught upon their power."[42] In a chapter entitled "Expenditures of Resources," Bates claimed that "if a man 'uses himself up' at every effort he makes in trying to build his imperial highway to fortune, that way will never be finished, nor the fortune secured." The most successful men in life's race, he went on, were those who kept themselves "well in hand" and kept "in reserve some extra power or ability, with which to meet emergencies and eclipse competing rivals."[43] The power of reserve depended on the ability to accumulate resources.

When old Dr. Bellamy was asked by a young clergyman for advice about the composition of his sermons, he replied: "Fill up the cask! Fill up the cask!, and then if you tap it anywhere you will get a good stream. But if you put in but a little, it will dribble, dribble, dribble, and you must tap, tap, tap, and then you get but a small stream, after all."[44]

The only solution to this dilemma in which man was expected to "sleep with his pistol under his pillow on full cock," "keep his resources well in hand," and avoid "going off unexpectedly like a rusty firearm," was to deploy that most masculine of all virtues, the power of will. In a chapter entitled "Will-Power," Owen lamented, "some of the most potent spirits that ever peered through flesh have been rendered effete and useless for lack of this one element." In another chapter entitled "Decision," he observed: "Unless man can erect himself above himself, how poor a thing is man."[45] Bates advised readers to "be firm" and cautioned that "without will, a man would be like the soft, flabby, nerveless mollusk or shell-fish in the ocean."[46] He elaborated:

> The will, considered without regard to direction, is simple constancy, firmness; and therefore, it will be obvious that everything depends upon right direction and motive. Directed toward the enjoyment of the senses, the strong will may be a demon, and the intellect merely its debased slave, but directed toward good, the strong will is king and the intellect is then minister of man's well being.[47]

Here, *will* symbolized the possibilities and dangers of masculine force and the male sexual drive—"constancy, firmness," a "demon" when "directed toward the enjoyment of the senses" and "king" when directed toward good. *Willpower* symbolized a man's ability to contain and direct an inner masculine force in productive ways; it represented the proper combination of potency and self-control.[48] The doctrine of sexual reserve power, a corollary to economic reserve power, transformed a constraining ideology of male sexual repression into an ideology of male potency and opportunity. Only the virile could succeed, and then only by holding their inner powers in reserve for use at just the right moment of conquest.

Success, then, demanded a special kind of man—he who possessed great sexual powers as well as the willpower to reserve these vital energies for expenditure in the battle of life. Success in the outside world was possible only for those who first won the battle within and conquered themselves and their unacceptable impulses and emotions. "Surely the world knows not always, indeed seldom imagines the struggles within, or the heroic discipline which at length confers upon man that greatest of all triumphs, the mastery of himself."[49] In the success manual, manhood was not only a symbol of man's mastery in the world, but just as important, manhood stood for self-mastery, mastery of the world within.

On one level, the sexual metaphor of the success manual may have at least subliminally expressed and addressed concerns and interests that were in fact quite literally about sex and sexuality. Victorian middle-class sexual culture confronted men with an especially difficult challenge. At the same time that sex and sexuality were deemed more important and opportunities for illicit sex were more plentiful,[50] admonitions against almost all forms of sexual expression, from masturbation to overexpenditure in sexual intercourse within marriage, became more intense.[51] In such an environment, advice literature addressed to young men that was couched in sexual innuendo and masculine self-aggrandizement must have had special poignancy. It would be a mistake to overlook the possibility that part of the success manual's appeal was the covert eroticism of advice laced with sexual references—heteroeroticism, homoeroticism, and especially autoeroticism. Note, for example, the pervasiveness of sexually oriented self-referential language insisting that men keep their reserve power "well in hand," etc. Paradoxically, success manuals' endless preaching about the importance of self-control and self-restraint may have provided a safe, unacknowledged forum for the celebration of male libido. Far from denying male sexuality, success writers covertly, perhaps unwittingly, acknowledged it and built it into their prescription for success. Here and elsewhere, success writers' ability to address, even subliminally, real concerns of their audience helps explain the appeal of success manuals and helps account for their popularity.

Though the sexualized language in success manuals may have gotten some men's attention by subtly teasing prurient interests, the overt message was, of course, just the opposite. The sexualizing of success in a doctrine of self-control was a way to encourage sexual sublimation—redirecting potentially disruptive sexual energy into economically productive activity. More importantly, by emphasizing body and mind, potency and control, these sexualized prescriptions for success focused readers' attention on the self. The power of "will"—with or without its sexual implications—was unequivocally about the individual man and his capacity for self-control. The sexualized language added a new level of intensity to an already intensely individualistic ideology of success, and in a striking way, it made the call for self-discipline both personal and immediate. Titillating words that called on a man to "erect himself above himself" both dramatized and aggrandized what might otherwise be seen as a somewhat uninspiring duty—the obligation to exercise self-restraint, to work hard, to be sober, prudent, frugal, and industrious. Put another way, the admonition to establish exacting control over body and mind in order to succeed in life was a way to press home the requirement that the individual internalize the rules and the discipline of the new economic order.[52] The sexualization of success, the celebration of willpower, and the presentation of self-mastery as the precondition for mastery in the world can be understood as one of the latter-day strategies in the ongoing nineteenth-century endeavor to "educate the character" and "instruct the conscience" of the nation's young men, to discipline themselves and internalize authority in a society in which the authority formerly vested in church and community had all but disappeared.[53] In the absence of outside authority, success manuals as well as other types of advice literature called on individual conscience to play the role of task master.[54] In the world of the success manual, willpower in the form of self-discipline was the most manly of traits, and the most essential in the battle for success. If a man was going to succeed in the new industrial order, he must voluntarily accept and live by its rules.

A MAGNIFICENT MANHOOD — GREATER THAN WEALTH, GRANDER THAN FAME

Manhood had yet another meaning in the world the success manual created — a significance that went beyond the search for masculine identity, beyond the call for self-control, and beyond the notion that manly qualities were the necessary means to achieving success in life. By insisting that "character was capital" and concluding that "manhood was everything," success writers raised the personal achievement of a truly manly character above the pecuniary gain and individual advancement that otherwise seemed to be the goal of most of their advice. According to this logic, manhood and the character and willpower upon which it was built were not only the means but also the end in the search for success; the achievement of a magnificent manhood was itself success. Success writers never claimed that all men could become millionaires. In *The Way to Win*, Dale explained that "when there is one millionaire, there must of necessity be thousands of men of moderate circumstances."[55] Success manuals offered consolation in the form of a higher type of success to those whose lives might not replicate the rags-to-riches saga. Crafts proclaimed that it was "better to be a man than merely a millionaire."[56] Marden reassured readers that manhood was "greater than wealth, grander than fame."[57] If manhood was higher than wealth, power, and position, what did it matter if all could not succeed by reaching the pinnacle of their profession? William Mathews claimed that some "have been successful as men, though they may have failed as lawyers, doctors, and merchants."[58] Owen concluded a discussion of occupations by remarking, "Let them labor with the hand or the head but busy themselves in the cultivation of manhood."[59] Marden quoted Rousseau in a chapter entitled "What Career": "Let him first be a man. Fortune may remove him from one rank to another as she pleases; he will be always found in his place."[60] Similarly, though Bates wrote under the rubric of "The Highway to Fortune and Success in Business Life," he too claimed that there was something higher than business success: the formation of a "manly character," in his words, was the "highest object of life."[61] And Haines and Yaggy urged the young man discouraged by failure not to despair, observing: "If he can make nothing by any work that presents itself now, he can at least make himself."[62]

Given that every man could not expect to achieve fame, power, or fortune and given success writers' determination to offer the promise of *success* to all men of character and willpower, Haines was suggesting the only logical conclusion: he consoled the discouraged with the prospects of "making themselves" by cultivating their manhood. Accordingly, the definition of the self-made man might be broadened. It could include not only those who, like the great industrialists, were alleged to have built their fortunes entirely by their own efforts but also those who had built a "magnificent manhood" entirely by their own efforts. For many, this may have been the only true meaning of the success manual maxim, "self-made if ever made."

"Manhood," then, could be seen as a nonmaterialistic alternative to a notion of success that focused narrowly on "getting ahead," and a rather exalted alternative at that. To anyone anxious about his prospects in the new industrial order, this "higher" idea of success had three definite advantages.

First, manhood, unlike wealth, represented a kind of success that was unlimited. If success meant wealth, fame, and position, only a few could succeed. This was the problem with the strictly entrepreneurial model of manhood. But if success meant the achievement of a noble manhood, potentially all who were willing to cultivate the character and willpower that made up manliness—all *men* that is—could become successful. Defining "success" in terms of "manhood" democratized success; just as in politics, any man could participate in the process if only he would.

Secondly, by this definition, each man was the sole judge of his own success. Wealth was quantifiable, manliness was not. Fame, fortune, and power often constituted the public measure of a man; manhood was a private matter—measurable only by the man himself. Manhood was a matter of self-esteem. If success was the achievement of a magnificent manhood, the embodiment of sterling character, even the man of modest means might define himself as a success. Thus a man determined his own status in the world—not only by his actions—but by self-definition or identity.

Thirdly, designating "manhood" as the definition of true success provided a common ground on which the haves and have-nots might unite. If the meaning of success was not wealth or position but personal virtue—

as conveyed by the idea that "character is capital" and "manhood is every-thing"—then economic differences among men and places could be mini-mized. In this view, the worthy—be they rich or poor, capitalists or laborers, great or small—might be joined together in a shared set of ideas about what it meant to be a man and about what it meant to be a success. The manly man was distinct not only from the feminine but from the lazy and profli-gate complainers who would not struggle, from the demagogues and critics of American society who wanted only to "fire cities and deprecate capital," and from the pretentious, dissipated rich who live by inherited wealth. True men, by this logic, be they the virtuous poor or the self-made millionaires, shared a harmony of beliefs that transcended a disharmony of interests. The true man did not complain of lack of opportunity or capital. He be-lieved that there was no failure for the man who invested character in every enterprise; he created opportunities out of difficulties; he was the one who knew that all men were "self-made if ever made." In the last analysis, true men sought not after wealth, power, and place; rather they were motivated by the desire to perform the "greatest amount of useful work and human duty."[63] In the world of the success manual, as in the world of the Puri-tan forefathers, fame and fortune were welcome but nonessential signs of a higher state of grace. In the modern instance, that state of grace took the form of the achievement of a magnificent manhood.

In a literature devoted to "getting on in life," this may seem like an odd conclusion and a strange definition of success. But from the perspective of the authors—and perhaps the readers—there was beauty in a book that at first glance seemed focused on advice about how to get rich but which ulti-mately insisted that true success was not necessarily wealth, but something higher, a type of manhood that could be won by those who may have failed utterly in business. The beauty was that these books offered a magnificent loophole in the otherwise unworkable theory that all could achieve success and live what later would be called "the American dream." The promise of this nonpecuniary version of success, after all, was much easier to deliver than the rags-to-riches scenario.

This broadly inclusive definition of success may have been very practi-cal for success writers who were looking to achieve success of their own—presumably of the pecuniary sort—through the sale of success manuals. In this regard, it might be useful to note that success manuals had something in common with another product that was marketed in the same period by these same methods—namely patent medicine.[64] Both were peddled door-to-door by traveling agents, in small towns and rural areas across the nation. The families that these salesmen canvassed were not likely to have had the spare cash to spend on either many books or many different medicines. The best patent medicine, therefore, promised to cure everything from syphilis to rheumatism and, likewise, the best success manual promised success to all customers—all male customers, that is—who were willing to follow the prescription carefully. In an anxious age, success manuals offered to the spirit what patent medicine offered to the body—an antidote for a multitude of ills.

Finally, by defining success and manliness in terms of personal virtues—especially duty to one's calling, willpower, self-control, and self-discipline—success writers did more than reassure worried readers and obscure class fissures. They laid the ideological foundation for a new model of manhood that paradoxically lacked both the fierce individualism of the entrepreneurial model of manhood and the militance and solidarity of labor's notion of manhood. This new economic man would work hard and contribute to the new industrial order while not demanding too much from it. He would identify his interests with the dominant social and economic order and voluntarily conduct himself in ways that were consistent with its triumph in the hopes of sharing some of its bounty. He could identify with the successes of the entrepreneur kings without having his manhood depend on achieving the same for himself. Here were the antecedents of the twentieth-century corporate "organization man." The heirs of this generation and of this way of seeing the world would become members of what C. Wright Mills called the "new middle class" of economically dependent, politically passive, white-collar workers.[65]

If, under the harsh light of the twentieth century, this model of manhood appears as a self-effacing capitulation to the powers that be, it must be remembered that success writers presented it to late-nineteenth-century readers as something very different. Success manuals flourished in a period of great economic and social upheaval and crisis. In trying times, success writers offered readers a view of the world—a way of thinking about and understanding the new social order and their place in it—that was more palatable and more hopeful than the apocalyptic predictions of Gilded Age radicals, dissenters, and critics. By making an exalted but achievable form of manhood the measure of success in a frightening yet promising new era, success writers offered those who feared they were being left behind a way to overcome their anxieties and uncertainty and to identify with the optimism and achievement of those at the pinnacle of the new industrial order. In offering men a way to rationalize their new and sometimes unwelcome circumstances, success writers helped to legitimize the new industrial order. And for those who could not muster that kind of enthusiasm about what the new order might bring, at the very least the ideology of manhood and success provided a graceful and respectable way to accommodate themselves to things they lacked the power to change. The success manual was an invitation to the ideological mainstream; the success ideology was the ultimate big tent—it welcomed all believers in the legitimacy of the new industrial order. In this light, the success manual provides evidence not of consensus about the efficacy of the new industrial order but rather a glimpse at the subtle ideological process whereby the *appearance* of consensus—or hegemony—was created.[66]

SHE HATH DONE WHAT SHE COULD

The world within the pages of success manuals was organized around polar opposites: success versus failure, virtue versus vice, and victory versus defeat in the proverbial battle of life. It was perhaps only natural that "manhood" also would be framed in terms of some notion of its opposite. These binary oppositions were valuative; the polarities not only represented "difference," they stood for positive and negative values.[67] Thus the idea of manhood was given force, poignancy, and positive meaning in part by counterpointing it with a pejorative notion of the feminine. Put another way, the equation that linked manhood with success was built upon a corollary equation that linked the feminine with failure, sometimes explicitly, but often implicitly, subtly, and probably unwittingly. For example, witness the change of gender at the end of the following quote. It comes from a success manual by William Owen entitled, *Success in Life, and How to Secure It: or Elements of Manhood and Their Culture*:

> Whatever you do, do it well. You need not be shy of your ambition: the world respects the man who is trying to make something out of himself. Let your aspirations out, give your inspiration full play. Be strictly honest; be above a mean act; be conscientious. Be pleasant with your superiors; be polite to your inferiors; be a gentleman. Read the newspaper; read good books; read the Bible. Advertise your business; deal with dispatch; pay your debts; don't idle; don't smoke; don't chew; don't swear; don't drink. Cultivate self-assertion: blow your own trumpet, to a moderate degree. Be as the Lord commanded Joshua, "very courageous." Pattern your morals after the world's model, the Nazarene. Concentrate your energies upon one aim. Never permit "give up" a place in your vocabulary. Work hard; be patient; hope for the best; and if you fail to reach the goal of your aspirations, you will possess the proud consciousness of having done your best, which after all, is the noblest "success in life." The highest praise bestowed by the Great Master was, "She hath done what she could."[68]

This concluding phrase, "she hath done what she could," comes from the book of Mark in the Bible. Jesus was in Bethany in the house of Simon the leper for the Passover feast when a woman entered with an alabaster box of the precious ointment spikenard, with which she anointed Jesus's head. When others present "murmured against her" for wasting this costly ointment that might instead have been sold to feed the poor, Jesus rebuked them and instead commended the woman, saying: "She hath done what she could."[69] In the most literal sense, the entire quote and the scriptural passage that concludes it make the point that is frequently made in success manuals: success is defined as doing one's best—whether or not the effort produces tangible results in terms of position, wealth, or fame. But on another level it gives an entirely different message. The quote begins with the assumption of masculine gender ("the world respects the man who is trying to make something of himself"). But at the moment that the possibility of failure is introduced ("if you fail to reach the goal of your aspirations") the gender switches from masculine to feminine (from the man trying to make something of himself to the woman of Bethany). In this shift of gender, failure to achieve in the real world was linked with the feminine. Despite the claim that "doing your best is the noblest success of all," the man who failed to achieve his aspiration was likened to a woman whose actions other men thought foolish, but whom Jesus defended because she had "done what she could." The shift to the feminine gender also expresses the success manual's ambivalence about the definition of success. It shows the tension between the idea that concrete achievement (such as the attainment of position, wealth, or fame) was the measure of success (and of the man) versus the more humble contention that it was the quality of the effort that really counted. Note, for example, that the commendation for "doing what she could" occurs as a feeble and "feminized" consolation for the man who, after trying everything, has "failed to reach the goal of [his] aspiration."

In the success manual, certain abstracted notions of "the feminine" were assumed to have a pejorative connotation for readers; "the feminine" was a "natural" and easily understood way to express the negative, the opposite of all that was to be admired in the true man. This tendency is most apparent in the use of terms like "effeminate" or "woman-like" as a kind of shorthand to label the failures in life and the attributes that lead to failure. In *Getting On in the World*, William Mathews wrote admiringly of a Scottish chieftain camping with his clan on a snowy night who kicked a pillow of snow from beneath his sleeping son's head because, as he explained, "the young rascal, by his degenerate effeminacy, would bring disgrace upon the clan."[70] Jermone Paine Bates claimed, in *The Imperial Highway*, that aid or advice of any kind could be "ruinous to character," making a man "weak, irresolute and effeminate."[71] Men who lacked decisiveness, it was said, "come and go like shadows, speak like women, sandwich their sentences with apologies, are overtaken by events while still irresolute, and let the tide ebb before they feebly push off."[72]

In another story, dependence on a woman marked the ultimate humiliation for a man who failed in business. Twin brothers worked in the same store, one "with a willing step and a smile, solicited customers and cared for his employer's interest. The other did what he was told to do but no more, quarreled about his wages, and whined." The first brother's success was distinguished by a promotion to partner in the wholesale house, while the other ended as a clerk in his wife's millinery shop.[73] Not only does this man fail to move from a lowly clerkship, he is reduced to working in the most feminine of businesses, a lady's hat shop. And to top it off, the shop is owned by his wife. Here was a parable calculated to make any true man shudder. It also illustrates a point developed more fully elsewhere, namely, that in the worldview articulated in the success manual the truly successful man was loyal to his employer's interests; the failures were the ones who bucked the system or were indifferent to its imperatives.[74] In this case of the two brothers, the failure is the one who quarreled about his wages and "whined" (whining, is of course, another pejorative, "feminine" term). Manhood and success were defined in terms of the man who complied with the demands of the establishment. The man who would not or could not comply was not only a failure, he was labeled effeminate and womanlike.

The phenomenon of using the masculine as a code for the positive and the feminine as a code for the negative is by no means unique to the success manual. In *Gender and the Politics of History*, Joan Scott argues that gender-related binary oppositions in language often function in powerful ways to make valuations and assign meanings.[75] Similarly, in the success manual, the use of an abstracted concept of "the feminine" was not about women or womanhood per se. It was rather about employing a diminished concept of the feminine to counterpoint and establish a strong, coherent, and very specific definition of manhood. This special definition of manliness was used not to distinguish men from women, but to distinguish one type of man from another—to define as "successful" the man who would work hard and identify his interests with the new industrial order. In this sense, "manhood" functions primarily as political ideology and only secondarily as gender ideology. The terms "manhood" and "manly" described the "successful" man, while the terms "feminine" and "effeminate" labeled and stigmatized the men who failed—or more specifically, the men who failed to conform to success writers' notions of manliness and success. In the world of the success manual, "the feminine" (in the form of the threat of being called a "sissy") played a special role; it became a coercive means to shame men into behaving in certain prescribed ways.[76]

The tendency of success manuals to associate failure with the feminine also made it possible to displace onto the feminine male anxiety about achieving success. This was nowhere more apparent than in the characterization of all kinds of obstacles to success as threatening allegorical female figures. Again, an abstracted concept of the feminine became a shorthand for the negative, for failure and the fear of failure. When William James Tilley discussed depression, worry, and "lack of enthusiasm," in *Masters of the Situation*, he "genderized" these obstacles to success, warning: "Care smothers the rising aspirations. The hollow-eyed goddess, haggard and wrinkled and wan, clutches the arm and shrivels the sinews of endeavor. One is amazed as he realizes how dull, and stupid, and aimless it is possible to be."[77] Bates employed the same tactic to illustrate the powerful hold "bad habits" could have on a man:

> Montaigne, in one of his essays, says of custom or habit "She is a violent and treacherous schoolmistress. She, by little and little, slyly and unperceived, slips in the foot of her authority, but having by this gentle and humble beginning with the aid of time, fixed and established it, she then unmasks a furious and tyrannic countenance, against which we have no more courage nor power so much as to lift up our eyes."[78]

The illusiveness of success is presented in the feminine. To Bates, hope is an "enchantress who ever smiles and waves her golden hair."[79] Likewise, when Mathews discussed the uncertainties of success, hope became a "deceitful enchantress" and success a "coy maiden . . . made saucy [by] the crowds of wooers, . . . now harder than ever to win."[80] In these examples, the assumed fickleness of women symbolically represents the precariousness of the struggle for success. Furthermore, the female is presented as both temptress and scapegoat: she plays Eve to a nineteenth-century Adam— she is alluring but dangerous and ultimately the cause of man's woes, worries, and failures.

The images of these threatening and withholding allegorical female figures, however, are worlds away from the official depictions of real women and womanhood in the success manual. When success writers wrote literally as opposed to figuratively about women, their views were squarely within the bourgeois Victorian mainstream that Barbara Welter has so aptly characterized as the "the cult of true womanhood": domesticity, piety, purity, and submissiveness.[81] In success manuals, women typically made up the supporting cast; they appear primarily as loyal, virtuous, and loving mothers, sisters, and wives. Especially the larger success manuals (prepared for the subscription trade) typically devoted a few chapters specifically to women and girls. These chapters had titles such as "Woman's Sphere and Mission" or the "Education of Girls." [82] In the *Royal Path of Life*, a chapter entitled simply "Man and Woman" outlined prescriptions for ideal womanhood and ideal manhood:

> Man is bold—woman is beautiful. Man is courageous—woman is timid. Man labors in the field—woman at home. Man talks to persuade—woman to please. Man has a daring heart—woman a tender, loving one. Man has power—woman taste. Man has justice—woman mercy. Man has strength—woman love; while man combats with the enemy, struggles with the world, woman is waiting to prepare his repast and sweeten his existence. He has crosses, and the partner of his couch is there to soften them; his day may be sad and troubled, but in the chaste arms of his wife he finds comfort and repose. Without woman, man would be rude, gross, solitary. Woman spreads around him the flowers of existence, as the creepers of the forest, which decorate the trunks of sturdy oaks with their perfumed garlands. [83]

In the same volume, a chapter entitled "Mother" focused on "the sacredness and power of a mother's tender love"; a chapter entitled "To Young Women" stressed the importance of cultivating inward as opposed to outward beauty and urged young women to "hold a steady moral sway over their male associates, so strong as to prevent them from becoming such lawless rowdies"; and in a chapter entitled "Daughters and Sisters" the daughter's duty to make her mother happy was second only to her duty to God, while the sister's most important charge was to "mollify, tame and refine" her brothers. [84] Women's role was defined primarily in terms of duties toward men—to comfort them, care for them, and morally guide and influence them.

Success writers did occasionally mention "successful" women who had careers outside the home, such as actress Charlotte Cushman, educator Mary Lyon, astronomer Marie Mitchell, nurse Florence Nightingale, and writer Harriet Beecher Stowe. [85] And they made sporadic references to the "successes" of courageous but unknown girls who accomplished heroic acts—the rescuer of a shipwrecked sailor or the exemplary girls who saved themselves from starvation by working day and night as dressmakers. [86] But those who broadened the definition of success enough to admit the triumphs of women quickly backtracked by assuring readers that "women's success" was of a separate sphere. Tilley, more progressive than most on the subject, wrote of the "wonderful revolution" that had taken place in the status of women and applauded the "self-supporting girls" of his era. [87] But the title of his chapter, "Self-Dependent Women," revealed that he was loath even to use the same language to describe women's and men's achievement. While the true man was above all else "self-reliant," a self-reliant woman, could be described—at best—as "self-dependent."

Success writers thus agreed that the right vocation for a woman and her true position and work in life was as wife and mother. Only in cases of dire need was it approved for women to seek gainful employment, and then with strictures against careers in the professions or business—the very areas that were recommended for aspiring males. Bates wrote that "women cannot hope to succeed in business life as well as a man," claiming they were "adapted to but few kinds of business." For women driven into the workforce by financial necessity, he suggested factory work, house cleaning, nursing, or teaching.[88] In a chapter entitled "A Talk to Girls," Dale offered advice on everything from "cheerful housekeeping" to the importance of cultivating a "pleasant, mild voice," but he also addressed the question of female employment. Like Tilley, he advised girls to prepare themselves to be "self-supporting" in case the need arose, but he warned them not to attempt to do "noble work" (the professions), "where there were too many dangers," or to attempt to achieve the "tempting fruits of honor and renown." In a chapter entitled "Woman's Sphere and Mission," he welcomed what he called "the radical change in women's work in the past fifty years that allowed women to be more than either 'drudge' or 'lady,'" observing that "formerly, cultivated intellect in woman was stigmatized as audacious and manlike." Yet he cautioned women not to go to the other extreme and ignore sex and womanly instinct or to regard men and women as on the "same plane," warning that "those women who long for public careers reap a bitter harvest."[89]

Such prescriptions about "woman's sphere" are, of course, nothing new. They are now a familiar part of the history of nineteenth-century women, researched especially in the last thirty years.[90] The task here is to probe the meaning of the appearance of the cult of true womanhood in success manuals. It is possible that the inclusion of chapters devoted to woman's place have no special significance beyond serving to pad these works enough to make them suitable for the subscription trade, widening the potential audience by broadening their appeal as a "family book." But given the importance of "the feminine" as an abstract, pejorative counterpoint to the ideal of manhood, it seems plausible that idealized womanhood might also have some special relevance. The persistence of the cult of true womanhood in the success manual at a point when it was under siege more generally may seem incongruous. But it is consistent with the larger worldview of the success manual. Success writers presented a very selective picture of reality, much of it ensconced in the values and the lifestyles of an earlier era. Part of the success manuals' message of reassurance depended on the denial of aspects of the modern world that could not be easily accommodated by their ideology of manhood and self-help. The insistence that women had a special role (which just happened to keep them behind the scenes) may have been another expression of a need to deny certain unsettling social changes.

With this in mind, one success writer's explanation for why women could not become doctors provides a clue about the meaning that the cult of true womanhood had in success literature. In Russell Conwell's *The New Day, or Fresh Opportunities: A Book for Young Men*, he observed that though women had important roles as helpers, nursing and cheering the sick, they weren't usually successful as doctors or at getting patients because women were "naturally timid, and shuddered at blood." Moreover, he added, "her sympathy, love and fear would unsettle her judgement and make her hand unsteady." He further argued that women should not be exposed to the disease of the general public. But since exposure to the public's disease did not seem to worry Conwell in regard to women's role of nursing and comforting the sick, probably his final objection was more to the point. He believed that women should not cause pain, as in the setting of a broken leg, remarking, "the man feels that her true place is somehow to nurse, soothe, and assuage pain, never to cause any." [91]

It seems possible that the kind of pain Conwell feared women doctors might cause men was more than physical. Success writer's admonitions against women in the professions may have expressed an underlying anxiety about the advent of the "New Woman" who pursued higher education, professional employment, and public careers, often eschewing the traditional domesticity of marriage, home, and family. [92] Were the men who wrote success manuals motivated by the fear that women would provide unwanted competition for men if they took up careers outside the home? This is part of the implications of Carroll Smith-Rosenberg's study "The New Woman as Androgyne," which documents male physicians' and social critics' "attacks upon [women's] right to enter the 'male' world and assume 'male' power." [93]

But the warnings against women taking up careers may have also reflected fears of yet another kind of pain—the fear that women would abandon the home and neglect their duties and their labor as the caretakers of husbands, sons, and brothers. In this respect, Mary Ryan's discoveries and observations in *Cradle of the Middle Class* are instructive. She makes the important point that the success of the so-called "self-made men" who made it into the middle class in mid-nineteenth-century Oneida County was, paradoxically, based on the intensification of effort by families that "cradled" and supported their sons through an extended adolescence. Specifically, the labor and the sacrifices of mothers and sisters (enhancing family income by taking in boarders, for example) made it possible for sons to acquire education and to remain home longer until they could secure a desirable position in the new middle class. In mid-nineteenth-century Oneida County, the "self-made man" referred to the young man who made his way without a traditional "start in life" in the form of land, capital, or a place in his father's trade or business. The transformation of work and of the economy—specifically, the move toward new categories of white-collar employment—meant that even sons from middle-class families (the old middle class) could not secure their class position (in the new middle class) by following in their father's footsteps. In this context, as Ryan points out, the emergence of an ethos of the self-made man amounted to "making a virtue out of necessity" and further constituted what she describes as the essential irony of nineteenth-century individualism: that "the vaunted autonomy and egotism of the nineteenth-century male was not a monument to self-reliance. Quite the contrary, it was conceived, cultivated, pampered, and protected within a revitalized American home." [94]

In *The Culture of Professionalism*, Burton Bledstein also writes of the sacrifices poor rural families made on behalf of their sons to provide them an education as a stepping stone into the middle class through professions such as the ministry.[95] Many success manual authors were ministers who were themselves the beneficiaries of just this type of family effort and were thus in a position to have a keen awareness of the important role played by the labor and sacrifices of women in creating opportunities for young men of their circumstances.[96] David Leverenz makes a point similar to that of Ryan in his examination of Ralph Waldo Emerson's preoccupation with manhood and self-reliance. Emerson—who was an important influence on the cohort of men who produced success manuals—wrote vividly (albeit painfully) of his father, while his mother appears as a nurturing but nearly anonymous presence. Her caretaking is important, but assumed. She is faceless; she has no personality beyond her function.[97]

If the anonymous, domestic labor of mothers, sisters, wives, and daughters was important to the success of the self-made man, as these examples suggest, and the cult of true womanhood defined femininity in terms of women's willingness to be the faceless, self-sacrificing nurturers of male ambition, then this ideal of womanhood had an important place in the success manual. Their celebration of women in the home and their abhorrence of women in the professions may have reflected both a desire that women continue to play the supporting role and a fear that they would abandon it.[98] Within the success manual, the cult of true womanhood fit perfectly both a *reality*, in which women's work in the home was crucial, *and* an *ideology*, in which men's dependence on women was to be denied. On one level, when success writers defined true womanhood in terms of domestic duty on behalf of men and warned women away from professional employment and public acclaim, they merely capitalized on the self-serving aspects of the dominant Victorian ideology for aspiring men. On another level, by promoting the cult of female domesticity, they revealed an unacknowledged belief in a blasphemous idea—the idea that the self-made man was dependent upon women. Men who would succeed in life were dependent on women's continued willingness to take a place in the supporting cast.

In this light, one element of success writers' rhetoric about self-reliance and the "self-made man" might be interpreted in terms of men's need to "deny" or compensate for their emotional and material dependence on women. The success manuals were addressed to boys and young men who came of age in a world increasingly bereft of much direct contact with fathers and the adult world of men's work. As factory and office replaced farm and workshop and men's work became physically removed from the home, child rearing came to be more exclusively the sphere of mothers, and home itself became a predominantly female realm.[99] While girls could become women by modeling themselves after their mothers, boys had to separate from mother and the world of women both physically and psychologically to become men. Success manuals—especially their emphasis on self-reliance and the stigma they attached to dependence on women—may have had special appeal and provided emotional guidance to boys and youths who had to deny the world of their mothers in order to join the world of their fathers.[100] This perspective may help explain the audacity of the success writer Wilbur Crafts, who seemed to suggest that men had volition even in their own births. He entitled chapter 1 of *Successful Men of Today* "Choosing a Birthplace."

In summary, "the feminine" helped to "make" the self-made man on two levels. First, an abstracted and pejorative notion of the feminine—the feminine linked with failure—was the necessary other half of the binary opposition that established the ideological equation of manhood and success. "The feminine," used figuratively and pejoratively in the language of success manuals, was part of the social construction of manhood and of the *idea* of the self-made man.

Second, on another level, as Ryan's study suggests, "the feminine" in the very literal form of women's labor helped create the *reality* of the self-made man or at least the potential for some degree of upward mobility; mothers and sisters worked and made sacrifices in order to provide opportunities for sons and brothers. When success manuals addressed real women (as opposed to an abstracted, pejorative concept of the feminine as a foil for manhood), they adopted the idealized, prescriptive language of the cult of true womanhood. Success writers exalted the angel at the hearth and applauded the selfless and anonymous nurture that women provided in the home, but they took pains to deny dependence of the true man on anyone but himself, and most especially to deny dependence on women. The cult of true womanhood might have at least partially disguised the contradictions of a world where true men saw "the feminine" and dependence on women as a code for failure while simultaneously depending on the love and labor of mothers, sisters, wives, and daughters for their own success.

When success writers wrote about women, whether figuratively or literally, they came to a consensus about neither the precise nature of women nor the exact way in which women differed from men. But they were in resounding agreement about one important point: they believed that there existed fundamental and far-reaching differences in attributes and abilities of the sexes; they all agreed that womanly accomplishments belonged on the periphery of a man's world. These beliefs placed success writers in the mainstream of nineteenth-century gender ideology. But in the context of the success manual, the maintenance of a sexually dimorphous view of human capabilities, and the notion that men and women were destined for separate and unequal spheres, had a special meaning. It was part of the rickety ideological framework upon which the success writers established an exalted notion of manhood as the key to success in the new industrial order.

"Manhood" and "womanhood," "the feminine" and "the manly," constitute neither the primary focus nor the main subject matter of the success manual. Yet concepts of the masculine and the feminine were critical to the meanings established in the success ideology. The success manuals employed gender—especially the manhood/success equation—to give power to ideas that have nothing intrinsically to do with gender. But genderized terms—even when used in nongender contexts—have implications for gender, for gender definitions, and for relations between men and women.[101] In the world of the success manual, men who did not conform to prescriptions for manhood and success were stigmatized as "effeminate," while any idea of female "success" outside the home became a casualty of a definition of success that equated success and manliness. Success in the world of business was a sign of manhood and manliness, a crown when won and worn by men but a sacrilege when worn or even aspired to by women. In such a world, it became hard to even imagine a "successful woman," and if a woman did "succeed" in the world outside the home, she stepped outside the circle of true womanhood; it became difficult to conceive of her as either "feminine" or "womanly."[102] Success writers employed gender to articulate a way of viewing the world that might ease men's anxieties about achieving success and finding a place for themselves in the new industrial order. In the process they reinforced an existing ideology of gender difference and inequality that narrowed the scope of socially sanctioned aspirations, behaviors, and values for both men and women.

8

Conclusion: Beyond Success

Much has been made of success writers' jubilant promise of success and progress, but the fear of poverty and the threat of failure played an equally important role in their message. These authors wrote with a keen awareness of the paradoxes of their age. They reflected aspects of the social reality around them, a reality not only of phenomenal economic growth and technological advancement but also of unprecedented waves of depression, rural dislocation, agrarian revolt, industrial unemployment, and labor strife. The popularity of success manuals coincided with an era in which a profound and far-reaching transformation was being effected in the everyday lives of ordinary men and women, particularly in regard to the way in which people were to make their livings. Industrialization and urbanization meant the decline of certain occupations and the emergence of others. As the place of work for many shifted from country to city, from farm and shop to factory and office, the nature and organization of work changed as well. Specialization and the division of labor meant, among other things, that the unity of mental and manual labor was undermined, and as self-employment increasingly gave way to wage and salaried work, valued ideals of independence and equal opportunity were threatened. Even those living in the small towns and lonely homesteads of the American hinterland were not immune to such change. The demand for labor in expanding areas of business, industry, trade, and transportation coupled with the relative decline of small-scale agriculture, particularly by the turn of the century, meant that more and more young men would break traditional patterns of father-to-son occupational continuity and leave home in search of work with which they and their fathers had no experience and very little familiarity.

Success writers addressed themselves to questions that most Americans faced with the transformation of the society around them, namely: what impact would these changes have on them? What was to be gained and what was to be lost? How would they and their children find their way in a new and uncertain era? These writers commiserated with readers about the difficulties of a competitive and hostile new era. They acknowledged the fact that all were not believers in the gospel of success; some had lost hope, while others rejected the rags-to-riches dream from the start. Success writers, by their own testimony, wrote with the intention of inspiring all to join the race, to assure every man that he had a chance in life, and to spread the news that there was room at the top for those who really tried.

They insisted not only that all could join the fray (all men, that is) but also that all were duty-bound to do so. They argued that it was of utmost importance to distinguish oneself through self-reliance and industry from both the lazy, spendthrift, and incendiary below, and the idle, dissipated and pretentious above. God wanted all to succeed, but he helped only those who helped themselves.

Success writers counseled adaptation to changing times, particularly in the matter of choosing an occupation. In order to find success, a young man had to be willing to seek a calling that suited him precisely, the advisors claimed, even if it meant pursing work different from that of his father. Yet they assured readers that a man need not go far to find his fortune, but needed only to cultivate the opportunities around him. The chances were as good if not better in the country as in the city, and the boy with no formal education could thrive and win just as well guided by the lessons he learned in the school of life. Every man had a calling, they argued, and his duty was to find it and fill it to the best of his ability. Though all would not be called to high places, success might be won in even the humblest of callings.

Success writers claimed that poverty was no barrier to success; on the contrary, boys born in poverty had the best chance for success. Why? Because character was capital. It was character forged in the battle of life, developed in the school of adversity, that won success, not genius, special talents, or inherited wealth or position. Far from being outmoded, it was precisely old-fashioned virtue that constituted the means of success in the new era.

In the final analysis, success writers defined true success as an exalted form of manhood, a self-made combination of character, virility, willpower, and self-discipline. Manhood, they claimed, was above wealth, fame, and title—mere millions dwindled in significance when seen in the light of this higher, more accessible form of success.

The popularity of success manuals reveals a sense of anxiety and uncertainty about the new social order. Their high sales reflected a search for reassurance and a need for guidance on the part of those who bought them. These books were, after all, primarily advice manuals. They clearly acknowledged the "vicissitudes of life" and offered a formula by which to overcome them. They responded to both the hopes and the fears generated by change, and they offered an explanation of many of the troubling conflicts and tensions that plagued the era. It is difficult to imagine that hundreds of thousands of Americans would be willing to pay handsomely for this advice and guidance if they had faced the prospects of getting on in life with confidence and certainty.

Success manual popularity, then, may have reflected a search for answers on the part of those who bought them, but what of the answers success writers offered? How did they pose and answer questions and what was the nature of their explanation of the difficulties of the period?

Nothing was more pervasive in success writers' portrayal of society than a bipolar view of the world, through which all could be understood in terms of conflict between opposing and antagonistic elements. The primary antagonism, as these advisors saw it, was of course that between success and failure — conflict expressed metaphorically in terms of a battle, a struggle, a climb, or a race in which there were winners and losers, pushers and pushed, top and bottom. But in the process of showing readers the way to succeed, success writers identified many more tensions in the social life of their times. They wrote of conflicts between old and new, country and city, independent self-employment and wage or salaried labor, manual and mental work, rich and poor, capital and labor, virtue and vice, and male and female. In this world of antagonism, all conflicts were not equal. Certain tensions — such as those between success and failure, virtue and vice, male and female — were presented as central in understanding how society operated, while other social tensions — such as those between rich and poor, and capital and labor — were acknowledged as misconceptions that required correction. The conflicts that success writers took pains to reinterpret and dismiss were those that revealed the most troubling features of industrial capitalism and pointed to some of the most irresolvable contradictions of the age, namely, (1) growing economic inequalities, particularly as expressed in the strife between capital and labor; (2) the decline of opportunity for self-employment and independence due to the rise of wage and salaried labor organized in factories and offices; and (3) the threat that a newer, more blatantly acquisitive ethic posed to time-honored values and old-fashioned virtues. It was no accident that these were the conflicts that success writers were most eager to minimize or eliminate from their view of the world, for they pointed to the problems that were the most difficult to reduce to the common denominator of individual success or failure. Success writers reinterpreted these three conflicts in the following ways.

First, success writers dealt with the problem of economic inequality by accepting the notion that there were two classes in the world but insisting that these two classes had no relationship to the current strife between capital and labor. They neatly substituted a class schema in which the distinguishing qualities of the successful were manhood and character rather than the ownership of property. Success writers claimed to be the champion of the common man, but they were no champions of democratic equalitarianism. They believed that the race of life was open to all runners, but they did not claim that a man had to progress up a ladder of *actual* economic and social status in order to achieve success.

What better way to minimize economic inequalities than to advocate respect for all labor and insist that success could be won in even the humblest rank by the manly performance of duty? What need of rank and position when a man might ennoble and dignify his place in life, however lowly, through his own efforts?

Secondly, success writers extolled the value of independence and often claimed that the goal of every working man should be not only self-employment but the employment of others as well. But they could take this position only insofar as they deflected attention away from the decline of real opportunity to become a self-made man in the traditional sense. They simply avoided the realities of the country's changing occupational structure by focusing on occupations of the preindustrial era. They mentioned only in derision the wage and salaried work that was the lot of more and more Americans.

Thirdly, success writers dealt with the onslaught of the modern ethic of fast living and a fast buck by defending the most cherished values of the past. Honesty, frugality, industry, self-reliance, and the simple, wholesome, pious virtues, they argued, were the very qualities essential in achieving success in the new order. Character, like capital, was something a man could trade on.

Though success writers can be seen as apologists of the new order, paradoxically the advice they offered amounted to a simultaneous defense of both the old and the new. They consistently assured readers of the value of older ways of thinking and living while at the same time heralding the opportunities and advantages of the new industrial age and urging all to join the race. It was again this bifurcated view of the world poised between virtue and vice that made it possible to bridge the gap between old and new, for the power of individual virtue was timeless and universal and could therefore solve the problems of one age as well as another. By placing character at the center of their worldview, success writers offered the old as a solution to the new—old-time virtue could solve the problems of industrial capitalism. Further, by making the combination of character and manhood not only the means to success but success itself, success came within the reach of the many rather than the few.

Insofar as success writers redefined many of the great conflicts of their day, dismissing some of the most indicting features of the new order and minimizing crucial differences between an older era and their own, the success manuals they wrote can be understood as a literature that offered advice about coping with change in part by denying its existence. Only by overlooking such change would it be possible to show "the way to win" while ushering Americans smoothly and uncritically into a new industrial order. Yet the very existence of such a surplus of advice proclaiming this message was itself a testimony to the fact the transition was neither smooth nor without criticism.

NOTES

Introduction

1   Dale, *The Way to Win, Showing How to Succeed in Life*; Marden, *Pushing to the Front, or Success under Difficulties*; Haines and Yaggy, *The Royal Path of Life, or Aims and Aids to Success and Happiness*; Thayer, *Onward to Fame and Fortune, or Climbing Life's Ladder*.

2   Louis B. Wright suggests this extensive market for the success manual in "Franklin's Legacy to the Gilded Age." I have located 144 book-length, didactic works published between 1870 and 1910 that belong within the success manual genre. See chapter 1 for more on circulation.

3   Examples of studies that look at the idea of success over time in multiple sources include Banta, *Failure and Success in America*; Cawelti, *Apostles of the Self-Made Man*; Huber, *American Idea of Success*; Rex Burns, *Success in America*; Weiss, *American Myth of Success*; Wyllie, *Self-Made Man in America*.

4   For example, Thernstrom, *The Other Bostonians*; and Blumin, *Emergence of the Middle Class*.

5   I am indebted to the late Warren Susman for encouraging me to study all aspects of success manuals and to view them as "artifacts" which taken together constitute a "cultural form" capable of revealing something about the culture that produced and used it. See also chapter 1.

6   See for example, Hartz, *Liberal Tradition in America*.

7   See notes 23 and 24 below and note 8 in chapter 4.

8   Welter, "Cult of True Womanhood."

9   Hilkey, "Masculinity and the Self-Made Man in America."

10 See, for example, Carnes, *Secret Ritual and Manhood in Victorian America*; Carnes and Griffen, *Meanings for Manhood*; Leverenz, *Manhood and the American Renaissance*; Stearns, *Be a Man!*

11 See, for example, Filene, *Him-Her Self*; Scott, *Gender and the Politics of History*; and Smith-Rosenberg, *Disorderly Conduct*.

12 Mather, *A Christian at His Calling*, 24.

13 See Rex Burns, *Success in America*, and Horatio Alger, *Struggling Upward, or Luke Larkin's Luck*, both in Rischin, *American Gospel of Success*, 67–89.

14 On the shift from character to personality, see Susman, *Culture as History*, chap. 14.

15 The work of Norbert Elias is suggestive here. He shows how a wide range of subtle forces gradually transform society and personality and rationalize the hegemony of the state. See Elias, *Power and Civility*, esp. part 2. See also C. Wright Mills, *White Collar: The American Middle Class.*

16 For useful discussions of hegemony and legitimation, see Gramsci, *Prison Notebooks*; Lears, "The Concept of Cultural Hegemony"; and Elias, *The Civilizing Process*. In Lears, see esp. his discussion of the concepts of "consent" and "legitimation":

> Consent, for Gramsci, involves a complex mental state, a "contradictory consciousness" mixing approbation and apathy, resistance and resignation. The mix varies from individual to individual; some are more socialized than others. In any case, ruling groups never engineer consent with complete success; the outlook of subordinate groups is always divided and ambiguous. (570)

> Whether one imagines hegemony to be relatively open or relatively closed, the essence of the concept is not manipulation but legitimation. The ideas, values, and experiences of dominant groups are validated in public discourse; those of subordinate groups are not, though they may continue to thrive beyond the boundaries of received opinion. . . . the line between dominant and subordinate cultures is a permeable membrane, not an impenetrable barrier. (577)

The success manual as well as the moral philosophy textbooks and the keystone college seminars in which they were used may be seen as a way of validating the ideas and values of the dominant group. See D. H. Meyer's insightful study, *The Instructed Conscience: The Shaping of the American National Ethic.*

17 Haskell, *Emergence of Professional Social Science*, 244. See also Lears, "The Concept of Cultural Hegemony," esp. 588.

18 Scott, "Deconstructing Equality-Versus-Difference," 36; and Scott, *Gender and the Politics of History*, 45–46.

19 Elias, *Power and Civility*, 254, 268.

20 See Leverenz's discussion of how an "intensified ideology of manhood is a compensatory response to fears of humiliation" in *Manhood and the American Renaissance*, 4.

21 See also Mosse, *Nationalism and Sexuality*; and Smith-Rosenberg, *Disorderly Conduct.*

22 Scott, *Gender and the Politics of History*, 48–49.

23 Trachtenberg, *Incorporation of America*, 3–4. I believe that Trachtenberg provides the best synthesis of this period since Robert Weibe's important and influential work, *The Search for Order, 1877–1920*. Trachtenberg gives a fuller sense of the real conflict that underlay the anxiety of the age, anticipating more recent criticism of Weibe for failing to explain how a new set of ideas "take the fort" and making the triumph of new ideas seem to have happened without a fight. Comments by Richard L. McCormick and Paula Baker, members of panel titled "Reconsideration: Robert H. Weibe's *The Search for Order*," Organization of American Historians Eighty-second Annual Meeting, St. Louis, Mo., April 8, 1989.

24 In addition to those by Trachtenberg and Weibe, a great many studies establish and analyze different aspects of the crisis and conflict of Gilded Age America. Works that I have found especially helpful include: Gutman, *Work, Culture and Society in Industrializing America*; Montgomery, *Workers' Control in America*; Fink, *Workingmen's Democracy*, esp. chaps. 1 and 8; Laurie, *Artisans into Workers*; Goodwyn, *The Populist Moment*; Salvatore, *Eugene V. Debs, Citizen and Socialist*; Ross, "Socialism and American Liberalism"; Lears, *No Place of Grace*, esp. chap. 1; Hall, *Organization of American Culture*, esp. chaps. 8–12; Haskell, *Emergence of Professional Social Science*; Bannister, *Social Darwin-*

ism, Science, and Myth, esp. chap. 7; Carter, *Spiritual Crisis of the Gilded Age*; Fellman and Fellman, *Making Sense of Self*; D'Emilio and Freedman, *Intimate Matters*, esp. parts 2 and 3. For contemporary accounts that capture this sense of crisis, see especially Beard, *American Nervousness*; and Strong, *Our Country, Its Possible Future and Its Present Crisis*.

25 Trachtenberg, *Incorporation of America*, 39.

26 C. Wright Mills, *White Collar: The American Middle Class*. I understand the idea of a "middle-class" as much in terms of worldview and "self-definition" as in terms of a category of socioeconomic standing. For a fuller discussion, see chapter 5. See also Bledstein, *Culture of Professionalism*; Ryan, *Cradle of the Middle Class*; Blumin, "The Hypothesis of Middle-Class Formation"; Blumin, *Emergence of the Middle Class*.

27 This is not intended to suggest that movements critical of the new order necessarily eschewed an ideology of upward mobility or the comforts of a middle-class home; there is plenty of evidence to the contrary. However, their ideas about both the means and the ends of these goals are defined in less individualistic terms compared to those of the dominant culture. See Fink, *Workingmen's Democracy*, 12; Levine, *Labor's True Woman*; Buhle, *Women and American Socialism*; Salvatore, *Eugene V. Debs*. What it does suggest is the source of some of the contradictory elements of the producer ideology that "pointed toward accommodation as well as resistance." Lears, "Concept of Cultural Hegemony," 575.

28 Published as articles in the *Home Missionary* beginning in the 1840s, *Our Country* was said to have had an impact comparable in intensity to that of *Uncle Tom's Cabin*. One hundred seventy thousand copies were sold before 1916. See editor's notes by Jurgen Herbst in Strong, *Our Country*.

Chapter One

1 For an evocative discussion of the elements of a genre or literary formula in popular works, see Cawelti, *Adventure, Mystery, and Romance: Formula Stories as Art and Popular Culture*.

2 Irwin G. Wyllie especially draws on such sources, in *The Self-Made Man in America*.

3 See, for example, Hunt, *Worth and Wealth*; and Freedley, *A Practical Treatise on Business*.

4 My study begins in 1870 because this is the decade in which the success manual becomes recognizable as a genre. It ends in 1910 because this decade marks the beginning of a gradual decline of this genre and its displacement by the emergence of a new type of success literature. The shift is primarily one from an emphasis on character to a focus on personality, applied psychology, and mind control; it reflects the turn-of-the-century shift from a producer-oriented society to a consumer- and sales-oriented, corporate society. The power *within* (virtue, character, and manhood) was no longer enough to win success; it needed bolstering with the power of personality, the power to sell one's self. Applied psychology was the art of projecting one's personality *outwardly* to others. Warren Susman makes this distinction in " 'Personality' and the Making of Twentieth-Century Culture," chap. 14 in *Culture as History*. Some of the most popular success writers of the older genre, such as Orison Swett Marden, actually made the transition to a new kind of advice, as is evident in the title of the book he published in 1921, *Masterful Personality*. One of the most widely circulated books of the early twentieth century, Frank Channing Haddock's *Power of Will: A Practical Companion Book for Unfoldment of Powers of Mind* (1907) represents the shift in success literature. In *Power of Will*, Haddock articulated a new pseudo-science of personal mind control as the key to success. In it,

the emphasis on *self-control* apparent in the late-nineteenth-century success manual is intensified and refined as *mind control*. These early-twentieth-century advice books prefigure the later, enormously popular works of Dale Carnegie (*How to Win Friends and Influence People*, 1936) and Norman Vincent Peale (*The Power of Positive Thinking*, 1952).

5 Warren I. Susman, personal conversation on "cultural forms," 1975.

6 As quoted in the back pages of Haines and Yaggy, *Royal Path of Life*.

7 Sheehan, *This Was Publishing*, chaps. 1 and 2.

8 U.S. Bureau of the Census, *Historical Statistics*, Series A195–209, 14.

9 Lehmann-Haupt, *The Book in America*, 250.

10 Sheehan, *This Was Publishing*, 189.

11 Lehmann-Haupt, *The Book in America*, 242–49.

12 Sheehan, *This Was Publishing*, 197. By the end of the century, mail order was known to be an important part of the book publishing business, but just how important it was statistically is impossible to know.

13 Several historians of the book trade document that subscription was the major sales method of the Gilded Age. See Compton, "Subscription Books," 889; Hill, *Mark Twain and Elisha Bliss*, chap. 1 (hereafter cited as Hill, *Twain and Bliss*); Lehmann-Haupt, *The Book in America*, 250; Sheehan, *This Was Publishing*, 190; Waldman, "Subscription Sets," 238.

14 For descriptions of the sales method, see Lehmann-Haupt, *The Book in America*, 252; Sheehan, *This Was Publishing*, 190, 194; and Barcus, *Philosophy of Canvassing*.

15 Compton, "Subscription Books," 889. A number of technological developments that began prior to the Civil War helped expand the market for books: the industrialization of the printing industry, improved lighting, affordable eyeglasses, and the ever expanding network of railroads, which made it possible for books (and book agents) to reach the hinterlands. See Zboray, "Antebellum Reading and the Ironies of Technological Innovation."

16 Compton, "Subscription Books," 889; Hill, *Twain and Bliss*, chap. 1.

17 Hill, *Twain and Bliss*, 5.

18 The publishing industry's awareness of the significance of this new development is reflected in the many complaints that the "regular" trade voiced about competition from the "subscription" trade in the book trade magazine, *Publishers' Weekly*. See, for example, July 2, 1881, 7; January 18, 1879, 48; March 8, 1879, 279.

19 Hill, *Twain and Bliss*, 4–5.

20 Sheehan, *This Was Publishing*, 190.

21 Hill, *Twain and Bliss*, 7; *Publishers' Weekly*, July 2, 1881, 7.

22 Sheehan, *This Was Publishing*, 190–92.

23 Ibid., 192–94; Hill, *Twain and Bliss*, 10.

24 Lehmann-Haupt, *The Book in America*, 251; Hill, *Twain and Bliss*, 10–13; Compton, "Subscription Books," 890.

25 Sheehan, *This Was Publishing*, 194; *Publishers' Weekly*, July 2, 1881, 7.

26 Sheehan, *This Was Publishing*, 192–94.

27 Compton, "Subscription Books," 889.

28 Sheehan, *This Was Publishing*, 169–71.

29 Compton, "Subscription Books," 890.

30 International Publishing Co., *General Agent's Guide to Success*; N. D. Thompson Publishing Co., *Success in Canvassing*.

31 See, for example, Browning, *O. A. Browning's Confidential Instructions, Rules and Helps for His Agents.*
32 Barcus, *Philosophy of Canvassing*, 90–91.
33 Hill, *Twain and Bliss*, 16.
34 "Book Sellers as Local Agents," *Publishers' Weekly*, vol. 15, no. 10 (Mar. 8, 1879), 279.
35 Twain, "Ledger of the American Publishing Co."
36 Sheehan, *This Was Publishing*, 192.
37 Tilley, *Masters of the Situation*, preface.
38 These numbers are based on the collective holdings of success manuals in the Library of Congress, New York Public Library, Columbia University Library, and the New-York Historical Society. This number does not necessarily represent the entire genre. Some books were not copyrighted and, as has been suggested above, success manuals were the last kind of books that libraries were encouraged to collect and preserve. But these collections do provide important evidence of both the size and growth pattern of the genre. The 144 works referred to here exclude the many pamphlets devoted to the success theme. The number includes only book-length works fitting the general description established above for the success manual.
39 On the extensiveness of this market, see Wright, "Franklin's Legacy to the Gilded Age."
40 Connolly, *Life Story of Marden*, 197–204.
41 Mott, *Golden Multitudes*, 103.
42 Ibid., 259, 303, 313, 320–23.
43 Wyllie, *Self-Made Man in America*, 127; Mathews, *Getting On in the World*, title page.
44 American Library Association, *National Union Catalog* (hereafter ALA, *National Union Catalog*); Mathews, *Getting On in the World*, title page; *U.S. Catalog of Books.*
45 Schaff and Jackson, *Encyclopedia of Living Divines and Christian Workers*, 43.
46 ALA *National Union Catalog*; *U.S. Catalog of Books.*
47 "Population in Urban and Rural Territory, by Size of Place: 1790–1950," in U.S. Bureau of the Census, *Historical Statistics*, Series A195–209, 14.
48 Lehmann-Haupt, *The Book in America*, 252.
49 Compton, "Subscription Books," 889.
50 Success Company's Branch Office, *Working Plans and How to Work Them*, 15.
51 Though references to success manuals in this study generally list only one (the first) city as the place of publication, it was very common for the title page of these works to list more than one city and sometimes several cities. For example, many would say New York and St. Louis, or include several more cities. The preponderance of New York as the place of publication in works cited here reflects (1) the fact that the research was conducted primarily in New York libraries, which would be more likely to have in their collections New York editions of books that may have been published simultaneously elsewhere, and (2) the tendency of some publishers to have New York offices along with Midwestern distribution points or agencies.
52 Conwell, *The New Day*, 38.
53 Mathews, *Getting On in the World*, 305.
54 Tilley, *Masters of the Situation*, 438.
55 Bok, *Keys to Success*, 108.
56 Dale, *Way to Win*, 558.
57 John Farwell, introduction to Dale, *Secret of Success*, vii.
58 N. D. Thompson Publishing Co., *Facts for Those Contemplating Book Agency*, 14.

59   Barcus, *Philosophy of Canvassing*, 90–91.

60   Pricing information was sometimes included in the manuals along with advertisements.

61   "Average Annual Earnings in All Industries and in Selected Industries and Occupations: 1890–1926," in U.S. Bureau of the Census, *Historical Statistics*, Series D603–617, 91–92. The same money bought a man's Sunday suit, a platform rocker, or an oak dining table from the 1897 *Sears, Roebuck and Company Consumers' Guide*.

62   Sheehan, *This Was Publishing*, 87.

63   Shove, "Cheap Book Production in the United States, 1870–1891," x, vii.

64   Sears, Roebuck, *Consumers' Guide*, 1897.

65   These were the kinds of comments found in the testimonials and endorsements in some editions of success manuals. See, for example, Haines and Yaggy, *Royal Path of Life*; or Marden, *Rising in the World*.

66   Barcus, *Philosophy of Canvassing*, 108–9.

67   Mott, *Golden Multitudes*, 103.

68   The average weekly earnings in 1894 was $7.69. "Average Annual Earnings in All Industries . . . 1890–1926," in U.S. Bureau of the Census, *Historical Statistics*, Series D603–617, 92.

69   This may be explained by the change in the use and meaning of the word "success." In its original usage, "success" had no set valuative meaning but required an adjective: "good" success or "ill" success. Not until the second half of the nineteenth century did the word take on its modern meaning of "favorable outcome" (*Oxford English Dictionary*). The fact that the word was so much used in Gilded Age America—in its sense of "favorable outcome"—and the fact that the term was applied to individual lives as well as to endeavors and events is another indicator of the society's preoccupation with competition, results, individual showings, and a heightened awareness that a favorable outcome might not be easily achieved. In the literature that Rex Burns refers to in his study *Success in America: The Yeoman Dream and the Industrial Revolution*, the word "success" rarely appears until the 1850s and after, and then almost always in the context of competition.

70   Thayer, *Onward to Fame and Fortune*; Tilley, *Masters of the Situation*.

71   Thayer, *Onward to Fame and Fortune*, 113, 42, 220.

72   Marden, *Rising in the World*, frontispiece; Thayer, *Onward to Fame and Fortune*, 62. Owen, *Success in Life*, frontal plate.

73   Harry A. Lewis, *Hidden Treasures*, 16, 18.

74   Haines and Yaggy, *Royal Path of Life*, frontispiece; Harry A. Lewis, *Hidden Treasures*, 480–81.

75   Dale, *Way to Win*, back pages.

76   Tilley, *Masters of the Situation*, back pages.

77   Haines and Yaggy, *Royal Path of Life*, back pages.

78   "The Subscription Book Trade," *Publishers' Weekly*, July 25, 1872, 93–94. The same perspective is reflected in current scholarship about the publishing industry. John Tebbel describes subscription books as "essentially fraudulent items," and devotes only 3 of his 466 pages to the subscription industry; see Tebbel, *Between Covers*, 166–69.

79   Pacific Northwest Library Association, "Points to Consider in Judging Subscription Books," 42–44.

80   Hill, "The Only Way to Sell a Book," chap. 1 in *Twain and Bliss*, 13.

81   Hill, *Twain and Bliss*, 13.

82   Wyllie, *Self-Made Man in America*, 128.

83   Bates, *Imperial Highway*, preface; Haines and Yaggy, *Royal Path of Life*, preface.

84 See, for example, Tilley, *Masters of the Situation*, preface.

85 Mathews, *Getting On in the World*, title page, attributed to Arthur Helps.

86 Quoted in Mathews, *Getting On in the World*, 180.

87 G. R. Hewitt, "Practice Secures Perfection," in King, *Portraits and Principles*, 327–28.

88 Bates, *Imperial Highway*, 168.

Chapter Two

1 Out of thirty-three success manual authors considered, there was no information, not even dates of birth and death and occupations, for thirteen of them. Some of the least known authors wrote some of the best-selling subscription success manuals.

2 See, for example, "Hale" in Burke and Howe, *American Authors and Books*.

3 Mott, *Golden Multitudes*, 103.

4 Sheehan, *This Was Publishing*, 90, 98.

5 Connolly, *Life Story of Marden*; Wyllie, *Self-Made Man in America*, 120; *National Cyclopaedia of American Biography*, 14: 269; Huber, *American Idea of Success*, 146–47 (reprint ed.).

6 Connolly, *Life Story of Marden*, 193–206; *National Cyclopaedia of American Biography*, 14: 269.

7 Connolly, *Life Story of Marden*, 278.

8 Marden, *Pushing to the Front*, iii (reprint ed.).

9 *National Cyclopaedia of American Biography*, 3: 29; Burr, *Russell H. Conwell*, esp. chap. 17.

10 Burke and Howe, *American Authors and Books*, 63; *National Cyclopaedia of American Biography*, 23: 41.

11 Bok, *Successward* and *Keys to Success*; Wyllie, *Self-Made Man in America*, 123.

12 Burke and Howe, *American Authors and Books*, 268–69; Kunitz and Haycraft, *American Authors*, 324–25.

13 Huber, *American Idea of Success*, 51.

14 Burke and Howe, *American Authors and Books*, 634.

15 Ibid., 411, 714; Kunitz and Hoycraft, *American Authors*, 518–19; *National Cyclopaedia of American Biography*, 11: 118; Weiss, *American Myth of Success*, 122.

16 *National Cyclopaedia of American Biography*, 14: 172; Schaff and Jackson, *Encyclopedia of Living Divines and Christian Workers*, 43; Huber, *American Idea of Success*, 62–63.

17 *Biographical Dictionary of American Congress*, 1601; Banta, *Indiana Authors*.

18 *National Cyclopaedia of American Biography*, 15: 163.

19 Barnum claimed that a half million copies were sold, but given that the book was reprinted for forty years and reissued several times after his death in 1891, it is likely that the total sales figures are substantially higher. In 1930, it was picked up again by Macmillan Company for inclusion in their Modern Reader Series. Other nonfiction best-sellers published between 1850 and 1920 were Haines and Yaggy's *The Royal Path of Life* (1876), Henry George's *Progress and Poverty* (1879), William Hope Harvey's *Coin's Financial School* (1884), and Frank Channing Haddock's *Power of Will* (1907). See Mott, *Golden Multitudes*, 168–70, 260, 303. See also listings in the ALA *National Union Catalog*.

20 The ALA *National Union Catalog* also shows that this work was handled by at least six different publishers; different editions ranged in length from 346 to 874 pages.

21 Bledstein, *Culture of Professionalism*, 277–79, 297.

22 Ibid., 277–78, 284–86; Ryan, *Cradle of the Middle Class*, 169–70.

23 Bledstein, *Culture of Professionalism*, 176.

24 Ross, "Socialism and American Liberalism," 55–56.

25 Josephson, *Robber Barons*, chap. 14, esp. 315–46.

26 Ibid., 322, 323.

27 Ross, "Socialism and American Liberalism," 56.

28 Ibid., 52.

29 Ibid., 48.

30 Ibid., esp. 55–60.

31 Hall, *Organization of American Culture*, chaps. 8–11, esp. 151–77.

32 Ibid., 182.

33 Ibid., 156; see also quotation from Samuel Atkins Eliot, 196–97.

34 Meyer, *Instructed Conscience*, vi–x, 13, 29, 66, 175.

35 Ibid., 66.

36 See Bledstein, *Culture of Professionalism*, 214–22.

37 Ibid., 218.

38 Ibid., 260.

39 Ibid.

40 Quoted in Leverenz, *Manhood and the American Renaissance*, 44–45.

41 Bledstein, *Culture of Professionalism*, 259.

42 See Leverenz, "Three Ideologies of Manhood, Four Narratives of Humiliation," chap. 3 in *Manhood and the American Renaissance*, 72–107. See also chapter 7 below.

43 Leverenz, *Manhood and the American Renaissance*, 43.

44 Bannister, *Social Darwinism: Science and Myth*, esp. 57–78.

45 Ibid., 59, 45, 47.

46 Mott, *Golden Multitudes*, 320–23.

Chapter Three

1 Marden, *Rising in the World*, iii.

2 H. A. Lewis, *Hidden Treasures*, vi.

3 Dale, *Way to Win*, preface; Tilley, *Masters of the Situation*, preface; King, *Portraits and Principles*, preface. Note also the full title of Tilley's book: *Masters of the Situation, or Some of the Secrets of Success and Power: A Volume Designed To Awaken in its Readers by Precept and Example a Realizing Sense of the Vast and Inspiring Possibilities of Human Achievement Which Lie Within the Reach of All.*

4 Thayer, *Onward to Fame and Fortune*, 25.

5 Tilley, *Masters of the Situation*, 397–99.

6 Smiles, *Self-Help*, 310–11.

7 H. A. Lewis, *Hidden Treasures*, iii.

8 King, *Portraits and Principles*, 404.

9 See, for example, Marden, *Pushing to the Front*, iii.

10 Bok, *Successward*, 7.

11 Tilley, *Masters of the Situation*, 502, 456.

12 Smiles, *Self-Help*, 75.

13 Marden, *Pushing to the Front*, 139.

14 Dale, *Way to Win*, 381, 390.

15 Tilley, *Masters of the Situation*, 273, 276, 272, 280–81.

16 Haines and Yaggy, *Royal Path of Life*, preface.

17 See, for example, Fellman and Fellman, *Making Sense of Self,* esp. 57–87; and Beard, *American Nervousness,* 5.

18 Lutz, *American Nervousness,* 20.

19 Trachtenberg, *Incorporation of America,* 47–48; Beard, *American Nervousness,* 5.

20 See Weibe's concept of "the distended society" in Weibe, *Search for Order,* 44.

21 Marden, *Pushing to the Front,* 109; Marden, *Rising in the World,* iv; King, *Portraits and Principles,* 3.

22 Mathews, *Getting On in the World,* 4.

23 King, *Portraits and Principles,* 3.

24 Ibid., 329–30.

25 Thayer, *Onward to Fame and Fortune,* 31; Tilley, *Masters of the Situation,* 618; King, *Portraits and Principles,* 401.

26 Thayer, *Onward to Fame and Fortune,* 253.

27 Mathews, *Getting On in the World,* 186.

28 Owen, *Success in Life,* 30.

29 Tilley, *Masters of the Situation,* 347–48, 414, 582.

30 Dale, *The Secret of Success,* 63; Mathews, *Getting On in the World,* 329–30; Haines and Yaggy, *Royal Path of Life,* 53.

31 Mathews, *Getting On in the World,* 227.

32 Smiles, *Self-Help,* 266–67.

33 Bok, *Successward,* 8.

34 Owen, *Success in Life,* 186–88.

35 Sharman, *Power of the Will,* 41.

36 Bates, *The Imperial Highway,* 75.

37 Joseph Cook, "The Power and Possibilities of Young Men," in King, *Portraits and Principles,* 337.

38 Examples of this type of missionary rhetoric can be seen in Josiah Strong's popular polemic *Our Country* (1885) and in Senator Albert J. Beveridge's speech in the Senate in 1900, which urged the U.S. to retain the Philippine Islands won from Spain in the Spanish-American War.

39 Lehmann-Haupt, *The Book in America,* 251; Mott, *Golden Multitudes,* 157; Compton, "Subscription Books," 889.

40 In *Social Darwinism, Science and Myth in Anglo-American Social Thought,* Robert C. Bannister attests to Herbert Spencer's "vogue" from the 1860s to the turn of the century, but he argues that even among conservative businessmen social Darwinism was embraced neither as widely nor as wholeheartedly as is commonly thought. Rather, the term "social Darwinism" was most often used by reformers as a pejorative label to describe what they saw as the materialism and avarice of business interests (see Bannister, 1–13, 59). Success writers adopted the language of social Darwinism to portray life as a battle. But their insistence that only the fittest survived was not a justification for the wealth and status of those at the top of the ladder. Rather, it was a call to action for those at the bottom, the assurance that there was "room at the top."

41 See, for example, Greene, *American Heroes: Changing Models of Success in American Magazines,* part 2; and Emerson, "Napoleon; or, The Man of the World."

42 Gorn, *Manly Art,* 179–206.

43 Lears, *No Place of Grace,* 100.

44 Ibid., 108–12. See also Gorn, *Manly Art,* 179–206.

45   Gorn, *Manly Art*, 144–45.
46   Mathews, *Getting On in the World*, 186; and Thayer, *Onward to Fame and Fortune*, 31.
47   Brown, *Top or Bottom—Which?*, 47; Thayer, *Onward to Fame and Fortune*, 216.
48   Owen, *Success in Life*, 30.
49   Tilley, *Masters of the Situation*, 367, 350.
50   Conwell, *The New Day*, 9–10.
51   Marden, *Pushing to the Front*, 328.
52   Sharman, *Power of the Will*, 34.
53   Mathews, *Getting On in the World*, 84.
54   See, for example, Crafts, *Successful Men of Today*, 31, 37.
55   Dale, *The Secret of Success*, 29; Marden, *Rising in the World*, 145; Dale, *Way to Win*, 29.
56   Thayer, *Onward to Fame and Fortune*, 25.
57   Conwell, *The New Day*, 11.
58   Tilley, *Masters of the Situation*, 352.

Chapter Four

 1   For evidence of the rural and small-town market for success manuals (most of which
     were produced and marketed by the subscription trade), see the handbooks produced by
     subscription publishers designed to teach book agents how, where, and to whom to sell:
     Browning, *O. A. Browning's Confidential Instructions, Rules and Helps for His Agents*; N. D.
     Thompson Publishing Co., *Success in Canvassing*; and International Publishing Co., *The
     General Agent's Guide to Success*. On Gilded Age movements of protest and dissent, see,
     for example, Goodwyn, *The Populist Moment*; Fink, *Workingmen's Democracy*; Salvatore,
     Eugene V. Debs; Laurie, *Artisans into Workers*; and Trachtenberg, *Incorporation of America*.
 2   Trachtenberg, *Incorporation of America*, 39.
 3   Ibid., 3–100; and Ross, "Socialism and American Liberalism," 9.
 4   Frank Luther Mott defines "best-sellers" as books "believed to have had a total sales
     equal to one percent of the population of the continental United States for the decade
     in which it was published." He excludes Bibles, hymnals, textbooks, almanacs, cook-
     books, doctor-books, how-to manuals (practical guides on topics such as letter writing
     and animal husbandry), and reference works. See Mott, *Golden Multitudes*, 303.
 5   Ibid., 241–42, 260. *The Royal Path of Life* is included as one of the success manuals
     considered in this study. *The Power of Will* is not included, as it marks a shift in the
     success genre away from the emphasis on character (one of the important hallmarks of
     nineteenth-century success manuals) and toward an emphasis on personality as the key
     to success (a theme more typical of the twentieth-century genre). See also note 22 in
     the introduction. For more on the subscription book industry and the price of books
     sold by subscription, see Tebbel, *Between Covers*, 166–69; Lehmann-Haupt, *The Book in
     America*, 190, 194; Sheehan, *This Was Publishing*; Barcus, *Philosophy of Canvassing*; and
     chapter 1 above.
 6   The other two nonfiction best-sellers of the period were John Richard Green's *A Short
     History of the English People* (1875), sold in paperback for as little as thirty-eight cents,
     and Hannah Whithall Smith's *The Christian Secret of a Happy Life* (1883), sold mostly by
     subscription. See Mott, *Golden Multitudes*, 241–71.
 7   Books were sold inexpensively in paperback through mail order, sometimes in series
     or "libraries," and were available also in dry goods and department stores. Works such

as *Progress and Poverty* and *Coin's Financial School* were also sold by organizations promoting their ideas. See Mott, *Golden Multitudes*, 167–71, and the works on the history of book publishing cited in note 5 above.

8 Thanks to the social and intellectual history of the last twenty years that has shown the extent to which Gilded Age America was "contested terrain" both socially and ideologically, there is a context to understand the defensiveness and the contentiousness of the success manuals and to see them as part of an important debate rather than simply a celebration of the American dream. In *The Incorporation of America*, Alan Trachtenberg synthesizes much of this newer research in his argument that the corporate order that achieved hegemony in the twentieth century was the product of a long, wrenching process of transformation that included a pitched battle over the future shape of the nation and the national ethic. The newer scholarship provides an antidote to the consensus school of historical interpretation exemplified by works such as Louis Hartz's *The Liberal Tradition in America* (1955) and to the sense of inevitability of Robert Weibe's *The Search for Order, 1877–1920* (1967). On Gilded Age conflict and crisis, see the secondary sources cited in note 1 above; see also Gutman, *Work, Culture and Society in Industrializing America*; Montgomery, *Workers' Control in America*; Ross, " Socialism and American Liberalism"; Lears, *No Place of Grace*, esp. chap. 1; Hall, *Organization of American Culture*; Haskell, *Emergence of Professional Social Science*; Carter, *Spiritual Crisis of the Gilded Age*; Meyer, *Instructed Conscience*; Smith-Rosenberg, *Disorderly Conduct*; Carnes and Griffen, *Meanings of Manhood*.

9 This is not to attribute the motives of either accommodation or legitimation to success writers. The process of legitimation and the establishment of a hegemonic socioeconomic order does not require conscious intention on the part of those producing the cultural forms that contribute to the process. For a discussion of the concepts of legitimation and hegemony, see Gramsci, *Prison Notebooks*; and Lears, "Concept of Cultural Hegemony." For studies that demonstrate how particular cultural forms contribute to the process of change and legitimation, see Elias, *Power and Civility*; and Meyer, *Instructed Conscience*.

10 James W. Cole, "Selecting an Occupation," in King, *Portraits and Principles*, 45.

11 Haines and Yaggy, *Royal Path of Life*, 1.

12 Quigley, *Success Is for You*, 1, 2.

13 Marden, *Rising in the World*, 147.

14 The success manual's bipolar view of the world, in which the choices offered are really no choice at all, might be seen as an exaggerated statement of the deconstructionist contention that "meaning is made through implicit or explicit contrasts, that a positive definition rests on the negation or repression of something repressed as antithetical to it" and further that "the interdependence is hierarchical with one term dominant or prior, the opposite term subordinate and secondary." Scott, "Deconstructing Equality-Versus-Difference," 36–37. Chapter 7 expands the list of these "binary oppositions" to include masculinity/femininity as corollaries to success/failure and virtue/vice.

15 Brown, *Top or Bottom — Which?*, 7.

16 Marden, *Rising in the World*, iv.

17 Owen, *Success in Life*, 135.

18 Bates, *Imperial Highway*, 89–90.

19 Cole, "Selecting an Occupation," in King, *Portraits and Principles*, 45.

20 Barnum, *Dollars and Sense*, 17–18.

21 Smiles, *Self-Help*, 282.

22 H. A. Lewis, *Hidden Treasures*, 100.

23 Ibid., x.

24 James Truax, "Danger of Being Side-Tracked," in King, *Portraits and Principles*, 57.

25 James W. Cole, "The Importance of Self-Mastery," in King, *Portraits and Principles*, 173–74.

26 Sharman, *Power of the Will*, 125–26.

27 James W. Cole, "The Dignity of Labor," in King, *Portraits and Principles*, 78.

28 Dale, *Way to Win*, 399, 339, 443.

29 Mathews, *Getting On in the World*, 89.

30 Smiles, *Self-Help*, 261–62.

31 Conwell, *The New Day*, 43.

32 Ibid., 42.

33 "Acres of Diamonds" was a sermon that Conwell delivered for the first time in 1861 and is reported to have given six thousand times in his life. First published in 1870, it was printed as a pamphlet, but also appeared as a part of Conwell's full-length success manuals. See Burr, *Russell H. Conwell*.

34 Conwell, *Acres of Diamonds*, 22.

35 Ibid., 23.

36 Conwell, *The New Day*, 42.

37 Ibid., 40–41.

38 Smiles, *Self-Help*, 180–82; Owen, *Success in Life*, 57.

39 Marden, *Rising in the World*, iv.

40 Conwell, *The New Day*, 43.

41 Ibid., 11.

42 Hale, *What Career?*, 6; see also Owen, *Success in Life*, 57.

43 Chamberlain, *Makers of Millions*, preface.

44 Conwell, *The New Day*, 22, 54.

45 Mathews, *Getting On in the World*, 20, 88.

46 Dale, *Way to Win*, 441.

47 Sharman, *Power of the Will*, 35.

48 Owen, *Success in Life*, 61.

49 Conwell, *Acres of Diamonds*, 22.

50 Dale, *Way to Win*, 441.

51 Barnum, *Dollars and Sense*, 59–60.

52 Conwell, *The New Day*, 117.

53 Ibid., 43.

54 Ibid., 117.

55 Tilley, *Masters of the Situation*, 425.

56 Mathews, *Getting On in the World*, 283.

57 Dale, *Way to Win*, 500–501.

58 Ibid., 500–501.

59 Tilley, *Masters of the Situation*, 616.

60 Ibid., 673.

61 Mathews, *Getting On in the World*, 329–30; Tilley, *Masters of the Situation*, 618; King, *Portraits and Principles*, 401; Dale, *Way to Win*, 433.

62 Crafts, *Successful Men of Today*, 53.

63 John Farwell, introduction to Dale, *The Secret of Success*, vii. Such expressions of nativism are part of the evidence that the success manual was directed to a native-born audience and not the new immigrant population.

64 Farwell, introduction to Dale, *The Secret of Success*, vii.

65 Tilley, *Masters of the Situation*, 766.

66 Quoted in Thayer, *Onward to Fame and Fortune*, 394.

67 Smiles, *Self-Help*, 303.

68 Dale, *Way to Win*, 560.

69 Smiles, *Self-Help*, 305.

70 Dale, *Way to Win*, 565.

71 Brown, *Top or Bottom — Which?*, 35.

72 See Carter, *Spiritual Crisis of the Gilded Age*.

73 James W. Cole, "Fruits of Industry," in King, *Portraits and Principles*, 91–93.

74 Dale, *Way to Win*, 559.

75 Mathews, *Getting On in the World*, 240.

76 Ibid., 281, 284.

77 Conwell, *Acres of Diamonds*, 11–12.

78 Bok, *Keys to Success*, 121.

79 Ibid., 369.

80 King, *Portraits and Principles*, 79.

81 Thayer, *Onward to Fame and Fortune*, 369.

82 Smiles, *Self-Help*, 252.

83 Owen, *Success in Life*, 34.

84 Matthew 25: 21, 26–30, King James Version.

85 See, for example, commentary accompanying chapter and verse in Thompson, *New Chain Reference Bible*.

86 Sharman, *Power of the Will*, 49.

87 Mathews, *Getting On in the World*, 25: 29.

88 Dale, *Way to Win*, 546.

89 Elbert Hubbard, *Message to Garcia*, 4.

90 Chapter 5 explores the tenacity of Jeffersonian agrarianism as the ideological backdrop for viewing a world of work that was rapidly changing. See Blumin, *Emergence of the Middle Class*; E. Anthony Rotundo, "Boy Culture: Middle-Class Boyhood in Nineteenth-Century America," in Carnes and Griffen, *Meanings for Manhood*; Smith-Rosenberg, *Disorderly Conduct*; Ryan, *Cradle of the Middle Class*; Gutman, *Work, Culture and Society in Industrializing America*; Kett, *Rites of Passage*; Rex Burns, *Success in America*; Horlick, *Country Boys and Merchant Princes*.

91 There is some evidence that employers attempted to use success manuals to inculcate their workers with these desirable traits. Certainly the success manuals' powerful admonition for self-discipline and internalization of the rules of the new industrial order is obvious. But this is not to say that success writers were cynical ideologues of the new employer class, consciously seeking to help them create a tractable, productive workforce. Success writers were true believers in the world they portrayed. But they lived in an era that Thomas L. Haskell has described as "an age in which an individual's acts generated unplanned consequences far beyond his range of vision, and in which the individual himself was subjected to influences not intended by others." Haskell, *Emergence of Professional Social Science*, 244.

Chapter Five

1 James W. Cole, "Selecting an Occupation," in King, *Portraits and Principles*, 47.

2 A. Lewis, *Manhood-Making*, 105, 108.

3 Russell Conwell is said to have delivered "Acres of Diamonds" 6,000 times in his lifetime. It was first published as a pamphlet in 1870 and was reissued as a part of Conwell's first full-length success manuals. The ALA *National Union Catalog* lists its first publication as follows: *Acres of Diamonds: How Men and Women May Become Rich . . . Advice and Examples Adapted to All Classes* (Philadelphia: S. Y. Huber Co., 1890). It is also included in a biography by Agnes Rush Burr, *Russell H. Conwell and His Work*, 405–38.

4 Conwell, "Acres of Diamonds," in Burr, *Russell H. Conwell*, 407–9.

5 Ibid., 409.

6 Ibid., 426–27.

7 Tilley, *Masters of the Situation*, 300.

8 Marden, *Pushing to the Front*, 8.

9 H. A. Lewis, *Hidden Treasures*, 100.

10 Marden, *Pushing to the Front*, 44.

11 Conwell, *Acres of Diamonds*, title page.

12 Tilley, *Masters of the Situation*, 549–62.

13 Dale, *Way to Win*, 517–22.

14 Marden, *Rising in the World*, 423–24.

15 The most important contemporary example was Josiah Strong's *Our Country, Its Possible Future and Its Present Crisis*, originally published in 1886; see editor Jurgen Herbst's introduction, xxiv–xxv, and Ross, "The Liberal Tradition Revisited and the Republican Tradition Addressed," 121–23. See also Sarah Burns, *Pastoral Inventions*, chap. 11; Weibe, *Search for Order*, preface, introduction, chap. 2, and p. 159; Smith, *Virgin Land*, chap. 11; Hofstadter, *Age of Reform*, parts 1 and 2.

16 Smith, *Virgin Land*, chap. 18.

17 Ibid., 190, 124–32, 155, 192–93, 259–60; Goodwyn, *The Populist Moment*, 69–72; Trachtenberg, *Incorporation of America*, 112–14; Hofstadter, *Age of Reform*, 46–59; Shannon, *The Farmer's Last Frontier*.

18 Laurie, *Artisans into Workers: Labor in Nineteenth Century America*, 124, 115.

19 Weibe, *Search for Order*, chap. 2, esp. 15–17.

20 Trachtenberg, *Incorporation of America*, 112–15.

21 Conwell, *The New Day*, 38.

22 Bledstein, *Culture of Professionalism*, 278, 297. Enrollment in institutions of higher learning rose from 52,000 in 1870 to 238,000 in 1900.

23 Kett, *Rites of Passage*, 128–29.

24 Ibid., 128–29, 151–52.

25 King, *Portraits and Principles*, 54.

26 Smiles, *Self-Help*, 328.

27 Ibid., 20–21.

28 Marden, *Rising in the World*, 5.

29 Kett, *Rites of Passage*, 154.

30 Bledstein, *Culture of Professionalism*, 278.

31 Laurie, *Artisans and Workers*, 122.

32 Ryan, *Cradle of the Middle Class*, 145–85; Kett, *Rites of Passage*, 144–72; Bledstein, *Culture of Professionalism*, 284.

33 King, *Portraits and Principles*, 154.

34 Dale, *Way to Win*, 357.

35 See, for example, Kirkland, "The Higher Learning," chap. 4 in *Dream and Thought in the Business Community 1860–1900*.

36 Tilley, *Masters of the Situation*, 415.

37 Owen, *Success in Life*, 279.

38 Marden, *Rising in the World*, 163–64.

39 Mathews, *Getting On in the World*, 304.

40 James W. Cole, "Not About Your Business," in King, *Portraits and Principles*, 100–101.

41 Owen, *Success in Life*, 38.

42 Crafts, *Successful Men of Today*, 221.

43 H. A. Lewis, *Hidden Treasures*, 493.

44 The phenomenon of the dead-end clerkship could be seen by midcentury, as evidenced in "The Tale of Two Clerks," in Horlick, *Country Boys and Merchant Princes*, 106–43.

45 Blumin, *Emergence of the Middle Class*, esp. chaps. 4, 8, and epilogue.

46 Conwell, *The New Day*, 40–41.

47 Tilley, *Masters of the Situation*, 406.

48 Conwell, *The New Day*, 40–41.

49 Marden, *Rising in the World*, 335.

50 Dale, *Secret of Success*, 156.

51 Blumin, *Emergence of the Middle Class*, 269 and chaps. 3 and 8; Trachtenberg, *Incorporation of America*, chap. 2.

52 According to Thomas Haskell, the "prevailing division of labor" in the nineteenth century "defined the professions as divinity, law and medicine." The success writers expanded this list somewhat. Haskell, *Emergence of Professional Social Science*, vii.

53 Trachtenberg, *Incorporation of America*, 64–65.

54 Ibid., 66.

55 Ibid., 67.

56 Ibid., 68.

57 Conwell, *The New Day*, 72–76.

58 Kett, *Rites of Passage*, 154.

59 Bledstein, *Culture of Professionalism*, 84–85.

60 Ibid., 184–88.

61 Ibid., 198, 175–77.

62 Josephson, *The Robber Barons*, 316–25; Ross, "Socialism and American Liberalism," 55–56; Bledstein, *Culture of Professionalism*, chap. 5; C. Wright Mills, *White Collar*, chap. 6.

63 Trachtenberg, *Incorporation of America*, 5; see also Weibe, *Search for Order*, chap. 2; and Haskell, *Emergence of Professional Social Science*, chap. 11.

64 On the ideal of the harmony of hand and head and the sense of dehumanization associated with the separation of mental and manual work, see Salvatore, *Eugene V. Debs*, 228–29; and Gorn, *The Manly Art*, 141–42.

65 See Braverman, *Labor and Monopoly Capital*; and Trachtenberg, *Incorporation of America*, 54–69.

66 Blumin, *Emergence of the Middle Class*, 258–75.

67 Owen, *Success in Life*, 155.

68 Smiles, *Self-Help*, 310.

69 Bates, *Imperial Highway*, 167.

70 Samuel Smiles, quoted in A. Lewis, *Manhood-Making*, 87.

71 Hold, *Phrase and Word Origins*, 200.

72 Crafts, *Successful Men of Today*, 31.

73 Marden, *Rising in the World*, 186.

74 Dale, *Secret of Success*, 63.

75 See Green, *Fit for America*; and Gorn, *The Manly Art*, chap. 6.

76 Smiles, *Self-Help*, 311.

77 Mathews, *Getting On in the World*, 54, 61.

78 Tilley, *Masters of the Situation*, 231.

79 Bates, *Imperial Highway*, 301.

80 Dale, *Way to Win*, 61.

81 Owen, *Success in Life*, 481.

82 King, *Portraits and Principles*, 197.

83 Thayer, *Onward to Fame and Fortune*, 277.

84 Tilley, *Masters of the Situation*, 233.

85 Marden, *Pushing to the Front*, 360.

86 Smiles, *Self-Help*, 315.

87 Mathews, *Getting On in the World*, 58.

88 Marden, *Pushing to the Front*, 359.

89 Owen, *Success in Life*, 491.

90 Crafts, *Successful Men of Today*, 33–34.

91 Mathews, *Getting On in the World*, 36.

92 Owen, *Success in Life*, 17–18.

93 Owen, *Success in Life*, 30.

94 Mathews, *Getting On in the World*, 350.

95 On the decline of the authority of church and community in nineteenth-century America and the attempt to replace external discipline with self-discipline through character education, see, for example, Hall, *Organization of American Culture*; Meyer, *Instructed Conscience*; Lears, *No Place of Grace*, esp. chap. 1; Ryan, *Cradle of the Middle Class*, 40–48, 126–29; D'Emilio and Freedman, *Intimate Matters*, xvii, 84.

96 Marden, *Pushing to the Front*, 91; Thayer, *Onward to Fame and Fortune*, 177.

97 Marden, *Pushing to the Front*, 84, 91.

98 Tilley, *Masters of the Situation*, 626.

99 Marden, *Pushing to the Front*, 74–75.

100 Cole, "Selecting an Occupation," in King, *Portraits and Principles*, 45.

101 Ibid., 45.

102 Tilley, *Masters of the Situation*, 405.

103 Owen, *Success in Life*, 78.

104 Dale, *Way to Win*, 477.

105 Bok, *Successward*, 30.

106 Owen, *Success in Life*, 78.

107 James W. Cole, "Our Noblest Birth Right," in King, *Portraits and Principles*, 26.

108 Crafts, *Successful Men of Today*, 223.

109 Rex Burns, *Success in America*, 180. On the tenacity of Jeffersonian agrarian ideology, see Smith, *Virgin Land*, 126–28, 250–60.

110 Trachtenberg, *Incorporation of America*, 70–75; Laurie, *Artisans into Workers*, 11.

111 Trachtenberg, *Incorporation of America*, 80.

112 Laurie, *Artisans into Workers*, 136.

113 Fink, *Workingmen's Democracy*, 3–15; Laurie, *Artisans into Workers*, 111–40; Trachtenberg, *Incorporation of America*, 70–75.

114 Dale, *Way to Win*, 477.

115 Smiles, *Self-Help*, 333, emphasis added.

116 Dale, *Way to Win*, 494, 496.

117 Ibid., 477.

118 Cole, "Our Noblest Birth Right," in King, *Portraits and Principles*, 28.

119 Thayer, *Onward to Fame and Fortune*, 30.

Chapter Six

1 See, for example, Bledstein, *Culture of Professionalism*, 214–22; Meyer, *Instructed Conscience*, esp. vii–x, 13, 29, 66, 175; and Hall, *Organization of American Culture*, 156–57.

2 Halttunen, *Confidence Men and Painted Women*; see esp. "Epilogue: The Confidence Man in Corporate America," 198–207.

3 Susman, "'Personality' and the Making of Twentieth-Century Culture," chap. 14 in *Culture as History*.

4 Marden, *Pushing to the Front*, 272.

5 Smiles, *Self-Help*, 396–97.

6 Marden, *Rising in the World*, iv.

7 Tilley, *Masters of the Situation*, 96.

8 Dale, *Way to Win*, 160.

9 Owen, *Success in Life*, 130.

10 Dale, *Way to Win*, 296.

11 H. A. Lewis, *Hidden Treasures*, 491.

12 Marden, *Rising in the World*, 252; see summary listed under "Rich without Money" in table of contents.

13 Ibid., 252.

14 Ibid., 152.

15 See, for example, Smith, *Virgin Land*, 124–32, 155, 190, 192–93, 259–60; Goodwyn, *The Populist Moment*, 69–72; Trachtenberg, *Incorporation of America*, 112–14; Hofstadter, *Age of Reform*, 46–59; Shannon, *Farmer's Last Frontier*.

16 See, for example, King, *Portraits and Principles*; Dale, *Way to Win*; Marden, *Rising in the World*; and Owen, *Success in Life*.

17 Mathews, *Getting On in the World*, 89.

18 Thayer, *Onward to Fame and Fortune*, 35.

19 Kent, *How to Achieve Success*, 95.

20 Marden, *Rising in the World*, 104.

21 Tilley, *Masters of the Situation*, 358.

22 Dale, *Way to Win*, 406.

23 Marden, *Pushing to the Front*, 304, 312.

24 Owen, *Success in Life*, 153.

25 Dale, *Way to Win*, 236–37.

26 Smiles, *Self-Help*, 368–69.

27 Dale, *Way to Win*, 502.

28 Mathews, *Getting On in the World*, 21 (reprint ed.).

29 Owen, *Success in the World*, 325.

30　Thayer, *Onward to Fame and Fortune*, 31.

31　Smiles, *Self-Help*, 258.

32　Mathews, *Getting On in the World*, 314, 310, 308.

33　Tilley, *Masters of the Situation*, 426, 431.

34　Smiles, *Self-Help*, 275.

35　George R. Hewitt, "Motive and Method," in King, *Portraits and Principles*, 411–13.

36　Mathews, *Getting On in the World*, 282 (reprint ed.).

37　Ibid., 282–83 (Toronto ed.).

38　Fink, *Workingmen's Democracy*, 3–15.

39　Kent, *How to Achieve Success*, 52.

40　Dale, *Way to Win*, 401.

41　Ibid., 400, 402.

42　King, *Portraits and Principles*, 385–86.

43　Conwell, *The New Day*, 89.

44　Tilley, *Masters of the Situation*, 460–74.

45　Lewis, *Hidden Treasures*, 508.

46　Dale, *Way to Win*, 345–47.

47　Bates, *Imperial Highway*, 487.

48　Dale, *Secret of Success*, 159.

49　Bok, *Successward*, 159.

50　Ibid., 112–17.

51　Smiles, *Self-Help*, 273.

52　John F. Kasson makes this point in *Rudeness and Civility: Manners in Nineteenth Century Urban America*; see, for example, pages 6 and 257. See also Halttunen, *Confidence Men and Painted Women*, xvi.

53　Smiles, *Self-Help*, 408.

54　Mathews, *Getting On in the World*, 153.

55　A. Lewis, *Manhood-Making*, 201.

56　Tilley, *Masters of the Situation*, 654.

57　Dale, *Way to Win*, 161.

58　Owen, *Success in Life*, 158.

59　Elias, *Power and Civility*, 268.

60　See, for example, Ross, "Socialism and American Liberalism," 47–56.

61　See Trachtenberg, "The Politics of Culture," chap. 5 in *Incorporation of America*, 140–80.

62　Smiles, *Self-Help*, 283.

63　Dale, *Way to Win*, 442.

64　See Blumin, "The Hypothesis of Middle-Class Formation in Nineteenth-Century America," 308–9; and Blumin, *Emergence of the Middle Class*.

65　See, for example, Gutman, *Work, Culture and Society in Industrializing America*.

66　On the concept of individual internalization of societal rules and authority, see Elias, *Power and Civility*, 229–80; Lears, *No Place of Grace*, esp. chap. 1; Hall, *Organization of American Culture*, esp. chaps. 8–12; Meyer, *Instructed Conscience*, vii–xiv, 3–11; and Ryan, *Cradle of the Middle Class*, 145–85.

67　Mary P. Ryan makes the observation that the attempt to reproduce a middle-class personality by teaching honesty, industry, frugality, temperance, and self-control produced not the daring, aggressive entrepreneur but the cautious, prudent small-business man. See Ryan, *Cradle of the Middle Class*, 161.

68　James W. Cole, "Self-Mastery," in King, *Portraits and Principles*, 175.

69 See Wright, "Franklin's Legacy to the Gilded Age," 276–77. The author of *Worth and Wealth* was Thomas L. Haines.

Chapter Seven

1 There exists a growing body of historical research exploring the theme of "manhood" and "manliness" in American society. See, for example, Barker-Benfield, *Horrors of the Half-Known Life*, esp. chap. 15, "The Spermatic Economy and Proto-Sublimation"; Filene, *Him-Her Self*; Stearns, *Be a Man!*; Smith-Rosenberg, *Disorderly Conduct*, esp. part 2, "Davy Crockett as Trickster: Pornography, Liminality, and Symbolic Inversion in Victorian America," 90–108; D'Emilio and Freedman, *Intimate Matters*; Leverenz, *Manhood and the American Renaissance*; Carnes, *Secret Ritual and Manhood in Victorian America*; Carnes and Griffen, *Meanings for Manhood*. My focus here is on the meaning of "manhood" as it appears in the success manual and as part of a success ideology. I first presented work on this topic in 1974 at the Second Berkshire Conference on the History of Women; see Hilkey, "Masculinity and the Self-Made Man in America, 1850–1900."

2 For studies of "women's sphere" as it evolved in nineteenth-century America, see Welter, "The Cult of True Womanhood"; Cott, *Roots of Bitterness* and *Bonds of Womanhood*; Ryan, *Womanhood in America* and *Cradle of the Middle Class*; Sklar, *Catherine Beecher*; and Kerber, "Separate Spheres, Female Worlds, Woman's Place."

3 Peter Filene was one of the first historians to look at these issues in nineteenth-century America. In *Him-Her Self* (1974), he wrote: "The concept of manliness was suffering strain in all of its dimensions—in work and success, in familial patriarchy, and in the dimensions Victorian Americans did not often discuss aloud, sexuality" (77). For other sources on manhood in nineteenth-century America, see note 1 above.

4 Theodore P. Greene documents the predominance of the Napoleon-businessman figure in popular American magazines of the 1890s; see Greene, *American Heroes: The Changing Models of Success in American Magazines*, 110–65. For a discussion of American entrepreneurs' tendency to focus on business as the defining experience of manhood, to the exclusion and detriment of their sexuality, see Kriegel, *On Men and Manhood*, 73–79. For other evidence of the centrality of money-making and entrepreneurship for the male ideal, see Filene, *Him-Her Self*, 83; and Stearns, *Be a Man!*, 128.

5 See Montgomery, *Workers' Control in America*, 13–16; and Salvatore, *Eugene V. Debs*, 61, 64, 79–81, 89, 124, and 228–29.

6 See, for example, Bates, *Imperial Highway*, 170, 304, 289; Owen, *Success in Life*, 416, 347.

7 Marden, *Rising in the World*, 44, 104, 5.

8 Ibid., 2.

9 Tilley, *Masters of the Situation*, 282.

10 Marden, *Rising in the World*, 4.

11 Owen, *Success in Life*, 57; Tilley, *Masters of the Situation*, 282.

12 See, for example, Dale, *Way to Win*, 322; and Smiles, *Self-Help*, 396–97.

13 Marden, *Rising in the World*, 334.

14 Bates, *Imperial Highway*, 289.

15 Dale, *Way to Win*, 313; Hale, *What Career?*, 230–31.

16 Tilley, *Masters of the Situation*, 393.

17 Mathews, *Getting On in the World*, 128.

18 Marden, *Rising in the World*, 59.

19 Smiles, *Self-Help*, 203, 205.

20 Tilley, *Masters of the Situation*, 393.

21 H. A. Lewis, *Hidden Treasures*, 484.

22 Marden, *Rising in the World*, 44.

23 Crafts, *Successful Men of Today*, 35.

24 Smiles, *Self-Help*, 208; Tilley, *Masters of the Situation*, 394.

25 See, for example, Crafts, *Successful Men of Today*, 37; and H. A. Lewis, *Hidden Treasures*, 485.

26 The story was first in print in 1910, titled "The Pony Engine," and first published as a book in 1930 under the title "The Little Engine that Could." However, some recall hearing the story being told as early as the 1880s. See Ord, "Watty Piper," 279–81. Thanks to Ulla Dydo for calling my attention to this reference.

27 George R. Hewitt, "The Man of Push," in King, *Portraits and Principles*, 119.

28 Marden, *Rising in the World*, preface.

29 Hewitt, in King, *Portraits and Principles*, 119.

30 Owen, *Success in Life*, 280.

31 Mathews, *Getting On in the World*, 17–18.

32 Marden, *Pushing to the Front*, 170.

33 Judith Bardwick uses the term "phallocentric" in chapter 1 of *Psychology of Women, A Study of Bio-Cultural Conflict*. For confirmation of this type of phallic symbolism in the vernacular of Victorian America, see D'Emilio and Freedman, *Intimate Matters*, 59 and 83, where they quote men's diary entries about their sexual experiences, in which the phrase "got my gun off" is used to describe ejaculation.

34 See, for example, Mathews, *Getting On in the World*, 280; Owen, *Success in Life*, 146, 339, 497; Marden, *Pushing to the Front*, 250.

35 Owen, *Success in Life*, 186–88.

36 Owen, *Success in Life*, 134.

37 Thayer, *Onward to Fame and Fortune*, 115.

38 Tilley, *Masters of the Situation*, 385.

39 Bates, *Imperial Highway*, 191.

40 Barker-Benfield, "The Spermatic Economy and Proto-Sublimation," chap. 15 in *Horrors of the Half-Known Life*.

41 Marcus, *The Other Victorians*, 22.

42 Mathews, *Getting On in the World*, 239.

43 Bates, *Imperial Highway*, 189.

44 Ibid., 191.

45 Owen, *Success in Life*, 345, 131.

46 Bates, *Imperial Highway*, 166–67.

47 Ibid., 168.

48 The dual use of the term "willpower," calling on men to exercise self-restraint in both the sexual and business realms of life, was common in other kinds of nineteenth-century advice, self-help, and medical literature. See D'Emilio and Freedman, *Intimate Matters*, 68; and Fellman and Fellman, *Making Sense of Self*, esp. chaps. 5–7.

49 Tilley, *Masters of the Situation*, 326.

50 See Stearns, *Be a Man!*, 59–63.

51 On the changing and conflicting ideas about male sexuality and male sexual conduct in Victorian America, see D'Emilio and Freedman, *Intimate Matters*, 55–88, 110–38, 172–202; Stearns, *Be a Man!*, 108–12; Fellman and Fellman, *Making Sense of Self*, 73–112; and

Barker-Benfield, *Horrors of the Half-Known Life*, esp. chap. 15, "The Spermatic Economy and Proto-Sublimation."

52 Elias, *Power and Civility*, esp. part 2.

53 Hall, *Organization of American Culture*; see, for example, 156–57, 182, 196–97. The moral philosophy texts used to "instruct the conscience" of students in nineteenth-century American colleges may have been one of the models and inspirations for the success manual. See D. H. Meyer's study of these texts, *The Instructed Conscience: The Shaping of the American National Ethic*, and chapter 2 above. On the crisis of authority in Gilded Age America and the burden it placed on the individual, also see Lears, *No Place of Grace*, chap. 1; Ryan, *Cradle of the Middle Class*, chap. 4; and Fellman and Fellman, *Making Sense of Self*, chaps. 1 and 7.

54 Fellman and Fellman, *Making Sense of Self*, 139.

55 Dale, *Way to Win*, 559.

56 Crafts, *Successful Men of Today*, 128.

57 Marden, *Pushing to the Front*, 95.

58 Mathews, *Getting On in the World*, 348.

59 Owen, *Success in Life*, 51.

60 Marden, *Pushing to the Front*, 95–96.

61 Bates, *Imperial Highway*, 289.

62 Haines and Yaggy, *Royal Path of Life*, 12.

63 Bates, *Imperial Highway*, 289.

64 See Young, *Toadstool Millionaires*.

65 C. Wright Mills, *White Collar*, part 1.

66 See Lears, "The Concept of Cultural Hegemony."

67 See Scott, "Deconstructing Equality-Versus-Difference." Scott's discussion of the importance of the concept of "difference" in poststructuralist analyses is useful here and worth quoting at length. This approach holds that

> [M]eaning is made through implicit or explicit contrast, . . . a positive definition rests on the negation or repression of something represented as antithetical to it. Thus, any unitary concept in fact contains repressed or negated material; it is established in explicit opposition to another term. . . . Oppositions rest on metaphors and cross-references, and often in patriarchal discourse, sexual difference (the contrast masculine/feminine) serves to encode or establish meanings that are literally unrelated to gender or the body. In that way, the meanings of gender become tied to many kinds of cultural representations, and these in turn establish terms by which relations between women and men are organized and understood. . . . Fixed oppositions conceal the extent to which things presented as oppositional are, in fact, interdependent—that is, they derive their meaning from a particularly established contrast rather than from some inherent or pure antithesis. Furthermore, according to Jacques Derrida, the interdependence is hierarchical with one term dominant or prior, the opposite term subordinate and secondary. The Western philosophical tradition, he argues, rests on binary oppositions: unity/diversity, identity/difference, presence/absence, and universality/specificity. The leading terms are accorded primacy; their partners are represented as weaker or derivative. Yet the first terms depend on and derive their meaning from the second to such an extent that the secondary terms can be seen as generative of the definition of the first terms. (36–37)

This perspective describes well the use of the feminine to establish a certain idea of the masculine within the success manual.

68 Owen, *Success in Life*, 30–31.

69 Mark 14:3–8, King James Version.

70 Mathews, *Getting On in the World*, 61.

71 Bates, *Imperial Highway*, 84.

72 Mathews, *Getting On in the World*, 135.

73 Owen, *Success in Life*, 248.

74 See especially chapters 4 and 6 above.

75 See Scott, *Gender and the Politics of History*, in particular her theoretical chapter, entitled "Gender: A Useful Category of Historical Analysis" (28–50, esp. 42–49), and the case studies in part 3, "Gender in History" (93–163). See also Scott, "Deconstructing Equality-Versus-Difference," 34–37.

76 See Norbert Elias on "stigmatization" and the powerful motive force of "the fear of loss of social prestige" in teaching the internalization of discipline or the "the transformation of constraints through others into self-restraints," in Elias, *Power and Civility*, 229–70 (quotes on 254 and 268). For other examples of the power of the taunt of "sissy," or "girl-boy," see E. Anthony Rotundo's essay "Boy Culture: Middle-Class Boyhood in Nineteenth-Century America," in Carnes and Griffen, *Meanings of Manhood*, 15–36, esp. 29; and Stearns's comments on the "unusual revulsion to the effeminate male" in the Western tradition, in Stearns, *Be a Man!*, 17. For examples from ethnographies from around the world, see Gilmore, *Manhood in the Making*.

77 Tilley, *Masters of the Situation*, 272.

78 Bates, *Imperial Highway*, 210.

79 Ibid., 293.

80 Mathews, *Getting On in the World*, 17.

81 Welter, "The Cult of True Womanhood."

82 Dale, *Way to Win*, 176; Bates, *Imperial Highway*, 468.

83 Haines and Yaggy, *Royal Path of Life*, 14.

84 Ibid., 29–36, 82–93.

85 See, for example, King, *Portraits and Principles*, 119, 533, 534, 574, 577, 360–68.

86 Smiles, *Self-Help*, 380.

87 Tilley, *Masters of the Situation*, 563–74.

88 Bates, *Imperial Highway*, 45, 47.

89 Dale, *Secret of Success*, 161–67, 176–79.

90 See, for example, Welter, "The Cult of True Womanhood"; Cott, *Roots of Bitterness* and *The Bonds of Womanhood*; Ryan, *Womanhood in America* and *Cradle of the Middle Class*; Sklar, *Catherine Beecher*; Kerber, "Separate Spheres, Female Worlds, Woman's Place."

91 Conwell, *The New Day*, 76–79.

92 See Smith-Rosenberg, "The New Woman as Androgyne: Social Disorder and Gender Crisis, 1870–1936," in *Disorderly Conduct*, 245–96.

93 Ibid., 265.

94 See Ryan, "Privacy and the Making of the Self-Made Man: Family Strategies of the Middle Class at Midcentury," chap. 4 in *Cradle of the Middle Class*, 145–85, esp. 166, 168, 173, 184–85.

95 Bledstein, *Culture of Professionalism*, 176.

96 See chapter 2 above.

97 Leverenz, *Manhood and the American Renaissance*, 61–71.

98 This conclusion is consistent with Carroll Smith-Rosenberg's observations that the attack on the New Woman was organized around two allegations: first, her presumed rejection of motherhood, and second, her presumed rejection of men. Smith-Rosenberg, "The New Woman as Androgyne," in *Disorderly Conduct*, 245–96.

99 See Rotundo, "Boy Culture," in Carnes and Griffen, *Meanings of Manhood*, esp. 32–33; and Smith-Rosenberg, "Bourgeois Discourse and the Age of Jackson," in *Disorderly Conduct*, esp. 88.

100 See Carnes, "Middle-Class Men and the Solace of Fraternal Ritual," in Carnes and Griffen, *Meanings for Manhood*; and Chodorow, *The Reproduction of Mothering*.

101 See Scott, *Gender and the Politics of History*, 42–49.

102 As Carroll Smith-Rosenberg has shown, by the turn of the century, this idea was being presented in a "scientific" context by sexologists who argued that "unmarried career women and political activists constituted an 'intermediate sex.'" Smith-Rosenberg, "The New Woman as Androgyne," in *Disorderly Conduct*, 265.

BIBLIOGRAPHY

Primary Sources

Alcott, William A. *The Young Man's Guide*. Boston: T. R. Marvin, 1845.

Alger, Horatio. *Struggling Upward, or Luke Larkin's Luck*. Philadelphia: Porter and Coates, 1890.

Barcus, J. S. *The Philosophy of Canvassing*. Chicago: Werner Co., 1894.

Barnum, P. T. *Dollars and Sense, or How to Get On: The Whole Secret in a Nutshell*. Chicago: People's Publishing Co., 1890.

Bates, Jerome Paine. *The Imperial Highway*. Chicago: George W. Borland & Co., 1881.

Bok, Edward William. *Successward: A Young Man's Book for Young Men*. New York: Fleming H. Revell Co., 1895.

———. *The Keys to Success*. Philadelphia: John D. Morris and Co., 1898.

Brown, Archer. *Top or Bottom—Which? A Study of the Factors Which Most Contribute to the Success of Young Men*. New York: privately printed, 1903.

Browning, O. A. *O. A. Browning's Confidential Instructions, Rules and Helps for His Agents*. Toledo: O. A. Browning, 1882.

Carnegie, Dale. *How to Win Friends and Influence People*. New York: Simon and Schuster, 1936.

Chamberlain, J. S., ed. *Makers of Millions, or Marvelous Success of America's Self-made Men*. Chicago: George M. Hill Co., 1899.

———. *Success, or the Triumphs and Achievements of Self-made Men*. Chicago: Merchants' Specialty Co., 1891.

Conwell, Russell H. *Acres of Diamonds*. 1870. Reprint, Philadelphia: John C. Winston Co., 1959.

———. *The New Day, or Fresh Opportunities: A Book for Young Men*. Philadelphia: Griffith & Roland, 1904.

———. *Present Successful Opportunities*. Philadelphia: Temple Press, 1902.

Crafts, Wilbur F. *Successful Men of Today and What They Say of Success*. New York: Funk & Wagnalls, 1883.

Craig, Adam, comp. *Room at the Top, or How to Reach Success, Happiness, Fame and Fortune*. Augusta, Me.: True and Co., 1884.

Dale, John T. *The Secret of Success, or Finger Posts on the Highway of Life*. New York: Fleming H. Revell, 1889.

———. *The Way to Win, Showing How to Succeed in Life*. Chicago: Hammond Publishing Co., 1891.

Davidson, John Thain. *Sure to Succeed*. New York: A. C. Armstrong and Co., 1889.

Dubbs, Joseph Henry. *Conditions of Success in Life*. Philadelphia: Reformed Church Publishing Board, 1870.

Emerson, Ralph Waldo. "Napoleon; or, The Man of the World." In *The Works of Ralph Waldo Emerson*. New York: The Nottingham Society, n.d.

Franklin, Benjamin. *The Autobiography and Other Writings*. Edited by Jesse L. Lemisch. New York: New American Library, 1961.

Freedley, Edwin Troxell. *A Practical Treatise on Business*. New York: Lippincott, Granbo and Co., 1852.

Garland, Hamlin. *Main-Traveled Roads*. New York: Harper and Row, 1899.

George, Henry. *Progress and Poverty: An Inquiry into the Causes of Industrial Depression and Increase of Want with Increase of Wealth the Remedy*. New York: U.S. Book Co., 1879.

Givens, Charles J. *More Wealth without Risk*. New York: Simon and Schuster, 1991.

———. *Wealth without Risk*. New York: Simon and Schuster, 1988.

Haddock, Frank Channing. *The Power of Will: A Practical Companion Book for Unfoldment of the Powers of Mind*. Meriden, Conn.: Pelton Publishing Co., 1907.

Haines, Thomas L. *Worth and Wealth*. Chicago: Haines Brothers, 1883.

Haines, Thomas L., and Levi W. Yaggy. *The Royal Path of Life, or Aims and Aids to Success and Happiness*. Cincinnati: Western Publishing Co., 1876. Reprint, Detroit: F. B. Dickerson and Co.; Chicago: Western Publishing Co., 1879.

Hale, Edward E. *What Career? Ten Papers on the Choice of a Vocation and the Use of Time*. Boston: Roberts Brothers, 1878.

Harvey, William Hope. *Coin's Financial School*. Chicago: Coin Publishing Co., 1894.

Horton, Robert F. *Success and Failure*. New York: Dodd Mead & Co., 1897.

Hubbard, Elbert. *A Message to Garcia*. East Aurora, N.Y.: Roycraft, 1899.

Hubbard, L. Ron. *Dianetics: The Modern Science of Mental Health*. New York: Bridge Publications, 1985.

Hunt, Freeman. *Worth and Wealth: A Collection of Maxims, Morals and Miscellanies for Merchants and Men of Business*. New York: Stringer and Townsend, 1856.

International Publishing Co. *The General Agent's Guide to Success*. Chicago and Philadelphia: International Publishing Co., 1896.

Kent, Charles H. *How to Achieve Success, A Manual for Young People*. New York: Christian Herald, 1897.

King, William C., ed. *Portraits and Principles of the World's Great Men and Women, with Practical Lessons on Successful Life*. Springfield, Mass.: King, Richardson, and Co., 1895.

Knox, George H. *Ready Money*. Des Moines, Iowa: Personal Help Publishing Co., 1905.

Korda, Michael. *Looking Out for Number One*. New York: Funk and Wagnalls, 1977.

———. *Power! How to Get It, How to Use It*. New York: Random House, 1975.

LaShire, Lovis A. *The Book Agent, A Farce in One Act*. Clyde, Ohio: Ames Publishing Co., 1908.

Lewis, Alexander. *Manhood-Making: Studies in the Elemental Principles of Success*. Boston: Pilgrim Press, 1902.

Lewis, Harry A. *Hidden Treasures, or Why Some Succeed While Others Fail*. New York: A. W. Richardson & Co., 1887.

Marden, Orison Swett. *He Can Who Thinks He Can*. New York: Thomas Y. Crowell, 1908.

———. *How They Succeeded*. Boston: Lothrop Publishing Co., 1901.

———. *Little Visits with Great Americans*. New York: The Success Company, 1905.

———. *Masterful Personality*. New York: Thomas Y. Crowell, 1921.

———. *Pushing to the Front, or Success under Difficulties*. New York: Thomas Y. Crowell, 1894. Reprint, Petersburg, N.Y.: The Success Company, 1911.

———. *Rising in the World, or Architects of Fate*. New York: The Success Company, 1897.

———, ed. *Talks with Great Workers*. New York: Thomas Y. Crowell, 1901.

Mather, Cotton. *A Christian at His Calling*. Boston, 1701. Reprinted in *The American Gospel of Success*. Edited by Moses Rischin. Chicago: Quadrangle, 1968.

Mathews, William. *Getting On in the World, or Hints on Success in Life*. Chicago: S. C. Griggs and Company, 1873. Reprint, Toronto: Belford Brothers, 1876.

Mills, James D. *The Art of Money Making, or the Road to Fortune: A Universal Guide for Honest Success*. New York: International Publishing Co., 1872.

N. D. Thompson Publishing Co. *Facts for Those Contemplating Book Agency*. New York: N. D. Thompson Publishing Co., 1886.

———. *Success in Canvassing: A Manual of Practical Hints and Instructions Specially Adapted to the Use of Book Canvassers of the Better Class*. New York and St. Louis: N. D. Thompson and Co., 1884.

Northrop, Henry Davenport. *Character Building, or Principles, Precepts and Practices Which Make Life a Success*. Philadelphia: National Publishing Co., 1896.

Owen, William Dale. *Conquering Success, or Life in Earnest*. Boston: Houghton, Mifflin and Co., 1903.

———. *The Genius of Industry, or How Work Wins and Manhood Grows*. Chicago: Northern Publishing Co., 1883.

———. *Success in Life, and How to Secure It: or Elements of Manhood and Their Culture*. 1878. Reprint, Chicago: Howe Watts and Company, 1882.

Peale, Norman Vincent. *The Power of Positive Thinking*. New York: Prentice-Hall, 1952.

Quigley, Dorothy. *Success Is for You*. New York: E. P. Dutton and Co., 1897.

Ransom, J. *The Successful Man in His Manifold Relations with Life*. Baltimore: Hill and Harvey, 1886.

Reade, H. L. *A Book for the People: Money and How to Make It*. Norwich, Conn.: Reade Publishing Co., 1882.

Ringer, Robert J. *Winning through Intimidation*. New York: Funk and Wagnalls, 1974.

Sears, Roebuck and Co. *Sears, Roebuck and Company Consumers' Guide*. Chicago: Sears, Roebuck and Co. 1897.

Sharman, H. Risborough. *The Power of the Will or Success*. Boston: Roberts Brothers, 1894.

Sizer, Nelson. *The Royal Road to Wealth*. New York: J. R. Anderson and H. S. Allen, 1882.

Smiles, Samuel. *Character*. New York: Harper and Brothers, 1872.

———. *Duty*. New York: Harper and Brothers, 1881.

———. *Self-Help, with Illustrations of Character and Conduct*. Reprint, New York: Thomas Y. Crowell, 1884. First published in the United States in 1860.

———. *Thrift*. Reprint, Chicago: Donohue, Henneberry and Co., 1890. First published in the United States in 1875.

Smith, Mathew Hale. *Successful Folks: How They Win*. Hartford, Conn.: American Publishing Co., 1878.

Spreng, Samuel Peter. *Rays of Light on the Highway to Success*. Cleveland: Forest City Publishing House, 1885.

Strong, Josiah. *Our Country, Its Possible Future and Its Present Crisis*. 1886. Reprint, Cambridge: Harvard University Press, 1963.

Success Company's Branch Office. *Working Plans and How to Work Them*. N.p., 1913.

Thayer, William Makepeace. *Onward to Fame and Fortune, or Climbing Life's Ladder.* New York: Christian Herald, 1897.

Thompson, Frank Charles, comp. and ed. *The New Chain Reference Bible.* 4th ed. Indianapolis: B. B. Kirkbridge, 1964.

Tilley, William James. *Masters of the Situation, or Some Secrets of Success and Power.* New York: N. D. Thompson Publishing Co., 1890.

Twain, Mark. *Papers, Ledger of the American Publishing Co., December 1, 1866–December 31, 1879.* Berg Collection, New York Public Library, New York, N.Y.

Whipple, Edwin Percy. *Success and Its Conditions.* Boston, 1871. Reprint, Houghton, Mifflin and Co., 1883.

Wiman, Erastus. *Chances of Success: Episodes and Observations in the Life of a Busy Man.* New York: American News Co., 1893.

Secondary Sources

American Book Trade Association. *Publishers' Weekly.* New York: Office of Publishers' Weekly. July 1872–January 1897 issues.

American Council of Learned Societies. *Dictionary of American Biography.* New York: Scribner, 1990.

American Library Association (ALA). *National Union Catalog, Pre-1956 Imprints Prior Series.* London: Mansell, 1968–1981.

Bannister, Robert C. *Social Darwinism, Science, and Myth in Anglo-American Social Thought.* Philadelphia: Temple University Press, 1971.

Banta, Martha. *Failure and Success in America: A Literary Debate.* Princeton: Princeton University Press, 1978.

Banta, Richard Elwell. *Indiana Authors and Their Books, 1816–1916.* Vol. 1. Crawford, Ind.: Wabash College, 1949.

Bardwick, Judith. *Psychology of Women: A Study of Bio-Cultural Conflict.* New York: Harper and Row, 1971.

Barker-Benfield, G. J. *The Horrors of the Half-Known Life: Male Attitudes toward Women and Sexuality in Nineteenth-Century America.* New York: Harper and Row, 1976.

Beard, George M. *American Nervousness: Its Causes and Consequences.* New York: G. P. Putnam's Sons, 1881.

Biographical Directory of the American Congress, 1774–1961. Washington, D.C.: U.S. Government Printing Office, 1961.

Bledstein, Burton, *The Culture of Professionalism, the Middle Class, and the Development of Higher Education in America.* New York: W. W. Norton, 1978.

Blumin, Stuart M. *The Emergence of the Middle Class: Social Experience in the American City, 1760–1900.* Cambridge: Cambridge University Press, 1989.

————. "The Hypothesis of Middle-Class Formation in Nineteenth-Century America: A Critique and Some Proposals." *American Historical Review* 90, no. 2 (April 1985): 299–338.

Bowden, Henry Warner, and Edwin S. Gaustad. *Dictionary of American Religious Biography.* Westport, Conn.: Greenwood, 1977.

Braverman, Harry. *Labor and Monopoly Capital: The Degradation of Work in the Twentieth Century.* New York: Monthly Review Press, 1974.

Buhle, Mari Jo. *Women and American Socialism, 1870–1920.* Urbana: University of Illinois Press, 1981.

Burke, W. F., and Will D. Howe, eds. *American Authors and Books, 1640 to the Present Day.* 3d rev. ed. Revised by Irving Weiss and Anne Weiss. New York: Crown, 1972.

Burns, Rex. *Success in America: The Yeoman Dream and the Industrial Revolution.* Amherst: University of Massachusetts Press, 1976.

Burns, Sarah. *Pastoral Inventions: Rural Life in Nineteenth-Century American Art and Culture.* Philadelphia: Temple University Press, 1989.

Burr, Agnes Rush. *Russell H. Conwell and His Work.* Philadelphia: John C. Winston Company, 1926.

Carnes, Mark C. *Secret Ritual and Manhood in Victorian America.* New Haven: Yale University Press, 1989.

Carnes, Mark C., and Clyde Griffen, eds. *Meanings of Manhood: Constructions of Masculinity in Victorian America.* Chicago: University of Chicago Press, 1990.

Carter, Paul A. *The Spiritual Crisis of the Gilded Age.* DeKalb: Northern Illinois University Press, 1971.

Cawelti, John G. *Adventure, Mystery, and Romance: Formula Stories as Art and Popular Culture.* Chicago: University of Chicago Press, 1976.

———. *Apostles of the Self-Made Man: Changing Concepts of Success in America.* Chicago: University of Chicago Press, 1965.

Chodorow, Nancy. *The Reproduction of Mothering: Psychoanalysis and the Sociology of Gender.* Berkeley: University of California, 1978.

Compton, F. E. "Subscription Books." *Bulletin of the New York Public Library* 43, no. 12 (December 1939): 879-94.

Connolly, Margaret. *The Life Story of Orison Swett Marden.* New York: Thomas Y. Crowell Co., 1925.

Cott, Nancy F. *The Bonds of Womanhood: "Woman's Sphere" in New England, 1780-1835.* New Haven: Yale University Press, 1977.

———, ed. *Roots of Bitterness: Documents of the Social History of American Women.* New York: E. P. Dutton, 1972.

Davidson, Cathy N., ed. *Reading in America: Literature and Social History.* Baltimore: Johns Hopkins University Press, 1989.

D'Emilio, John, and Estelle B. Freedman. *Intimate Matters: A History of Sexuality in America.* New York: G. P. Putnam's Sons, 1880.

Elias, Norbert. *Power and Civility,* vol. 2 of *The Civilizing Process.* Translated by Edmund Jephcott. Reprint, New York: Pantheon, 1982. First published in German in 1939.

Fellman, Anita Clair, and Michael Fellman. *Making Sense of Self: Medical Advice Literature in Late-Nineteenth-Century America.* Philadelphia: University of Pennsylvania Press, 1981.

Filene, Peter. *Him-Her Self: Sex Roles in Modern America.* New York: Harcourt, Brace, Jovanovich, 1974.

Fink, Leon. *Workingmen's Democracy: The Knights of Labor and American Politics.* Urbana: University of Illinois Press, 1983.

Gilmore, David D. *Manhood in the Making: Cultural Concepts of Masculinity.* New Haven: Yale University Press, 1990.

Goodwyn, Lawrence. *The Populist Moment: A Short History of the Agrarian Revolt in America.* Oxford: Oxford University Press, 1978.

Gorn, Elliot J. *The Manly Art: Bare-Knuckle Prize Fighting in America.* Ithaca: Cornell University Press, 1986.

Gramsci, Antonio. *Selections from the Prison Notebooks.* Edited and translated by Quentin

Hoare and Geoffrey Norwell Smith. London: Lawrence and Wishhart, 1971. First published in Italian, 1948–51.

Green, Harvey. *Fit for America: Health Fitness, Sport, and American Society*. New York: Pantheon, 1986.

Greene, Theodore P. *American Heroes: The Changing Models of Success in American Magazines*. New York: Oxford University Press, 1970.

Gutman, Herbert G. *Work, Culture, and Society in Industrializing America*. New York: Vintage, 1977.

Hall, Peter Dobkin. *The Organization of American Culture, 1700–1900: Private Institutions, Elites, and the Origins of American Nationality*. New York: New York University Press, 1982.

Halttunen, Karen. *Confidence Men and Painted Women: A Study of Middle-Class Culture in America, 1830–1870*. New Haven: Yale University Press, 1982.

Hartz, Louis. *The Liberal Tradition in America: An Interpretation of American Political Thought since the Revolution*. New York: Harcourt Brace, 1955. Reprint, San Diego: Harvest/HBJ Books, 1983.

Haskell, Thomas L. *The Emergence of Professional Social Science: The American Social Science Association and the Nineteenth-Century Crisis of Authority*. Urbana: University of Illinois Press, 1977.

Herbert, Miranda C., and Barbara McNeil. *Biography and Genealogy Master Index*. Detroit: Gale Research Corp., 1980.

Hilkey, Judy. "Masculinity and the Self-Made Man, 1850-1900." Paper delivered at the Second Berkshire Conference on the History of Women, Radcliffe College, Cambridge, Mass., October 26, 1974.

———. " 'The Way to Win': The Search for Success in a New Industrial Order, 1870-1910." Ph.D. diss., Rutgers University, 1980.

Hill, Hamlin. *Mark Twain and Elisha Bliss*. Columbia: University of Missouri Press, 1964.

Hofstadter, Richard. *The Age of Reform, from Bryant to FDR*. New York: Vintage, 1955.

Hold, Alfred H. *Phrase and Word Origins*. New York: Dover, 1961.

Horlick, Stanley. *Country Boys and Merchant Princes: The Social Control of Young Men in New York*. Lewisburg, Pa.: Bucknell University Press, 1975.

Huber, Richard M. *The American Idea of Success*. New York: McGraw Hill, 1971. Reprint, Wainscott, N.Y.: Pushcart Press, 1987.

Josephson, Matthew. *The Robber Barons: The Great American Capitalists, 1861-1901*. New York: Harcourt, Brace and World, 1964.

Kasson, John F. *Rudeness and Civility: Manners in Nineteenth-Century Urban America*. New York: Hill and Wang, 1990.

Kelly, James. *American Catalogue 1861-1871*. New York: P. Smith, 1938.

Kerber, Linda. "Separate Spheres, Female Worlds, Woman's Place: The Rhetoric of Women's History." *Journal of American History* 75 (1988): 9–39.

Kett, Joseph. *Rites of Passage: Adolescence in America, 1790 to the Present*. New York: Basic, 1977.

Kirkland, Edward Chase. *Dream and Thought in the Business Community 1860-1900*. Chicago: Quadrangle, 1964.

Kriegel, Leonard. *On Men and Manhood*. New York: Hawthorn, 1979.

Kunitz, Stanley J., and Howard Haycraft, eds. *American Authors 1600-1900: A Biographical Dictionary of American Literature*. New York: N. W. Wilson Co., 1938.

Laurie, Bruce. *Artisans into Workers: Labor in Nineteenth-Century America*. New York: Noonday, 1989.

Lears, T. J. Jackson. "The Concept of Cultural Hegemony: Problems and Possibilities." *American Historical Review* 90, no. 3 (June 1985): 567–93.

———. *No Place of Grace: Antimodernism and the Transformation of American Culture, 1880–1920*. New York: Pantheon, 1981.

Lehmann-Haupt, Hellmut. *The Book in America: A History of the Making and Selling of Books in the United States*. New York: R. R. Bowker Co., 1939.

Leverenz, David. *Manhood and the American Renaissance*. Ithaca: Cornell University Press, 1989.

Levine, Susan. *Labor's True Woman: Carpet Weavers, Industrialization, and Labor Reform in the Gilded Age*. Philadelphia: Temple University Press, 1984.

Lutz, Tom. *American Nervousness, 1903: An Anecdotal History*. Ithaca: Cornell University Press, 1991.

Marcus, Steven. *The Other Victorians: A Study of Sexuality and Pornography in Mid-Nineteenth-Century England*. New York: Basic, 1964.

Meyer, D. H. *The Instructed Conscience: The Shaping of the American National Ethic*. Philadelphia: University of Pennsylvania Press, 1972.

Mills, C. Wright. *White Collar: The American Middle Class*. New York: Oxford University Press, 1956.

Montgomery, David. *Workers' Control in America: Studies in the History of Work, Technology, and Labor Struggles*. New York: Cambridge University Press, 1979.

Mosse, George L. *Nationalism and Sexuality: Respectability and Abnormal Sexuality in Modern Europe*. New York: Howard Fertig, 1985.

Mott, Frank Luther. *Golden Multitudes: The Story of Best Sellers in the United States*. New York: Macmillan, 1947.

National Cyclopaedia of American Biography Editorial Staff, comp. *National Cyclopaedia of American Biography*. New York: James T. White and Co., 1910.

New York Times Co. *New York Times Index*. New York: New York Times Co., 1851–1912.

Ord, Priscilla A. "Watty Piper." In *American Writers for Children, 1900–1960*. Vol. 22 of *Dictionary of Literary Biography*. Detroit: Gale, 1983.

Pacific Northwest Library Association, Subscription Book Committee. "Points to Consider in Judging Subscription Books." *Cumulated Bulletin* (1925): 42–44.

Publishers' Trade List Annual. New York: R. R. Bowker Co., 1873–1903.

Rischin, Moses, ed. *The American Gospel of Success*. Chicago: Quadrangle, 1968.

Rode, C. R., ed. *American Publishers' Circular and Literary Gazette*. Philadelphia, 1856–72.

Ross, Dorothy. "The Liberal Tradition Revisited and the Republican Tradition Addressed." In *New Directions in American Intellectual History*, 116–31. Baltimore: Johns Hopkins University Press, 1979.

———. "Socialism and American Liberalism: Academic Social Thought in the 1880s." *Perspectives in American History* 12 (1977–78): 7–79.

Ryan, Mary P. *Cradle of the Middle Class: The Family in Oneida County, New York, 1790–1865*. New York: Cambridge University Press, 1981.

———. *Womanhood in America*. New York: New Viewpoints, 1975.

Salvatore, Nick. *Eugene V. Debs, Citizen and Socialist*. Urbana: University of Illinois Press, 1982.

Schaff, Philip, and Samuel Macauley Jackson, eds. *Encyclopedia of Living Divines and Christian Workers of All Denominations in Europe and America* (supplement to Schaff-Herzog *Encyclopedia of Religious Knowledge*). New York: Funk and Wagnalls, 1887.

Scott, Joan Wallach. "Deconstructing Equality-Versus-Difference: or, The Uses of Poststructuralist Theory for Feminism." *Feminist Studies* 14, no. 1 (Spring 1988): 33–50.

———. *Gender and the Politics of History*. New York: Oxford University Press, 1985.

Shannon, Fred A. *The Farmer's Last Frontier, 1860–1897*. New York: 1945.

Sheehan, Donald. *This Was Publishing: A Chronicle of the Book Trade in the Gilded Age*. Bloomington: Indiana University Press, 1952.

Shove, Raymond Howard. "Cheap Book Production in the United States, 1870-1891." Unpublished master's thesis, Library School, University of Illinois, 1937.

Sklar, Katherine Kish. *Catherine Beecher: A Study in American Domesticity*. New Haven: Yale University Press, 1973.

Smith, Henry Nash. *Virgin Land: The American West as Symbol and Myth*. Cambridge: Harvard University Press, 1950.

Smith-Rosenberg, Carroll. *Disorderly Conduct: Visions of Gender in Victorian America*. New York: Oxford University Press, 1985.

Stearns, Peter N. *Be a Man! Males in Modern Society*. 2d ed. New York: Holmes and Meier, 1990.

Susman, Warren I. *Culture as History: The Transformation of American Society in the Twentieth Century*. New York: Pantheon, 1984.

Tebbel, John. *Between Covers: The Rise and Transformation of American Publishing*. New York: Oxford University Press, 1987.

Thernstrom, Stephen. *The Other Bostonians: Poverty and Progress in the American Metropolis, 1880–1970*. Cambridge: Harvard University Press, 1973.

Trachtenberg, Alan. *The Incorporation of America: Culture and Society in the Gilded Age*. New York: Hill and Wang, 1982.

U.S. Bureau of the Census. *Historical Statistics of the United States, Colonial Times to 1957*. Washington, D.C.: U.S. Department of Commerce, 1960.

United States Catalog of Books. New York: H. W. Wilson Company, 1902 and 1912.

Waldman, Milton. "Subscription Sets." *American Mercury* 4, no. 14 (1925): 237-43.

Wallace, William Stewart, comp. *A Dictionary of North American Authors Deceased before 1950*. Toronto: Ryerson, 1951.

———, ed. *Macmillan Dictionary of Canadian Biography*. Toronto: Macmillan, 1978.

Weibe, Robert. *The Search for Order, 1877–1920*. New York· Hill and Wang, 1967.

Weiss, Richard. *The American Myth of Success from Horatio Alger to Norman Vincent Peale*. New York: Basic, 1969.

Welter, Barbara. "The Cult of True Womanhood, 1820-1860." *American Quarterly* 18 (Summer 1966): 151-74.

Who Was Who in America, 1607–1896 and 1897–1942. Chicago: Marquis-Who's Who., 1963.

Wilson, General James Grant, and John Fiske. *Cyclopedia of American Biography*. New York: Press Association, 1918.

Wright, Louis B. "Franklin's Legacy to the Gilded Age." *Virginia Quarterly Review* 22, no. 2 (Spring 1946): 268-79.

Wyllie, Irvin G. *The Self-Made Man in America*. New York: Free Press, 1954.

Young, James Harvey. *The Toadstool Millionaires: A Social History of Patent Medicines before Federal Regulation*. Princeton: Princeton University Press, 1961.

Zboray, Ronald J. "Antebellum Reading and the Ironies of Technological Innovation." In *Reading in America: Literature and Social History*, edited by Cathy N. Davidson, 180-97. Baltimore: Johns Hopkins University Press, 1989.

INDEX